Korea:
Cold War and Limited War

PROBLEMS IN
AMERICAN CIVILIZATION

Under the editorial direction of
Edwin C. Rozwenc
Amherst College

Korea: Cold War and Limited War

Second Edition

Edited and with an introduction by

Allen Guttmann
Amherst College

D.C. HEATH AND COMPANY
Lexington, Massachusetts Toronto London

DS
919
G8

68814

Published simultaneously in Canada.

Printed in the United States of America.

International Standard Book Number: 0–669–82693–6

Library of Congress Catalog Card Number: 72–5150

CONTENTS

INTRODUCTION

The language of military strategy seems very abstract when compared to televised images of napalm-struck villages in flames and wounded men whose life's blood spurts away from shrapnel-severed arteries. Nonetheless, the abstract language is necessary. Without it, neither the Korean War of 1950–1953 nor the present war in Vietnam nor any other war is comprehensible.

We are all aware of the rapid development of modern weaponry; we all have some notion of the implications of intercontinental ballistic missiles armed with thermonuclear warheads. But the current revolution in military thought is less widely understood. While experts in the Pentagon or the Rand Corporation planned for a variety of strategic and tactical alternatives, most Americans continued to think in terms of one end of the spectrum—total war. Too many Americans still continue to imagine conflicts clearly won by the victorious and humbly acknowledged by the vanquished. Meanwhile, the strategists have gone back to the eighteenth century for the study of limited war, and to the early nineteenth century for the concepts of the military thinker Karl von Clausewitz. Theorists of limited war assume—to simplify a good deal—that military action is always in response to some political need and that the political implications of military action must always be considered.[1]

Disagreement about the validity of the theory of limited war, and about its application in the Korean War, brought the United States to the most severe crisis in civil-military relations in its entire history. It was over the limitation of the war that President Truman and Gen-

[1] "Political need" in this sense means not partisan politics but rather such matters as defense of treaty rights or even of national independence.

eral MacArthur came to disagree so violently that the former felt impelled to charge the latter with insubordination and to relieve him from his command. In the political turmoil that ensued, supporters of General MacArthur condemned President Truman in language usually reserved for men convicted of treason. No one who was alive then mistook the seriousness of the controversy. What has only recently begun to emerge, however, is the significance of the tumultuous partisan struggle.

The readings which follow are an attempt to clarify the significance of the Korean War as a case-study in civil-military relations and in limited warfare. The readings are divided into three main sections. The first is a series of basic documents supplemented with editorial notes to provide continuity. The documents and notes together are a skeleton history of the Korean War from its inception until the conclusion of the Congressional investigation that followed MacArthur's dismissal. Studying these documents and notes, one can encounter the questions that troubled the original participants. What were the capabilities and intentions of the North Koreans, and what could the UN forces do to carry out their mission? What exactly was that mission? Would the Chinese enter the war and, if they did, were the soldiers of MacArthur's command ready for them? How far should a field commander be allowed to go in the formation of policy? What was his responsibility to the Commander in Chief and to the Joint Chiefs of Staff, and what was theirs to him?

The problem of civil-military relations, unavoidably present in the original documents, is specifically examined in Part II of the readings. Was MacArthur the potential military dictator that the Founding Fathers feared, or was he, as he himself insisted, merely an obedient soldier attempting to carry through some remarkably ambiguous orders under extraordinarily difficult conditions? Had MacArthur infringed upon the prerogatives of the President and the Secretary of State? Had the civilians in the Truman Administration improperly interfered in military operations and thus hampered the general in his attempt to carry out their directives? The break between MacArthur and Truman was bitter. Was it unavoidable? Which of them bears the heavier responsibility for the clash that convulsed the American political system? Is the American system of government one that makes recurrences of the controversy likely?

Still other questions relate to the problems of limited war. The readings of Part III are retrospective attempts to analyze in a systematic fashion issues very much in the consciousness of contemporary participants. What exactly were the limitations imposed in the Korean War? Were they the result of studied plans or did they emerge from the day-to-day necessities of combat? Was American intervention a hasty response to unexpected aggression or was the Korean War but another example, as revisionists have argued, of a war of national liberation frustrated by American imperialism? Were American policies justified, or were they tragically mistaken?

Finally, stepping back a little from the readings, one can ask still more basic questions. Is a democratic society capable of the kind of reasoned restraint implied in the theory of limited war? Is it possible, on the other hand, that the whole concept of limited war is faulty? Is it possible, in other words, that the tragedy of the Korean War ran its full course because no one—neither Truman nor MacArthur, nor their many advisors—knew how to ask the right questions, questions that go beyond considerations of limited or unlimited wars?

The questions are urgent. Writing in 1960, Martin Lichterman pointed out that "the Korean War has been the only experience Americans have had with limited war in the nuclear age."[2] For that reason, he argued, the Korean War has immense historical importance. Now, American involvement in Vietnam in a second and perhaps even more serious nuclear-age, limited war makes the test-case of Korea even more important. Large numbers of Americans have lost faith in their own country. The framework of democratic government shows signs of strain. In this prolonged crisis, it is essential for us to understand the significance of the Korean War. We, as a nation, might not survive the consequences of a miscalculation of the uncertain dividing line between limited war and the irreversible escalation into total war.

[2] "Korea: Problems in Limited War," in Gordon B. Turner and Richard Challener, eds., *National Security in the Nuclear Age* (New York, 1960), p. 31.

The Clash of Issues

General Douglas MacArthur, Commander of the UN forces in Korea, disregards the ban on political actions by field commanders, calls upon the enemy commander to enter into negotiations with him, and is relieved by President Truman:

> MacArthur left me no choice—I could no longer tolerate his insubordination.

General MacArthur denies the President's allegations:

> I have been a soldier for fifty-two years. I have in that time, to the best of my ability, carried out every order that was ever given to me. No more subordinate soldier has ever worn the American uniform.

Returning to Washington, the general repeats his challenge to the limitations placed upon the conduct of the war:

> Once war is forced upon us, there is no other alternative than to apply every available means to bring it to a swift end. War's very object is victory—not prolonged indecision. In war, indeed, there can be no substitute for victory.

The chairman of the Joint Chiefs of Staff rebuts him:

> In the opinion of the Joint Chiefs, [General MacArthur's] strategy would involve us in the wrong war, at the wrong place, at the wrong time, and with the wrong enemy.
>
> GEN. OMAR BRADLEY

The war, which was not expanded, ended in a deadlock. For some historians, the outcome was little less than disaster:

> What Americans objected to was not the fact that the war was kept limited . . . but rather the fact that its limitations whittled down the real superiority of the United States. Since American policy-makers had posed a false dilemma—either a protracted stalemate or all-out war—popular opinion within the United States tended to conclude that American conventional forces had been misused in Korea. . . .
>
> ALVIN J. COTTRELL AND JAMES E. DOUGHERTY

But other historians take the opposite view:

> In sticking to a Clausewitzian policy of waging limited war as an instrument of policy, the Truman Administration [kept the Atlantic] coalition intact, repelled the Communist aggression and strengthened Western defenses. . . . In retrospect this is the major Western political achievement since 1945.
>
> DAVID REES

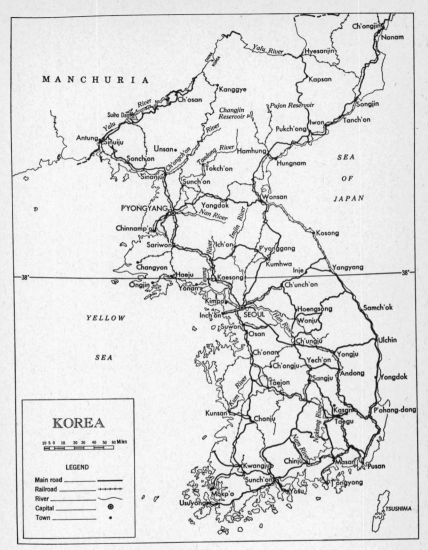

KOREA

10 5 0   10   20 30   40   50   60 Miles

LEGEND

Main road _____
Railroad _____ +++++
River _____
Capital _____ ◉
Town _____ •

Army Map Service, Corps of Engineers

I. THE CONTEMPORARY DEBATE

Harry S Truman

STATEMENT ON THE KOREAN CONFLICT

A little before dawn on June 25, 1950 (local time) Premier Kim Il Sung of the Democratic People's Republic of Korea (North Korea) sent seven infantry divisions, an armored brigade, and additional support units across the 38th Parallel into the territory of the Republic of Korea (South Korea). The South Korean army was unable to defend itself against the Communist forces. President Syngman Rhee requested American aid and forced upon President Truman one of the most momentous decisions of the postwar period.

American foreign policy, preoccupied with the "containment" of communism in Europe, was based on the assumption that any war would be a total war waged largely with nuclear weapons. On the basis of this assumption, the military establishment was drastically reduced in size—to the point where the Joint Chiefs of Staff began to wonder about their ability to defend Alaska. The Republican-dominated 80th Congress cut President Truman's defense budget by almost 20 percent. The Joint Chiefs of Staff decided, in 1947, that Korea was not vital to American security. In a speech delivered in January of 1950, Secretary of State Acheson very pointedly excluded South Korea from our main perimeter of defense in the Far East.[1] Japan itself was garrisoned with a skeleton force of four divisions, and these divisions were reduced to 70 percent of strength by defense economies. The United States, therefore, was unprepared both militarily and psychologically for the attack on South Korea.

Nonetheless, President Truman decided that the United States had to act. His first response was to request action by the United Nations. Meeting in emergency session, the Security Council called upon the North Koreans to cease their attack and to withdraw their armed forces to the 38th Parallel. (The Soviet delegate, Jacob Malik, was unable to veto the resolution because the Soviet Union had boycotted the UN when that body refused to seat Communist China in place of Nationalist China.) The North Koreans, arguing that they had been attacked by the "puppet Syngman Rhee," continued to move south. On the day that Seoul, the capital of South Korea fell, President Truman broadcast a statement of American policy.

In Korea the government forces, which were armed to prevent border raids and to preserve internal security, were attacked by

---

From US Senate, *The Military Situation in the Far East: Hearings before the Committee on Armed Services and the Committee on Foreign Relations,* 82nd Congress, 1st Session, 1951, p. 3369. Hereafter, *Hearings.*

[1] General MacArthur had also publicly excluded Korea from our defense perimeter. See David Rees, *Korea: The Limited War* (New York, 1964), p. 15.

invading forces from North Korea. The Security Council of the United Nations called upon the invading troops to cease hostilities and to withdraw to the 38th Parallel. This they have not done, but on the contrary have pressed the attack. The Security Council called upon all members of the United Nations to render every assistance to the United Nations in the execution of this resolution. In these circumstances I have ordered United States air and sea forces to give the Korean Government troops cover and support.

The attack upon Korea makes it plain beyond all doubt that communism has passed beyond the use of subversion to conquer independent nations and will now use armed invasion and war. It has defied the orders of the Security Council of the United Nations issued to preserve peace and security. In these circumstances the occupation of Formosa by Communist forces would be a direct threat to the security of the Pacific area and to United States forces performing their lawful and necessary functions in that area.

Accordingly I have ordered the Seventh Fleet to prevent any attack on Formosa. As a corollary of this action I am calling upon the Chinese Government on Formosa to cease all air and sea operations against the mainland. The Seventh Fleet will see that this is done. The determination of the future status of Formosa must await the restoration of security in the Pacific, a peace settlement with Japan, or consideration by the United Nations.

I have also directed that United States forces in the Philippines be strengthened and that military assistance to the Philippine Government be accelerated.

I have similarly directed acceleration in the furnishing of military assistance to the forces of France and the associated states in Indochina and the dispatch of a military mission to provide close working relations with those forces.

I know that all members of the United Nations will consider carefully the consequences of this latest aggression in Korea in defiance of the Charter of the United Nations. A return to the rule of force in international affairs would have far-reaching effects. The United States will continue to uphold the rule of law.

I have instructed Ambassador Austin, as the representative of the United States to the Security Council, to report these steps to the Council.

United Nations Security Council
RESOLUTION OF JUNE 27, 1950

Thanks again to the absence of the Soviet delegate, who would have vetoed the resolution had he been present, the Security Council sanctioned American intervention.

Resolution concerning the complaint of aggression upon the Republic of Korea, adopted at the four hundred and seventy-fourth meeting of the Security Council, on June 27, 1950:

The Security Council,

Having determined that the armed attack upon the Republic of Korea by forces from North Korea constitutes a breach of the peace,

Having called for an immediate cessation of hostilities, and

Having called upon the authorities of North Korea to withdraw forthwith their armed forces to the 38th Parallel, and

Having noted from the report of the United Nations Commission for Korea that the authorities in North Korea have neither ceased hostilities nor withdrawn their armed forces to the 38th Parallel and that urgent military measures are required to restore international peace and security, and

Having noted the appeal from the Republic of Korea to the United Nations for immediate and effective steps to secure peace and security,

Recommends that the Members of the United Nations furnish such assistance to the Republic of Korea as may be necessary to repel the armed attack and to restore international peace and security in the area.

(*Voting for the resolution:* United States, United Kingdom, France, China, Norway, Ecuador, and Cuba. *Voting against:* Yugoslavia, *Abstention:* Egypt, India [two days later India accepted the resolution]. *Absent:* Soviet Union.)

From *Hearings*, p. 3371.

Douglas MacArthur

LETTER TO THE VETERANS OF FOREIGN WARS, AUGUST 17, 1950

On June 29, President Truman authorized American ground forces to join our air and naval forces already in combat in Korea. Two companies of the Twenty-fourth Infantry Division reached Pusan, South Korea's southernmost port, on July 1st and were rushed immediately into action. The buildup of American forces was rapid enough for General Walton H. Walker, commander of the Eighth Army, to stop the North Korean offensive on a perimeter extending in an arc from fifty to a hundred miles around Pusan. By the middle of September, the UN forces were secure enough in the southwest corner of the peninsula to plan a counteroffensive.

While the fighting stabilized in Korea, the political tensions arising from the conduct of the war created a growing crisis of civil-military relations in the United States. On July 31, General MacArthur and his most trusted aides flew to Formosa and conferred with Generalissimo Chiang Kai-shek. The next day, Chiang issued a communique in which he looked forward to collaboration once again with his "old comrade in arms, General MacArthur." President Truman, fearing that American acceptance of the troops which Chiang offered might bring the Chinese Communists into the Korean War (and alienate our allies in the UN) sent Averell Harriman to Tokyo to explain to MacArthur the reasons for American policy vis-à-vis Nationalist China. General MacArthur complained to the Defense Department that he had been misunderstood, but Secretary of Defense Louis Johnson was unsympathetic. MacArthur then took an opportunity to let his view be known when the Veterans of Foreign Wars invited him to send a message to its annual convention.

Your inspiring message of the 17th has moved me deeply and I trust that you will convey to all of my comrades-in-arms of the Veterans of Foreign Wars assembled on the occasion of our Fifty-first Annual National Encampment my assurance that their confidence and support will give this command much added strength to meet the tests of battle which lie immediately ahead.

Tell them that I am happy to report that their successors in arms now engaging the enemy along our battle lines in South Korea are exemplifying that same high standard of devotion, fortitude, and

From *Hearings*, pp. 3477–3480.

valor which characterized their own march to victory when they themselves engaged in combat in the field.

From senior commanders down through all ranks, their tactical skill, their invincible determination, and their fighting qualities against a fanatical foe, well trained, expertly directed and heavily armed, have upheld our country's finest traditions.

Toward victory, however difficult the road, they are giving an account of themselves which should make every American heart beat with pride and infinite satisfaction.

In view of misconceptions currently being voiced concerning the relationship of Formosa to our strategic potential in the Pacific, I believe it in the public interest to avail myself of this opportunity to state my views thereon to you, all of whom, having fought overseas, understand broad strategic concepts.

To begin with, any appraisal of that strategic potential requires an appreciation of the changes wrought in the course of the past war. Prior thereto the western strategic frontier of the United States lay on the littoral line of the Americas with an exposed island salient extending out through Hawaii, Midway, and Guam to the Philippines.

That salient was not an outpost of strength but an avenue of weakness along which the enemy could and did attack us. The Pacific was a potential area of advancement for any predatory force intent upon striking at the bordering land areas.

All of this was changed by our Pacific victory. Our strategic frontier then shifted to embrace the entire Pacific Ocean, which has become a vast moat to protect us as long as we hold it.

Indeed, it acts as a protective shield to all of the Americas and all free lands of the Pacific Ocean area we control to the shores of Asia by a chain of islands extending in an arc from the Aleutians to the Marianas held by us and our free Allies. From this island chain we can dominate with air power every Asiatic port from Vladivostok to Singapore and prevent any hostile movement into the Pacific.

Any predatory attack from Asia must be an amphibious effort. No amphibious force can be successful with our control of the sea lanes and the air over these lanes in its avenue of advance. With naval and air supremacy and modern ground elements to defend bases, any major attack from continental Asia toward us or our friends of the Pacific would come to failure.

Under such conditions the Pacific no longer represents menacing avenues of approach for a prospective invader—it assumes instead the friendly aspect of a peaceful lake. Our line of defense is a natural one and can be maintained with a minimum of military effort and expense.

It envisions no attack against anyone nor does it provide the bastions essential for offensive operations, but properly maintained would be an invincible defense against aggression. If we hold this line we may have peace—lose it and war is inevitable.

The geographic location of Formosa is such that in the hand of a power unfriendly to the United States it constitutes an enemy salient in the very center of this defensive perimeter, 100 to 150 miles closer to the adjacent friendly segments—Okinawa and the Philippines—than any point in continental Asia.

At the present time there is on Formosa a concentration of operational air and naval bases which is potentially greater than any similar concentration of the Asiatic mainland between the Yellow Sea and the Strait of Malacca. Additional bases can be developed in a relatively short time by an aggressive exploitation of all World War II Japanese facilities.

An enemy force utilizing those installations currently available could increase by 100 percent the air effort which could be directed against Okinawa as compared to operations based on the mainland and at the same time could direct damaging air attacks with fighter-type aircraft against friendly installations in the Philippines, which are currently beyond the range of fighters based on the mainland. Our air supremacy at once would become doubtful.

As a result of its geographic location and base potential, utilization of Formosa by a military power hostile to the United States may either counter-balance or overshadow the strategic importance of the central and southern flank of the United States front-line position.

Formosa in the hands of such a hostile power could be compared to an unsinkable aircraft carrier and submarine tender ideally located to accomplish offensive strategy and at the same time checkmate defensive or counter-offensive operations by friendly forces based on Okinawa and the Philippines.

This unsinkable carrier-tender has the capacity to operate from ten to twenty air groups of types ranging from jet fighters to B-29 type bombers as well as to provide forward operating facilities for short-range coastal submarines.

In acquiring this forward submarine base, the efficacy of the short-range submarine would be so enormously increased by the additional radius of activity as to threaten completely sea traffic from the south and interdict all sea lanes in the Western Pacific. Submarine blockade by the enemy with all its destructive ramifications would thereby become a virtual certainty.

Should Formosa fall and bases thereafter come into the hands of a potential enemy of the United States, the latter will have acquired an additional "fleet" which will have been obtained and can be maintained at an incomparably lower cost than could its equivalent in aircraft carriers and submarine tenders.

Current estimates of air and submarine resources in the Far East indicate the capability of such a potential enemy to extend his forces southward and still maintain an imposing degree of military strength for employment elsewhere in the Pacific area.

Historically, Formosa has been used as a springboard for just such military aggression directed against areas to the south. The most notable and recent example was the utilization of it by the Japanese in World War II. At the outbreak of the Pacific War in 1941, it played an important part as a staging area and supporting base for the various Japanese invasion convoys. The supporting air forces of Japan's army and navy were based on fields situated along southern Formosa.

From 1942 through 1944 Formosa was a vital link in the transportation and communication chain which stretched from Japan through Okinawa and the Philippines to Southeast Asia. As the United States carrier forces advanced into the Western Pacific, the bases on Formosa assumed an increasingly greater role in the Japanese defense scheme.

Should Formosa fall into the hands of a hostile power, history would repeat itself. Its military potential would again be fully exploited as the means to breach and neutralize our Western Pacific defense system and mount a war of conquest against the free nations of the Pacific basin.

Nothing could be more fallacious than the threadbare argument by those who advocate appeasement and defeatism in the Pacific that if we defend Formosa we alienate continental Asia.

Those who speak thus do not understand the Orient. They do not grant that it is in the pattern of the Oriental psychology to respect and follow aggressive, resolute and dynamic leadership—to quickly turn on a leadership characterized by timidity or vacillation—and they underestimate the Oriental mentality. Nothing in the last five years has so inspired the Far East as the American determination to preserve the bulwarks of our Pacific Ocean strategic position from future encroachment, for few of its people fail accurately to appraise the safeguard such determination brings to their free institutions.

To pursue any other course would be to turn over the fruits of our Pacific victory to a potential enemy. It would shift any future battle area 5,000 miles eastward to the coasts of the American continents, our own home coast; it would completely expose our friends in the Philippines, our friends in Australia and New Zealand, our friends in Indonesia, our friends in Japan, and other areas, to the lustful thrusts of those who stand for slavery against liberty, for atheism as against God.

The decision of President Truman on June 27 lighted into flame a lamp of hope throughout Asia that was burning dimly toward extinction. It marked for the Far East the focal and turning point in this area's struggle for freedom. It swept aside in one great monumental stroke all of the hypocrisy and the sophistry which has confused and deluded so many people distant from the actual scene.

United Nations General Assembly
RESOLUTION OF OCTOBER 7, 1950

The political difficulties between General MacArthur and the Administration did not, apparently, hinder the progress of the war. In the very first week of the Korean War, MacArthur had seen that an amphibious landing at the port of Inchon (a little west of Seoul) would completely destroy the North Korean lines of communication and supply. Pointing out that strong tides and mud flats made amphibious landing possible only two days of the year and that twelve hours would lapse between the first wave of troops and their reinforcements, General MacArthur's staff and two members of the Joint Chiefs of Staff (General J. Lawton Collins and Admiral Forrest Sherman) advised against the extremely risky maneuver. MacArthur himself admitted that the odds were 5,000 to 1 against him. Nevertheless, he went ahead with his plans.

On September 15, the landing craft of X Corps rode in on the tides. Marine and Army troops scaled sea walls with ladders, waded up beaches, and won what has since been known as an "impossible victory." The X Corps quickly seized the port. By September 27, Seoul was recaptured and the North Korean army was in full retreat before a second offensive was launched from the Pusan perimeter. On October 1, South Korean troops crossed the 38th Parallel. The fragmented forces of North Korea were in full flight.

At this moment, General MacArthur's United Nations Command had achieved the goals set forth by the Security Council in its June resolutions. Now, in compliance with American requests, the British delegate to the UN, Kenneth Younger, introduced a new resolution, which the General Assembly passed on October 7. (The vote was 47–5, with 8 abstentions.)

Recalling the General Assembly declaration of 12 December 1948 that there has been established a lawful government (the Government of the Republic of Korea) having effective control and jurisdiction over that part of Korea where the United Nations Temporary Commission on Korea was able to observe and consult and in which the great majority of the people of Korea reside; that this government is based on elections which were a valid expression of the free will of the electorate of that part of Korea and which were observed by the Temporary Commission; and that this is the only such government in Korea,

From *The Record on Korean Unification: 1943–1960: Narrative Summary with Principal Documents* (Washington: US Government Printing Office, 1960), pp. 105–107.

Wide World Photos

Having in mind that United Nations armed forces are at present operating in Korea in accordance with the recommendations of the Security Council of 27 June 1950, subsequent to its resolution of 25 June 1950, that Members of the United Nations furnish such assistance to the Republic of Korea as may be necessary to repel the armed attack and to restore international peace and security in the area,

Recalling that the essential objective of the resolutions of the General Assembly referred to above was the establishment of a unified, independent and democratic Government of Korea,

1. *Recommends that*
   (a) All appropriate steps be taken to ensure conditions of stability throughout Korea;
   (b) All constituent acts be taken, including the holding of elections, under the auspices of the United Nations, for the establishment of a unified, independent and democratic government in the sovereign State of Korea;
   (c) All sections and representative bodies of the population of Korea, South and North, be invited to cooperate with the organs of the United Nations in the restoration of peace, in the holding of elections and in the establishment of a unified government;
   (d) United Nations forces should not remain in any part of Korea otherwise than so far as necessary for achieving the objectives specified in sub-paragraphs (a) and (b) above;
   (e) All necessary measures be taken to accomplish the economic rehabilitation of Korea. . . .

Joint Chiefs of Staff

MESSAGE TO GENERAL MACARTHUR, DECEMBER 6, 1950

On the day the General Assembly passed its new resolution, patrols of the Eighth Army crossed the 38th Parallel. Five days earlier, Chou En-lai, foreign minister of Communist China, summoned the Indian ambassador to China, K. M. Panikkar, to a conference at which Chou warned that China would enter the war if American forces continued north of the 38th Parallel. President Truman and his advisors had already begun to worry about this eventuality. Now President Truman called MacArthur, whom he had never met, to a conference at Wake Island, in the middle of the Pacific. The two men met on October 15. No official transcript was made of the conversations,

From *Hearings*, p. 3536.

and accounts of the conference vary with the political position of the narrator. The Armed Services and Foreign Relations Committees of the Senate published in 1951 a document entitled Substance of Statements made at Wake Island Conference, *compiled by General Omar Bradley, Chairman of the Joint Chiefs of Staff. In that document, President Truman asks, "What are the chances for Chinese or Soviet interference?" General MacArthur answers, "Very little. Had they interfered in the first or second months it would have been decisive. We are no longer fearful of their intervention." MacArthur then expatiates on his answers.*

MacArthur's partisans have, however, given a very different account. General Courtney Whitney, for instance, argues that Truman called the conference for political reasons: to make use of MacArthur's prestige for the mid-term elections, and to make MacArthur seem responsible if the Chinese did, indeed, intervene. In his biography, MacArthur: His Rendezvous with Destiny, *Whitney's account of MacArthur's answer, taken from MacArthur's notes, differs from Bradley's:*

"MacArthur promptly replied [when asked about the chances of Chinese or Russian intervention] that his answer would be purely speculative, but that his guess would be 'very little.' He then explained this viewpoint. Obviously he could only speak from a military standpoint, with its manifest limitations, on a question that revolved fundamentally around a political decision. But as a backdrop to his military speculation, MacArthur proceeded from the premise . . . that there was no evidence from Peiping even suggesting that Red Chinese intervention was under serious consideration. No such intimation had ever been communicated to him by the Defense Department, the State Department, or the Central Intelligence Agency, MacArthur's only sources of political intelligence on which alone such estimates could be made."

At the very time MacArthur and the President were conferring, Chinese troops under the commands of General Chen Yi and General Lin Piao had begun to cross the Yalu River from Manchuria into North Korea.

On October 24, General MacArthur ordered all commanders to drive for the Yalu River. The Joint Chiefs of Staff immediately reminded General MacArthur that they had authorized him, on September 27, to use only South Korean troops in the zone that stretched approximately half-way between the 38th Parallel and the Yalu. General MacArthur reminded the Joint Chiefs that the new Secretary of Defense, General George C. Marshall, had sent him the following message on September 29: "We want you to feel unhampered strategically and tactically to proceed north of the 38th Parallel." Furthermore, argued General MacArthur, South Korean forces were simply inadequate to do the job. The Joint Chiefs acquiesced in MacArthur's interpretation of his orders.

The next day, South Korean soldiers came into contact with Chinese "volunteers" and actually captured one of them. Units of the X Corps were attacked by the Chinese at the same time, and then again in the first week of November. Then the Chinese disappeared.

United Nations forces pressed forward. Elements of the South Korean army reached the Yalu on October 26; patrols from the Seventh Infantry Division of US X Corps reached the river on November 21st. Three days later, MacArthur ordered a full-scale offensive. The next day, November 25, United Nations forces were attacked by 300,000 Chinese soldiers. The retreat that followed—275 miles—was one of the greatest military disasters ever suffered by an American army. It was an entirely new war.

As the military situation worsened, political pressures approached the boiling point. On December 1, MacArthur was interviewed by the editors of U. S. News and World Report. He was asked, "Are the limitations which prevent unlimited pursuit of large Chinese forces and unlimited attack on their bases regarded by you as a handicap to effective military operations?" MacArthur answered, "An enormous handicap, without precedent in military history." The same day, he sent a message to Hugh Baillie, president of the United Press, that included the same complaint: "From the initiation of the North Korean aggression against the Republic of Korea until the total defeat of the North Korean armies, support from the Communist Chinese from behind the privileged sanctuary of neutral boundaries was open and notorious and all-inclusive." There was, insisted MacArthur, a failure in Europe, "intentional or from misinformation, to comprehend the mission prescribed for this command by resolutions of the United Nations. . . ."

Among the specific grievances which MacArthur had in mind when he spoke of "privileged sanctuary" were the inability of UN planes to strike Manchurian airfields, and (after a clash of opinion early in November) to bomb the bridges over the Yalu River.

The Joint Chiefs of Staff promptly set forth the President's response in a directive to MacArthur.

1. The President, as of 5 December, forwarded a memo to all Cabinet members.

> In the light of the present critical international situation, and until further written notice from me, I wish that each one of you would take immediate steps to reduce the number of public speeches pertaining to foreign or military policy made by officials of the departments and agencies of the Executive Branch. This applies to officials in the field as well as those in Washington.
>
> No speech, press release, or other public statement concerning foreign policy should be released until it has received clearance from the Department of State.
>
> No speech, press release, or other statement concerning military policy should be released until it has received clearance from the Department of Defense.
>
> In addition to the copies submitted to the Departments of State or Defense for clearance, advance copies of speeches and press releases

General Douglas MacArthur (center, arms akimbo) is briefed on fighting in the Inchon area by a front-line Marine corps officer. Bodies of three North Korean soldiers are in gully at right. (*Wide World Photos*)

concerning foreign policy or military policy should be submitted to the White House for information.

The purpose of this memorandum is not to curtail the flow of information to the American people, but rather to insure that the information made public is accurate and fully in accord with the policies of the United States Government.

2. He also forwarded the following to the Secretary of State and Secretary of Defense:

In addition to the policy expressed in my memorandum of this date to the heads of departments, concerning the clearance of speeches and statements, I wish the following steps to be taken:

Officials overseas, including military commanders and diplomatic representatives, should be ordered to exercise extreme caution in public statements, to clear all but routine statements with their departments, and to refrain from direct communication on military or foreign policy with newspapers, magazines or other publicity media in the United States.

3. The above is transmitted to you for guidance and appropriate action.

Douglas MacArthur

REPLY TO THE JOINT CHIEFS OF STAFF, DECEMBER 30, 1950

MacArthur's dissatisfaction with Administration policy grew increasingly intense. Realizing that MacArthur's operation directives dated back to September, Truman, Acheson, Marshall, and Bradley conferred to dispatch revised orders. The new directive, dated December 29, ordered MacArthur to maintain his hold on South Korea if this were possible without heavy losses: "A successful resistance to the Chinese-North Korean aggression at some position in Korea and a deflation of the military and political prestige of the Chinese Communists would be of great importance to our national interest." The general's response was a policy proposal of his own.

Any estimate of relative capabilities in the Korean campaign appears to be dependent upon political-military policies yet to be formulated regarding Chinese military operations being conducted against our forces. It is quite clear now that the entire military resources of the Chinese nation, with logistic support from the Soviet, is committed to a maximum effort against the United Nations Command. In implementation of this commitment, a major concentration of Chinese force in the Korean-Manchurian area will increasingly leave China vulnerable to areas from which troops to support Korean operations have been drawn. Meanwhile, under existing restrictions, our naval and air potential are being only partially utilized and the great potential of Chinese Nationalist force on Formosa and guerilla action on the mainland are being ignored. Indeed, as to the former, we are

From *Reminiscences* by Douglas MacArthur, pp. 378–380. Copyright © 1964 by Time, Inc. Used by permission of McGraw-Hill Book Company.

preventing its employment against the common enemy by our own naval force.

Should a policy determination be reached by our government or through it by the United Nations to recognize the state of war which has been forced upon us by the Chinese authorities and to take retaliatory measures within our capabilities, we could: (1) blockade the coast of China; (2) destroy through naval gunfire and air bombardment China's industrial capacity to wage war; (3) secure reinforcements from the Nationalist garrison on Formosa to strengthen our position in Korea if we decide to continue the fight for that peninsula; and (4) release existing restrictions upon the Formosan garrison for diversionary action, possibly leading to counter-invasion against vulnerable areas of the Chinese mainland.

I believe that by the foregoing measures we could severely cripple and largely neutralize China's capability to wage aggressive war and thus save Asia from the engulfment otherwise facing it. I believe furthermore that we could do so with but a small part of our overall military potential committed to the purpose. There is no slightest doubt but that this action would at once release the pressure upon our forces in Korea, whereupon determination could be reached as to whether to maintain the fight in that area or to effect a strategic displacement of our forces with the view to strengthening our defense of the littoral island chain while continuing our naval and air pressure upon China's military potential. I am fully conscious of the fact that this course of action has been rejected in the past for fear of provoking China into a major effort, but we must now realistically recognize that China's commitment thereto has already been fully and unequivocally made and nothing we can do would further aggravate the situation as far as China is concerned.

Whether defending ourselves by way of military retaliation would bring in Soviet military intervention or not is a matter of speculation. I have always felt that a Soviet decision to precipitate a general war would depend solely upon its own estimate of relative strengths and capabilities with little regard to other factors. If we are forced to evacuate Korea without taking military measures against China proper as suggested in your message, it would have the most adverse effect upon the people of Asia, not excepting the Japanese, and a material reinforcement of the forces now in this theatre could be mandatory if we are to hold the littoral defense chain against determined assault. Moreover, it must be borne in mind that evacuation of our forces from Korea under any circumstances would at once release the bulk of the Chinese forces now absorbed by that campaign for action elsewhere—quite probably in areas of far greater importance than Korea itself.

I understand thoroughly the demand for European security and fully concur in doing everything possible in that sector, but not to the point of accepting defeat anywhere else—an acceptance which I am sure could not fail to insure later defeat in Europe itself. The use of force in the present emergency in the Far East could not in any way prejudice this basic concept. To the contrary, it would ensure thoroughly seasoned forces for later commitment in Europe synchronously with Europe's own development of military resources.

Douglas MacArthur

NO SUBSTITUTE FOR VICTORY

MacArthur's message, in the words of one historian of the Korean War, "caused consternation in Washington." On January 9, the Joint Chiefs of Staff rejected MacArthur's proposals. MacArthur, the following day, replied that his men "are embittered by the shameful propaganda which has falsely condemned their fighting qualities and courage in misunderstood retrograde maneuver, are tired from a long and difficult campaign, and unless the political basis upon which they are asked to trade life for time is clearly delineated, fully understood, and so impelling that the hazards of battle are accepted cheerfully, their morale will become a serious threat to their battle efficiency." Under the limitations imposed upon him, the military position of his command was, in the long run, "untenable." He could hold out for a time, but only with "attendant hazard to Japan's security."

On January 13, Truman sent MacArthur a personal letter in which he urged that, at the very worst, UN forces be withdrawn to the offshore islands. Even in that case the world must understand "that that course was forced upon us by military necessity and that we shall not accept the result politically or militarily until the aggression has been rectified." The President also

From *Hearings*, pp. 3543–3544.

reminded the general that the main threat to American security came from the Soviet Union rather than from Communist China.

Fortunately, General Matthew B. Ridgway, who became commander of the Eighth Army after the death of General Walker, was able to rally the UN troops and, on January 25, 1951, resume the offensive. (General Walker was killed when a truck forced his jeep into a rice paddy, December 23. General Ridgway took over the command on December 26.) By March 14, Seoul was recaptured once again.

The military improvement coincided with complete political deterioration. On March 8, Representative Joseph W. Martin, Minority Leader of the House, sent MacArthur a copy of a speech in which he called for Chiang Kai-shek's opening of a "second Asiatic front to relieve the pressure on our forces in Korea." Representative Martin requested MacArthur's opinions and MacArthur sent them in the form of the letter reprinted below, which Martin read to the House of Representatives on April 5.

Dear Congressman Martin: I am most grateful for your note of the 8th forwarding me a copy of your address of February 12. The latter I have read with much interest, and find that with the passage of years you have certainly lost none of your old-time punch.

My views and recommendations with respect to the situation created by Red China's entry into war against us in Korea have been submitted to Washington in most complete detail. Generally these views are well known and clearly understood, as they follow the conventional pattern of meeting force with maximum counter-force as we have never failed to do in the past. Your view with respect to the utilization of the Chinese forces on Formosa is in conflict with neither logic nor this tradition.

It seems strangely difficult for some to realize that here in Asia is where the Communist conspirators have elected to make their play for global conquest, and that we have joined the issue thus raised on the battlefield; that here we fight Europe's war with arms while the diplomats there still fight it with words; that if we lose the war to communism in Asia the fall of Europe is inevitable, win it and Europe most probably would avoid war and yet preserve freedom. As you pointed out, we must win. There is no substitute for victory.

Harry S Truman

OUR AIMS IN KOREA

Four days after MacArthur wrote to Representative Martin, but before Martin made the letter public, the general called upon the commander-in-chief of the Communist forces to enter into negotiations "in the earnest effort to find any military means whereby realization of the political objectives of the United Nations in Korea, to which no nation may justly take exception, might be accomplished without further bloodshed." (For more of this communiqué see below, p. 78.) Truman's response was characteristically vigorous: "By this act MacArthur left me no choice—I could no longer tolerate his insubordination." After consultations with the Joint Chiefs, with Secretary of Defense Marshall and Secretary of State Acheson, Truman decided to relieve MacArthur of his command and to appoint General Ridgway in his place. Six days after MacArthur's letter to Martin was read in the House, Truman informed the nation of his decision.

We do not want to see the conflict in Korea extended. We are trying to prevent a world war—not to start one. The best way to do that is to make it plain that we and the other free countries will continue to resist the attack.

But you may ask why can't we take other steps to punish the aggressor. Why don't we bomb Manchuria and China itself? Why don't we assist Chinese Nationalist troops to land on the mainland of China?

If we were to do these things we would be running a very grave risk of starting a general war. If that were to happen, we would have brought about the exact situation we are trying to prevent.

If we were to do these things, we would become entangled in a vast conflict on the continent of Asia and our task would become immeasurably more difficult all over the world.

What would suit the ambitions of the Kremlin better than for our military forces to be committed to a full-scale war with Red China?

It may well be that, in spite of our best efforts, the Communists may spread the war. But it would be wrong—tragically wrong—for us to take the initiative in extending the war.

The dangers are great. Make no mistake about it. Behind the North Koreans and Chinese Communists in the front lines stand additional

From *Hearings*, pp. 3550–3552.

millions of Chinese soldiers. And behind the Chinese stand the tanks, the planes, the submarines, the soldiers, and the scheming rulers of the Soviet Union.

Our aim is to avoid the spread of the conflict.

The course we have been following is the one best calculated to avoid an all-out war. It is the course consistent with our obligation to do all we can to maintain international peace and security. Our experience in Greece and Berlin shows that it is the most effective course of action we can follow.

First of all, it is clear that our efforts in Korea can blunt the will of the Chinese Communists to continue the struggle. The United Nations forces have put up a tremendous fight in Korea and have inflicted very heavy casualties on the enemy. Our forces are stronger now than they have been before. These are plain facts which may discourage the Chinese Communists from continuing their attack.

Second, the free world as a whole is growing in military strength every day. In the United States, in Western Europe, and throughout the world, free men are alert to the Soviet threat and are building their defenses. This may discourage the Communist rulers from continuing the war in Korea—and from undertaking new acts of aggression elsewhere.

If the Communist authorities realize that they cannot defeat us in Korea, if they realize it would be foolhardy to widen the hostilities beyond Korea, then they may recognize the folly of continuing their aggression. A peaceful settlement may then be possible. The door is always open.

Then we may achieve a settlement in Korea which will not compromise the principles and purposes of the United Nations.

I have thought long and hard about this question of extending the war in Asia. I have discussed it many times with the ablest military advisers in the country. I believe with all my heart that the course we are following is the best course.

I believe that we must try to limit the war to Korea for these vital reasons: To make sure that the precious lives of our fighting men are not wasted, to see that the security of our country and the free world is not needlessly jeopardized and to prevent a third world war.

A number of events have made it evident that General MacArthur did not agree with that policy. I have, therefore, considered it essential to relieve General MacArthur so that there would be no doubt or confusion as to the real purpose and aim of our policy.

It was with the deepest personal regret that I found myself compelled to take this action. General MacArthur is one of our greatest military commanders. But the cause of world peace is more important than any individual.

The change in commands in the Far East means no change whatever in the policy of the United States. We will carry on the fight in Korea with vigor and determination in an effort to bring the war to a speedy and successful conclusion.

The new commander, Lieut. Gen. Matthew Ridgway, has already demonstrated that he has the great qualities of leadership needed for this task.

We are ready, at any time, to negotiate for a restoration of peace in the area. But we will not engage in appeasement. We are only interested in real peace.

Real peace can be achieved through a settlement based on the following factors:

1. The fighting must stop.
2. Concrete steps must be taken to insure that the fighting will not break out again.
3. There must be an end to the aggression.

A settlement founded upon these elements would open the way for the unification of Korea and the withdrawal of all foreign forces.

In the meantime, I want to be clear about our military objective. We are fighting to resist an outrageous aggression in Korea. We are trying to keep the Korean conflict from spreading to other areas. But at the same time we must conduct our military activities so as to insure the security of our forces. This is essential if they are to continue the fight until the enemy abandons its ruthless attempt to destroy the Republic of Korea.

That is our military objective—to repel attack and to restore peace.

In the hard fighting in Korea, we are proving that collective action among nations is not only a high principle but a workable means of resisting aggression. Defeat of aggression in Korea may be the turning point in the world's search for a practical way of achieving peace and security.

The struggle of the United Nations in Korea is a struggle for peace.

The free nations have united their strength in an effort to prevent a third world war.

That war can come if the Communist rulers want it to come. But this Nation and its allies will not be responsible for its coming.

We do not want to widen the conflict. We will use every effort to prevent that disaster. And in so doing, we know that we are following the great principles of peace, freedom, and justice.

Douglas MacArthur

OLD SOLDIERS NEVER DIE

The public uproar that followed MacArthur's relief was immense. Senator Joseph McCarthy denounced Truman in a speech full of personal vilification, and Senator William E. Jenner proclaimed that the nation was "in the hands of a secret inner coterie which is directed by agents of the Soviet Union." Richard Rovere and Arthur Schlesinger, Jr., comment ironically on the times: "All in all, it was an eventful period in the history of the Presidency: booed in public and publically burned in effigy, the incumbent had been described by responsible officials as an assassin, a rumpot, a son of a bitch, a plotter, and a heedless sacrificer of American lives; he had been characterized in the Congressional Record as a fish, a pig, a stupidity, a B. and a traitor."

MacArthur, on the other hand, was invited to address Congress. After reviewing the military situation in the Far East, his address ended with the following peroration.

Once war is forced upon us, there is no other alternative than to apply every available means to bring it to a swift end. War's very object is victory—not prolonged indecision. In war, indeed, there can be no substitute for victory.

There are some who for varying reasons would appease Red China. They are blind to history's clear lesson. For history teaches

From *Hearings*, pp. 3553–3558.

with unmistakable emphasis that appeasement but begets new and bloodier war. It points to no single instance where the end has justified that means—where appeasement has led to more than a sham peace. Like blackmail, it lays the basis for new and successively greater demands, until, as in blackmail, violence becomes the only other alternative. Why, my soldiers asked of me, surrender military advantages to an enemy in the field? I could not answer. Some may say to avoid spread of the conflict into an all-out war with China; others, to avoid Soviet intervention. Neither explanation seems valid. For China is already engaging with the maximum power it can commit and the Soviet will not necessarily mesh its actions with our moves. Like a cobra, any new enemy will more likely strike whenever it feels that the relativity in military or other potential is in its favor on a world-wide basis.

The tragedy of Korea is further heightened by the fact that as military action is confined to its territorial limits, it condemns that nation, which it is our purpose to save, to suffer the devastating impact of full naval and air bombardment, while the enemy's sanctuaries are fully protected from such attack and devastation. Of the nations of the world, Korea alone, up to now, is the sole one which has risked its all against communism. The magnificence of the courage and fortitude of the Korean people defies description. They have chosen to risk death rather than slavery. Their last words to me were "Don't scuttle the Pacific."

I have just left your fighting sons in Korea. They have met all tests there and I can report to you without reservation they are splendid in every way. It was my constant effort to preserve them and end this savage conflict honorably and with the least loss of time and a minimum sacrifice of life. Its growing bloodshed has caused me the deepest anguish and anxiety. Those gallant men will remain often in my thoughts and in my prayers always.

I am closing my 52 years of military service. When I joined the Army even before the turn of the century, it was the fulfillment of all my boyish hopes and dreams. The world has turned over many times since I took the oath on the plain at West Point, and the hopes and dreams have long since vanished. But I still remember the refrain of one of the most popular barracks ballads of that day which proclaimed most proudly that—"Old soldiers never die; they just fade away." And like the old soldier of that ballad, I now close my military career and just fade away—an old soldier who tried to do his duty as God gave him the light to see that duty.

Good-by.

Douglas MacArthur

TESTIMONY BEFORE THE SENATE ARMED SERVICES AND FOREIGN RELATIONS COMMITTEES

Early in May, when the tumult of MacArthur's return had subsided somewhat, the Senate began an inquiry into the military situation in the Far East. As Senator Richard Russell during the hearings put it, "Today we are opening hearings on momentous questions. These questions affect not only the lives of every citizen, but they are vital to the security of our country and the maintenance of our institutions of free government."

The first witness was General MacArthur. Although the questions covered a variety of subjects, two themes were prominent. The first covered below is the question of insubordination.

Senator Styles Bridges. General MacArthur, do you question the right of the President of the United States to dismiss you? Did you or do you now?

General MacArthur. You mean to recall me?

Senator Bridges. Yes.

General MacArthur. Not in the slightest. The authority of the President to assign officers or to reassign them is complete and absolute. He does not have to give any reasons therefor or anything else. That is inherent in our system.

Senator Bridges. How did you first receive word of your recall?

General MacArthur. I received it from my wife. One of my aides had heard the broadcast and instantly told her, and she informed me.

From *Hearings,* pp. 26–28, 98–100, 102, 282–283; and 39–45, 67–68, 138–139, 146–147, 167–168, 259–260.

Senator Bridges. You received it via the radio before you had any official notice?

General MacArthur. Yes, sir.

Senator Bridges. How long after your aide had told Mrs. MacArthur that he had heard it on the radio did you receive your official communication?

General MacArthur. Oh, I should say within 30 minutes, perhaps, or an hour. I couldn't tell you.

Senator Bridges. Were you recalled with the action to take effect summarily, immediately?

General MacArthur. The order relieved me of the command upon receipt.

Senator Bridges. Is that a customary procedure?

General MacArthur. I have never known it in the American army, and I know of no precedence anyplace. Being summarily relieved in that way made it impossible to carry out directives that I was working on at that moment. I had to turn them over to my successor, an admirable officer in every respect, General Ridgway, who was 350 miles away on the Korean front.

I don't think there is any question that the interest of the United States was jeopardized in such a summary mode of turning over great responsibilities which involve the security of the country.

Senator Bridges. And is it customary in the recall of a commander, to do it in such a manner that he will be able to turn over his command to his successor and brief him upon the current status of the operation?

General MacArthur. Unquestionably.

Senator Bridges. Have you ever, to your knowledge, refused to carry out a military order given you?

General MacArthur. Senator, I have been a soldier for 52 years, I have in that time, to the best of my ability, carried out every order that was ever given me. No more subordinate soldier has ever worn the American uniform.

I would repudiate any concept that I wouldn't carry out any order that was given me. If you mean to say that the orders I have carried out I was in agreement with, that is a different matter.

Many of the orders that I have received, I have disagreed with them, both their wisdom and their judgment; but that did not affect in the slightest degree my implementing them to the very best and maximum of my ability.

Any insinuation by anyone, however high his office, that I have ever in any way failed, to the level of my ability, to carry out my instructions, is completely unworthy and unwarranted.

Senator Wayne Morse. Do you think it would be a fair statement that the disagreement if any which arises between you and the Administration is that apparently some in the Administration feel that we cannot take a chance now that Russia will not become involved in the war until more time has elapsed for the strengthening of our defenses both in Asia and in Europe? Is it your understanding that that is the attitude of some in the Administration?

General MacArthur. I really couldn't speak for the Administration, Senator.

Senator Morse. Let me put the question this way. Is it your understanding that one of the reasons why you did not get authorization to broaden the Korean War was because it was felt that such action at this time might bring Russia into the war?

General MacArthur. It is quite possible.

Senator Morse. Have you heard it said, General, that that was one of the reasons for your recall?

General MacArthur. Senator, I do not know why I was recalled. The only statement that I have seen on it is the order for my recall.

Senator Morse. Well, what I said is, Was it your understanding that that was one of the reasons?

General MacArthur. That statement was of a nature which expressed the President's belief that I could not give wholehearted support to the policies of the United States and of the United Nations in the Far East.

So far as I know, I have completely implemented, to the best of my ability, every directive, every policy that was given to me, but there is no possible charge that I have failed to carry out and implement or even to take exception to any announced policy that the United States or the United Nations has made.

I can only interpret that order that the Administration, knowing the views I held, was going to act in a very contrary way, and believed it was advisable not to place any strain upon my loyalty, if you might put it that way, and relieved me of the command.

Senator Morse. As I said the other day—

General MacArthur. It must have been based upon what they had in mind for the future. It could not possibly have been based upon anything in the past.

I had made certain recommendations, most of which—in fact, practically all, as far as I know—were in complete accord with the military recommendations of the Joint Chiefs of Staff, and all other commanders.

Now, I have no knowledge whatsoever, today, as to why I was relieved, except the orders of the President.

I have said before that the President is under no obligation to explain his actions. He acted within his complete authority, and his responsibility, and I don't challenge either, in any way, shape, or manner.

Senator Morse. I think you have made an—

General MacArthur. But, as to the reasons of my recall, I am still completely uninformed, because the reasons contained in the order are not valid.

If the President had given a decision which was exactly contrary to the recommendations I had made, I would, to the best of my ability, have carried them out completely and absolutely.

My recommendations were seeking decisions, seeking policy directives. I felt that the position I was in, the military position, was untenable without having some directive, some mission which was more realistic than that which existed at the time; and I felt, in all conscience, I could not go on ordering men to their deaths by the thousands, in such a complete vacuum of policy decision.

There is nothing that I am aware of, of the slightest tinge of insubordination, or of dictation or anything that conflicted with any decision that has been made.

I merely first asked for decisions, and when they were not forthcoming, I gave my own recommendations.

Now, many of those, as I said, are completely in accord with the military and professional opinions that at that time were given by the Joint Chiefs of Staff.

Now, the opinion that the President expressed, as I read the order, and try to interpret it, is that something was in mind, that the Administration had in mind, that was so violative of the concept that

I had that it was thought best to relieve me, rather than charge me with their execution.

There has no charge ever been made to me, or publicly, that I know of, that I failed in any respect to try to carry out the directives I received; or any charge that I had disagreed with what had been decided upon. . . .

*   *   *

[*During MacArthur's testimony a second theme emerged and eventually became dominant: Why was MacArthur at odds with the Truman Administration? What were the two concepts of war adhered to by the two sides in the controversy?*]

Senator Leverett Saltonstall. General MacArthur, might I ask you about three or four questions that appear to me as important?

Now, what it seems to me that we are trying to do is to get security for our country, our own country, and to get a peace and a policy in the Far East.

I have been very much worried to try to find out what is our policy in the Far East, particularly with relation to Korea; and I read your speech in Chicago where, I think, you asked that same question twice.

Now, on April 15, the Assistant Secretary of State, Dean Rusk, in a television and press broadcast, stated, in part—and this is the pertinent part of his speech, as I read it:

> *What we are trying to do is to maintain peace and security without a general war. We are saying to the aggressors, "You will not be allowed to get away with your crime. You must stop it."*
>
> *At the same time, we are trying to prevent a general conflagration which would consume the very things we are now trying to defend.*

I would appreciate it very much, with your knowledge of the Far East, if you will give me your opinion of that statement, and if that is a practical policy.

General MacArthur. That policy, as you have read it, seems to me to introduce a new concept into military operations—the concept of appeasement, the concept that when you use force, you can limit that force.

The concept that I have is that when you go into war, you have exhausted all other potentialities of bringing the disagreements to an end.

As I understand what you read, that we would apply to the military situation in Korea certain military appeasements—that is, that we would not use our air forces to their maximum extent, only to the limited area of that Korea; that we would not use our navy, except along the borderlines of Korea.

To me, that would mean that you would have a continued and indefinite extension of bloodshed, which would have limitless—a limitless end.

You would not have the potentialities of destroying the enemy's military power, and bringing the conflict to a decisive close in the minimum of time, and with a minimum of loss.

It seems to me the worst possible concept, militarily, that we would simply stay there, resisting aggression, so-called, although I do not know what you mean by "resisting aggression."

The very term of "resisting aggression," it seems to me that you destroy the potentialities of the aggressor to continually hit you.

If that is the concept of a continued and indefinite campaign in Korea, with no definite purpose of stopping it until the enemy gets tired or you yield to his terms, I think that introduces into the military sphere a political control such as I have never known in my life or have ever studied.

Senator Saltonstall. In other words, you feel that the Korean situation, having gone into an armed conflict, it should be brought to an end in the quickest possible way through a military victory.

General MacArthur. I do, Senator, exactly; and I believe if you do not do that, if you hit soft, if you practice appeasement in the use of force, you are doomed to disaster.

I believe that if you continue that way, you are inviting the very thing that you desire to stop—the spread of the conflict.

Senator Saltonstall. Then assuming that your four recommendations, as made in your address to Congress, were all adopted, what do you visualize as the result?

General MacArthur. I believe that if you carry that out, you stand the best chance that is possible of ending this war in the quickest time and with the least cost in blood.

In fact, I haven't seen any other proposal as to how you would expect to bring it to an end except by agreeing to the enemy's terms.

Senator Saltonstall. And you think that if your four recommendations were carried into effect, it would not necessarily spread the war into Manchuria and China, but by quick and effective action of our power, it would be sufficiently limited to Korea as to be brought to an end in that general vicinity?

General MacArthur. I don't think that if you apply the measures that I advocate, which were the measures that the Joint Chiefs of Staff recommended on January 12, that you will necessarily confine the area of the conflict to Korea; but I believe it will give you an opportunity to hit the enemy where he is assembling to hit you.

Senator Saltonstall. Now, may I ask this question on a slightly different subject. In this so-called Wake Island conference statement on page 8, on the printed copy, the President is quoted as saying this:

> *General MacArthur and I have talked fully about Formosa. There is no need to cover that subject again. The general and I are in complete agreement.*

I believe that was also the purport of a communiqué issued at that time. Is that a fair statement of the President's and your position when you conferred on Formosa, if you care to say? That was a private communication, of course.

General MacArthur. I don't think the communiqué had any reference to Formosa, Senator, and I think that when the President said that he and I were in agreement about Formosa, that he meant the agreement was that both of us had dropped the question of discussing it there at Wake Island, or at any other time.

The strategic situation of Formosa, its value, and its general relativity to security in the Far East was not discussed by me with the President.

Now, I would not feel at liberty to reveal what was discussed by the President with me in our conference before the main conference.

Senator Saltonstall. I respect that.

General MacArthur. But I do offer that explanation of what I am sure the President had in mind when he made that statement.

Senator Saltonstall. I respect your position with relation to your conference with the President.

I would say, most respectfully, that I would think that that statement, the interpretation of an ordinary person, particularly in Congress, would give that statement, "We are in complete accord," would lead to a different inference.

General MacArthur. I agree with you 100 percent, Senator; and the same concept hit me in Tokyo, and the next day I issued a statement through the spokesman in Tokyo stating that there had been absolutely no change on my part in any views I held as to the strategic value of Formosa.

Senator Saltonstall. May I ask you, sir, one more question. In your address to the Congress you stated that you felt that military necessity and the conduct of the war—and I think I quote you accurately from here on—"removal of restrictions on the forces of the Republic of China on Formosa with logistical support to contribute to their effective operation against the Chinese mainland."

My question is: Just what do you visualize this logistical support would amount to in the way of men, materiel, and ships, as well as air support?

General MacArthur. The quotation from my statement is incorrect, Senator. What I said was not with reference to the Chinese mainland, but what I said was against the common enemy. As I explained this morning—or tried to—the use of troops, the Chinese Nationalist troops—should be left to the judgment of the Chinese commander in chief; and I tried to explain the various ways in which he might use those troops.

It is an absolutely incorrect statement, which I have great difficulty in comprehending why it was made, because I gave a copy of my statement to the Clerk of the Senate or the House, whoever was there, and it was recorded and you will find that there was a misquotation on it.

What I said was against the common enemy. I did not attempt to limit the use of the Chinese troops on the mainland.

Senator Saltonstall. The misquotation on my part—

General MacArthur. What we have recommended there, as I said this morning, I appointed a commission that went down there with the approval of Washington, who made a full report after two months of study of what materiel was necessary to place the troops, the Nationalist troops on Formosa, in a condition of general preparedness for fighting.

That report has been in general approved, and as I understand, is being carried out now.

Senator Saltonstall. Mr. Chairman, I thank the General. I have no more questions now. I would like to reserve the right to perhaps ask questions at a future time.

Senator Theodore Green. General, in the first place I would like to join with Senator Smith in thanking you for your kind hospitality in Tokyo in 1949.

General MacArthur. We still remember that visit with great pleasure out there, Senator.

Senator Green. What I would like to ask is a question which seems to me to go to the basis of the whole difference that has been developed. It is this:

The theory that we could win a quick victory in China simply by lending logistic support to the Chinese troops now in Formosa and in bombarding the coast cities and in establishing blockage would, in the first place, would it not, indicate we would proceed alone and not with any help from the other United Nations?

General MacArthur. I can give you no testimony about the United Nations, Senator.

Senator Green. What would be your expectation?

General MacArthur. My hope would be of course that the United Nations would see the wisdom and utility of that course, but if they did not, I still believe that the interest of the United States being the predominant one in Korea, would require our action.

Senator Green. Alone?

General MacArthur. Alone, if necessary. If the other nations of the world haven't got enough sense to see where appeasement leads after the appeasement which led to the Second World War in Europe, if they can't see exactly the road that they are following in Asia, why then we had better protect ourselves and go it alone.

Senator Green. Then why do you think that the Chinese now in Formosa, even with that help and without our ground forces in China, could achieve a victory when Chiang Kai-shek suffered such a severe defeat previously?

General MacArthur. I don't believe that the Chinese Nationalist forces alone, Senator, could achieve any such victory, but using them in conjunction with our own forces in accordance with the recommendations the Joint Chiefs of Staff made January 12, I believe that we would achieve a victory within a reasonable period of time.

I believe that the Chinese, the potential of China to wage modern war, is limited. She lacks the industrial base upon which modern war is based.

She is unable herself to turn out an air force or to turn out a navy. She is unable to supply herself with some of the heavier munitions.

I believe that the minute the pressure was placed upon her distributive system, the minute you stop the flow of strategic materials which has been going on so extensively since the Korean War started, that she would be unable to maintain in the field even the armies that she has now.

What I mean to say is if she has now an army of four or five million men, after the blockade, after the breaking up of her distributive systems due to her enormous poverty, due to the fact that she is only a couple of jumps ahead of starvation at any time at all, that that pressure of blockade and of concentrated attack upon her supply lines would make it impossible for her to maintain anything like four million men in the field. Perhaps a million men, perhaps half that.

She, I believe, has the inherent weaknesses for modern war of relying entirely upon ground forces and not having the industrial system to even supply them.

I believe that against the modern scientific methods of the United Nations, the potential of the United Nations, of the United States, if you would have it so, is sufficient to force the Chinese to stop their aggression in Korea.

We have no desire to destroy China, quite the contrary. You know from your own erudite and long experience of the innate friendship between the two countries. But we do have a great desire to make her stop her aggressive attacking in Korea.

I believe when you hit her base potential that way she would be forced to stop her aggression in Korea. I believe under those conditions she would talk a reasonable cease-fire procedure.

Senator Green. You do not think then that she would further call upon America for ground forces as well as air and sea forces?

General MacArthur. I don't know whether anybody would call on the United States for ground forces, but I do know it would be utterly reckless and foolish for the United States to even consider it. I do not believe it would be necessary.

Senator Green. The last experience they had in China when the Japanese attacked with air, sea, and land forces, was that China successfully resisted, although not so well equipped then as the Nationalist troops would be now.

General MacArthur. The objective of Japan and our objective, Senator, is different as day and night. The objective of Japan was to conquer, occupy, control and exploit all of China. Our only objective is to force the Chinese to stop their attacks in Korea on our troops. The two things are entirely different.

Senator Green. Well, are not masses of China now, the population of China, as much opposed to Chiang Kai-shek's forces as they were then to the Japanese invasion?

General MacArthur. I couldn't tell you Senator.

Senator Green. If that were true, then why would not the result be the same?

General MacArthur. The general reports from China, of course, are growing restlessness under the slavery of totalitarian rule. Just how far that may have gone, I don't know. The Chinese on Formosa will tell you it has gone a long way. The reports that come in indicate that. But without the intimate knowledge that would come from personal presence, I wouldn't attempt to act as a seer and answer such basic questions as that.

I do say unhesitatingly that with the power that we could bring against her with our air and navy, with the assistance of the ground forces that the Nationalists might summon, that I believe we can force her to stop her aggression in Korea, which is the only objective as far as I see it, that we would have in such a conflict.

Now you speak of American forces being sucked into China, ground forces. I invite your attention to the fact that hundreds of thousands of American Ground Forces have already been committed in Korea, and if you keep on this indecisive fighting, hundreds of thousands of more of them will go there.

Our losses already, the battle casualties, are approaching 65,000. This conflict in Korea has already lasted almost as long as General

Eisenhower's decisive campaign which brought the European war to an end. And yet the only program that I have been able to hear is that we shall indecisively go on resisting aggression, whatever that may mean. And if you do, you are going to have thousands and thousands and thousands of American lives that will fall, and in my own opinion events finally will catch up with you, so that you will have to stop it in some way; and then the great question is—Where does the responsibility of that blood rest?

This I am quite sure—It is not going to rest on my shoulders.

Senator Green. As I understand it, the pressure that could be brought in the south, you count upon to reduce the pressure in Korea to such an extent that it would be a quick victory in Korea?

General MacArthur. What I said, Senator, was that if you use the Chinese forces on Formosa for a diversionary effect, and force the enemy to operate on another front, you will unquestionably diminish the pressure upon our forces in Korea, and thereby you will save American blood and American efforts.

Senator Green. I understand how it might save that in Korea, but would it not increase it in China by more than what you save in Korea? If you get or you could get thereby a quick victory in Korea, it does not assure, or does it assure, you of a quick victory in China? Have we not substituted a greater problem for a lesser one? That is the thing that bothers me, and that is the reason I am asking these questions.

General MacArthur. I believe that if you will hit the Chinese and stop their potentials for war, you will bring peace not only to Korea but you will bring peace to China—that is as far as you can bring it.

Senator Green. Well, there is one other—

General MacArthur. The great problem, as I see it, in Korea, the great problem is to stop this sacrifice of American blood that has not got any definite end to it, as I see it.

Senator Green. There is one other phase to the question which applies to both Korea and China, which you touched upon, and that is this: You have dealt with these questions in both countries on a purely military basis. But isn't our government required to give consideration and decide upon it on both a military and a political basis? Can you separate them so distinctly and say that a military victory is a political victory?

General MacArthur. I think that it is quite impossible to draw a line of differentiation and say this is a political and this is a military situation.

The American Government should have such coordination so that the political and military are in coordination.

The general definition which for many decades has been accepted was that war was the ultimate process of politics; that when all other political means failed, you then go to force; and when you do that, the balance of control, the balance of concept, the main interest involved, the minute you reach the killing stage, is the control of the military. A theater commander, in any campaign, is not merely limited to the handling of his troops; he commands that whole area politically economically, and militarily. You have got to trust at that stage of the game when politics fails, and the military takes over, you must trust the military, or otherwise you will have the system that the Soviet once employed of the political commissar, who would run the military as well as the politics of the country.

*   *   *

General MacArthur. The only way I know, when a nation wars on you, is to beat her by force. I do not know of any argument that will bring an end to this thing.

War, in itself, is the application of superior force, and as we chose that path, and have entered upon that path, it seems to me that we must end it in some way.

Now, there are only three ways that I can see, as I said this morning: Either to pursue it to victory; to surrender to an enemy and end it on his terms; or, what I think is the worst of all choices, to go on indefinitely and indefinitely, neither to win nor lose, in that stalemate; because what we are doing is sacrificing thousands of men while we are doing it.

If you could just say that this line stops aggression, and we didn't lose the men, that would be a different thing; but every day over there you have this terrific and savage conflict, the most savage I ever fought in; and you are losing the very flower of our youth, and if you keep on month after month, and month after month, why, these losses are going to mount up to figures which would stagger the imagination.

Now, in that third process of merely continuing, as has been projected in some circles, that leads to an indefinite sacrifice of lives.

Senator Morse. Will the general let me say that—

General MacArthur. Now, war never before in the history of the world has been applied in a piecemeal way, that you make half war, and not whole war.

Now, that China is using the maximum of her force against us is quite evident; and we are not using the maximum of ours against her, in reply.

The result is—we do not even use, to the maximum, the forces at our disposal, the scientific methods, and the result is that for every percentage you take away in the use of the air and the navy, you add a percentage to the dead American infantrymen.

It may seem emotional for me to say that, but I happen to be the man that had to send them into it. The blood, to some extent, would rest on me; and with the objectives, I believe I could stop them—it seems terrific to me that we should not attempt something.

The inertia that exists. There is no policy—there is nothing, I tell you, no plan, or anything.

When you say, merely, "we are going to continue to fight aggression," that is not what the enemy is fighting for.

The enemy is fighting for a very definite purpose—to destroy our forces in Korea.

We constantly, every day, run that risk, without the potential of defeating him, and stopping him—to come again.

He attacks today. We resist it. We fall back. We form a new line, and we surge back.

Then, he is right back, within a week, maybe, up to the battle front with his inexhaustible supply of manpower. He brings in another hundred thousand, or another half-million men, and tosses them at these troops constantly.

That is a new concept in war.

That is not war—that is appeasement.

* * *

Senator William Fulbright. . . . Certainly if we should accept your basic philosophy of war, and that is to proceed to victory without any dilly-dallying along, without any what you call appeasement, without anything short of a decisive victory, then there is no stopping point once we become committed. Then what happens to us? As to my own thinking, I am a little more worried about Russia not coming in than I am of her coming in [to help] China, because if we become committed there, it seems to me she really is given a free hand in Europe and in the rest of the world. What really bothers us is the situation in the Middle East and Europe, if we really become committed to the point of having to supply very large forces of ground troops, and particularly air power in China.

I think that central question of whether or not this can be done in a relatively quick and definite decisive way is the key point to many other problems. That was why I was hoping you would develop it in a little fuller way, because this precedent of Japan's recent experience in that area makes it rather difficult to accept that it would be an easy sort of undertaking.

General MacArthur. The alternative Senator, is to sacrifice thousands and thousands and thousands of American boys month after month after month.

Not only that, but you will have sacrificed, if you keep on indefinitely, the entire Korean nation and people. The high moral reason for our intervention in Korea was to save Korea. If you do not continue and save her, you are going to destroy her.

She is pretty well destroyed now. This question of stopping halfway, of completely destroying the moral tone which caused us to intervene in Korea, completely ignoring the enormous bloodshed which goes on there month after month, that very concept shocks me, old soldier as I am. If these risks that you speak of were so real and so compelling, why did we intervene in Korea?

There is nothing that has happened that has changed those risks or increased those risks. The whole moral tone of the world resounded when in its nobility the United States and the United Nations following them intervened to save Korea.

At one stroke you would abandon that, at one stroke. You don't pay the slightest attention to that 30 millions of people in Korea, and that great nation and our own boys by the thousands and thousands.

I have been here two days now, and I have heard no proposition yet, outside of the ones that the Joint Chiefs made and myself, which would offer any hope for a successful conclusion of the Korean struggle.

I believe it would mean that if you don't attempt to bring this thing to a short and honorable conclusion, it means not only the indefinite sacrifice of life, but it means what is almost equally important, the complete degradation and sacrifice of our moral tone.

Senator Fulbright. . . . There is one other idea, General, that I think many of us are confused about. That is the idea that anything short of a complete victory in an all-out effort to end it by force of arms in the Orient would be called appeasement.

In other words, the word "appeasement" has come to have a sort of all-inclusive meaning. It does not seem to me that a negotiated peace, for example, is necessarily appeasement. Do you think so?

General MacArthur. Senator, I have my own definition of appeasement that might disagree with yours. I believe when you enter into war, you should use sufficient force to impose your will upon the enemy. The only purpose we have in the Korean conflict is to make the enemy stop his depredations. It isn't his conquest. It hasn't got an ounce of imperialism in it at all.

I believe that we do have the power to do so without sacrificing any of our other interests, and I do not believe in doing so that we in the slightest degree prejudice the beginning of another world war. On the contrary, I have said repeatedly I believe that it would have the opposite effect.

Senator Fulbright. Well, I understood at one time that you were willing to have a cease-fire in Korea. Wasn't that short of an all-out victory?

General MacArthur. I would be glad to have a cease-fire in Korea on honorable terms at any time. I have had no other thought and hope in the last ten months than to bring it to an honorable end with the least bloodshed that is possible.

Every recommendation I have made is to that end and to that purpose and none other. The glorification of a so-called overall victory or conquest, as you put it, has never entered my thoughts. What I am anxious to do is to bring the enemy to a round-table discussion on an honorable basis which will cause him to stop his depredation.

He is the aggressor without cause or reason. He is the one that sprung that foul blow on us. It's to stop that that we fight, and I say that anything that does not tend to stop that is in my lexicon appeasement.

Senator Fulbright. Well, I think that puts a little different light on it from what I had understood before. I mean that the only way would be, in effect, unconditional surrender. By the way, did you feel that the policy of—

General MacArthur. I don't know what you mean by "unconditional surrender," Senator. The only thing that the United Nations and the United States as its agent has ever demanded is a liberated, unified Korea.

Never by word or deed [have] they indicated that they had any other concept. The enemy, on the other hand, has openly announced its purposes which involve the complete destruction of our forces, the complete occupation of Korea, the forcing upon Korea of a totalitarian system of government.

All of those things have been announced, but the only purpose that we have as I see it, is to stop the depredation of the Chinese Communist forces in North Korea, and their allies, the North Koreans.

I have endeavored to the best of my ability to suggest a discussion of honorable terms to end this war. We have been met at every turn by that, by the introduction of other political efforts, the recognition of Red China, which has nothing to do with the Korean conflict, the turning over of Formosa, which has nothing to do with the Korean conflict. Those are the insistence of the enemy before he sits down.

Those, if they were accepted, would again fit my definition of appeasement.

Senator Fulbright. Well, do you feel our government has accepted those principles that you have just mentioned?

General MacArthur. Do I feel that our government has accepted them?

Senator Fulbright. Yes.

General MacArthur. No, sir. Those are the demands of the enemy, and as I said today, the Joint Chiefs of Staff within the month have recommended that in the discussion of cease-fire terms, that neither of those appeasement policies should be acceptable even for discussion. What the attitude of our government is, I don't know, but I would doubt very much that it would consider such terms.

Senator Morse. You say, General, that you are opposed to a limited war in Korea, but some are saying that, in effect, what you are really proposing is a limited war in China. Do you think that is a fair evaluation of your proposal?

General MacArthur. I do not, sir. I do not call it a fair evaluation of my concept in any way, shape, or manner. I said that we should put such pressure on Red China as would force her to stop her war in North Korea.

Senator Morse. That is my next question.

General MacArthur. It has nothing to do with geographical limitations of introducing war into China, except to put such pressure on her as would bring her Korean adventure to a cessation.

Senator Morse. That goes to my next question, in part in repetition, but I think it needs to be clarified.

If the program which you have outlined to us, which in essence, as I understand it, is first an ultimatum and then a deliverance on that ultimatum—bombing of the sources of supply—does not in fact stop the aggression in Korea, how much further do you think we ought to go with the war in China?

General MacArthur. I believe that the methods I have proposed will be completely effective. I believe that we can bring a sufficient blockade and air attack to unquestionably force China to diminish her effort in North Korea.

I believe—I wouldn't attempt to predict the exact time that that would be accomplished but, applied long enough, I believe its results would be a certainty.

I do not believe you need to go any further than those provisions. The length of time that you have to apply those provisions is problematical, but apply them. Sooner or later they will bring the results in my opinion.

Senator Morse. Is it fair to say, General, if—I am sorry I have to talk in terms of so many "if's"—if, after whatever you considered to be a reasonable time for applying those pressures, the Chinese aggression continued, either because they are supplied with more and more material from Soviet Russia or with other assistance from Soviet Russia, or for whatever cause, would you then, in carrying out the principle that we must meet this resistance until we have a victory over it, say we would have to then enlarge our military operations against China?

General MacArthur. No, sir. I say and repeat that I believe the application of that force, continued long enough, would accomplish completely the purpose I have in mind. If the Chinese continued to resist, we would continue to apply those forces until the time would come when those forces would force her to cease her campaign in North Korea.

In my belief that time would come as a certainty. It would be the continuation of that pressure until it produced the results.

Now, if the implication that the question implies—do I believe that we should introduce ground troops to support that movement in continental China—the answer is conclusively in the negative.

Senator Morse. I didn't have that in mind, because I think you made perfectly clear time and time again in the record that you are opposed to the introduction of ground forces—

General MacArthur. Completely.

Senator Morse. In China, and on the basis of my understanding of the military problems that would be involved in a ground war in China, I certainly agree because I doubt if you can win that kind of war, but I will tell you what I had in mind. I was going to ask it in the next question.

Although I realize you think it is a matter of certainty that you would win that way, I would like to find out what we might then have to do if you might be proven wrong about that and we didn't win that way. Would we then be justified in issuing an ultimatum to China that we would use the atomic bomb unless she stopped her aggression in Korea?

General MacArthur. Of course, when you get on the atomic bomb, you have gotten on territory that I can't comment on. The President of the United States has reserved the control or, so far as I know, the discussion of the use of the bomb within his own hands. It would be a matter at his own discretion, whether he wished to supplement the bombing attacks on China by the use of the atomic bomb.

I have never, of course, discussed the use of the bomb with him in any way, shape, or manner; so I wouldn't be able to give you any information whatsoever on that subject.

Senator Morse. As I understand your position, I respectfully point out that, however, as a people, in the event of the possibility that I referred to coming to pass, that we couldn't win an ultimate victory in the Korean War along the lines that you recommend, we as a people then have the right to make clear what we think ought to be done to end it; and on the basis of that assumption, I raise my question.

I meant to imply would it not be better to resort to stronger bombing methods, including atomic warfare, than to risk the lives of millions of American soldiers on the soil of China?

General MacArthur. The use of the atomic weapon would certainly represent a great reserve potential which we could exercise at the discretion of the Commander in Chief.

George C. Marshall
TESTIMONY BEFORE THE ARMED SERVICES AND FOREIGN RELATIONS COMMITTEES

Before his appointment as Secretary of Defense, General Marshall had been, among other things, Chief of Staff of the US Army during World War II and Secretary of State during the postwar period. Marshall and General Eisenhower (then in Europe as NATO commander) were the only American military leaders comparable in prestige to MacArthur. Marshall's testimony began on May 7 with a prepared statement, and continued, with one day's interruption, through May 14. The published text from which the following excerpts are taken occupies four hundred pages.

General Marshall. From the very beginning of the Korean conflict, down to the present moment, there has been no disagreement between the President, the Secretary of Defense, and the Joint Chiefs of Staff that I am aware of.

There have been, however, and continue to be basic differences of judgment between General MacArthur, on the one hand, and the President, the Secretary of Defense, and the Joint Chiefs of Staff, on the other hand.

In his testimony last week, General MacArthur indicated that, in

From *Hearings*, pp. 323–326, 644–646.

his understanding, there had been at least two instances in which the Joint Chiefs of Staff had been overruled by the Secretary of Defense or by higher authority.

One of these instances related to the views expressed by the Joint Chiefs of Staff with respect to the disposition of Formosa and the seating of the Communist Chinese Government in the United Nations.

In his testimony of May 4, General MacArthur suggested that I as Secretary of Defense had overruled the Joint Chiefs of Staff in their opposition to turning Formosa over to Communist China and seating Communist China in the United Nations.

At the time I became Secretary of Defense last September, the established policy of the United States was to deny Formosa to Communist China and to oppose the seating of the Communist Chinese in the United Nations.

There has been no deviation from that policy whatsoever. At no time have I entertained the opinion that there should be any deviation. These two issues were to be excluded from any armistice terms.

When the time comes for the negotiation of a settlement of the conflict in Korea, the questions of Formosa and the seating of the Chinese Communists in the United Nations will undoubtedly be raised by other parties to the discussion.

The position which the United States has taken in the United Nations in connection with such negotiations is that this government will not oppose discussion of these questions. In such discussions, however, I am confident that the United States will continue to adhere to its present position, namely, that it will oppose any settlement of the Korean conflict which would reward the aggressor in any manner whatever, and it will oppose the attempt of any nation or regime to shoot its way into the United Nations.

The second instance referred to by General MacArthur, of a supposed overruling or veto of the views of the Joint Chiefs of Staff, relates to the courses of action proposed by the Joint Chiefs of Staff in a memorandum addressed by them to the Secretary of Defense under date of January 12, 1951. Of 16 courses of action enumerated in the memorandum, the following 4 were quoted by General MacArthur in his testimony of May 3:

Continue and intensify now an economic blockade of trade with China.

> *Prepare now to impose a naval blockade of China and place it into*
> *effect as soon as our position in Korea is stabilized, or when we have*
> *evacuated Korea, and depending upon circumstances then obtaining.*
> *Remove now restrictions on air reconnaissance of China coastal areas*
> *and of Manchuria.*
> *Remove now the restrictions on operations of the Chinese Nationalist*
> *forces and give such logistic support to those forces as will contribute to*
> *effective operations against the Communists.*

At the time this memorandum was prepared, we were faced with the very real possibility of having to evacuate our forces from Korea. The proposals advanced by the Joint Chiefs of Staff, which I have just quoted, were put forward as tentative courses of action to be pursued if and when this possibility came closer to reality.

I transmitted this memorandum to the National Security Council for its consideration. At about this time, however, the situation in Korea began to show signs of improvement.

General Collins who, with General Vandenberg, had left for Korea to obtain a first-hand view of the situation, reported back from Tokyo on January 17, stating that he had just returned from Korea where he had found that the Eighth Army was in good shape and was improving daily.

Thereafter, the situation of our forces in Korea continued to improve and during the latter half of January the enemy forces remained on the defensive. Throughout February and March our forces maintained the initiative against the enemy.

As the result of this change in the military situation from that which prevailed during the early part of January, it became unnecessary to put into effect all of the courses of action outlined in the Joint Chiefs' memorandum of January 12.

None of these proposed courses of action were vetoed or disapproved by me or by any higher authority. Action with respect to most of them was considered inadvisable in view of the radical change in the situation which originally had given rise to them.

Now, as to the basic differences of judgment which exist between General MacArthur on the one hand, and the Joint Chiefs of Staff, the Secretary of Defense, and the President, on the other hand.

Our objective in Korea continues to be the defeat of the aggression and the restoration of peace. We have persistently sought to confine the conflict to Korea and to prevent its spreading into a third world war. In this effort, we stand allied with the great majority of our fellow-members of the United Nations. Our efforts have succeeded in thwarting the aggressors, in Korea, and in stemming the tide of aggression in Southeast Asia and elsewhere throughout the world. Our efforts in Korea have given us some sorely needed time and impetus to accelerate the building of our defenses and those of our allies against the threatened onslaught of Soviet imperialism.

General MacArthur, on the other hand, would have us, on our own initiative, carry the conflict beyond Korea against the mainland of Communist China, both from the sea and from the air. He would have us accept the risk involvement not only in an extension of the war with Red China, but in an all-out war with the Soviet Union. He would have us do this even at the expense of losing our allies and wrecking the coalition of free peoples throughout the world. He would have us do this even though the effect of such action might expose Western Europe to attack by the millions of Soviet troops poised in Middle and Eastern Europe.

This fundamental divergence is one of judgment as to the proper course of action to be followed by the United States. This divergence arises from the inherent difference between the position of a field commander, whose mission is limited to a particular area and a particular antagonist, and the position of the Joint Chiefs of Staff, the Secretary of Defense, and the President, who are responsible for the total security of the United States, and who, to achieve and maintain this security, must weigh our interests and objectives in one part of the globe with those in other areas of the world so as to attain the best overall balance.

It is their responsibility to determine where the main threat to our security lies, where we must fight holding actions, and where and how we must gain time to grow stronger. On the other hand, the responsibilities and the courses of action assigned to a theater commander necessarily apply to his own immediate area of responsibility. It is completely understandable and, in fact, at times commendable that a theater commander should become so wholly wrapped up in his own aims and responsibilities that some of the directives received by him from higher authority are not those that he would have written for himself. There is nothing new about this sort of thing in our military history. What is new, and what has brought about the necessity for General MacArthur's removal, is the wholly unprecedented situation of a local theater commander publicly expressing his displeasure at and his disagreement with the foreign and military policy of the United States.

It became apparent that General MacArthur had grown so far out of sympathy with the established policies of the United States that there was grave doubt as to whether he could any longer be permitted to exercise the authority in making decisions that normal command functions would assign to a theater commander. In this situation, there was no other recourse but to relieve him.

*   *   *

Senator Fulbright. . . . General MacArthur made a statement that was received with much enthusiasm that there is no substitute for victory. Now if it is an ideological crusade, I think the idea that you just can't compromise with sin fits very well, but if it is a continuation of the age-old struggle between tyranny in one form or another and the forces of law and order as we believe they are, it seems to me that there is room for qualifying the thought that there is no substitute for victory. Here is what I have in mind. We had unconditional victory in the last war, did we not?

Secretary Marshall. Yes, sir.

Senator Fulbright. We defeated Germany and Japan unconditionally.

Secretary Marshall. Yes, sir.

Senator Fulbright. I would not say that the result has been entirely satisfactory, has it?

Secretary Marshall. It wouldn't seem so, sir.

Senator Fulbright. So it looks as if we are justified in examining that idea of unconditional surrender, does it not?

Secretary Marshall. Yes, sir.

Senator Fulbright. Isn't that what you really are approaching in your policy in Korea? You are seeking a way that you can compromise—compromise is a bad word. It has come to have a meaning perhaps that is difficult to explain, like the word "appeasement," which used to be a very respectable word but now has become a word which you don't dare to use in any connection. So we will leave those two words out. Aren't we trying in Korea essentially not to go for all-out victory in the sense we did in the last war, partly because we found that not to be effective to achieve our purposes, but to do something short of that which in this instance is to avoid a war as long as we possibly can, with the hope that we may never have an all-out war? Isn't that what your real objective is?

Secretary Marshall. That is the objective to the extent that it first appeared necessary to destroy the aggressor considering the geographical situation and the continued menace which would follow for the South Korean Government if that aggressor from North Korea remained in organized being.

Now, as I understood the application of the United Nations action in the matter and our own procedure in connection with it, we were trying to bring to a halt any idea of aggression, of any people who attempt that sort of action, and particularly recognizing that this was an aggression which was undoubtedly stimulated, organized, by the Soviet Union.

Senator Fulbright. Yes. I grant that is certainly an essential and, you might say, primary purpose—to prevent the expansion of Russian power, to prevent aggression. But I cannot quite agree, nor do I think you mean to say, that that is all of it, that it is purely negative. It seems to me that we at the same time are trying to establish the machinery by which these international disputes may be settled by some kind of persuasion or reason rather than this idea of complete victory, unconditional surrender.

To put it another way: Do you not think we would be perhaps faced with a difficult situation assuming we completely defeated China and Russia? What would we do with them? Would we not have the same situation on a bigger scale than we have had with Germany and Japan—a very difficult situation with regard to administration? We do not have the people. We would not want to go in and administer. I mean that idea of complete victory does not entirely solve the situation, does it? What we really want is for them to give up their aggression and to accept the United Nations, is it not, which would bring a machinery for settling our differences by peaceful means rather than by force? Would you not say that is really our objective?

Secretary Marshall. I think our real desire is to have them establish the practice of acting like a decent nation should.

Senator Fulbright. That is right, through the United Nations. That is the way we have suggested.

Secretary Marshall. That is our machinery—

Senator Fulbright. That is the machinery we have accepted—

Secretary Marshall. For that action.

Senator Fulbright. It seems to me that this idea there is no policy in Korea, that there is no objective is one that is not sound, even though this objective is a new kind of objective and one that is not surrounded by all the glamor and emotional connections that the old-fashioned victory is surrounded with. It is much easier to appeal to most people's emotions by talking with language and concepts we used a century ago, but it seems to me this objective is just as real, albeit it is a new one, a new kind of objective. But it is one we consciously wanted new because we are not satisfied with the old way of having a war every 25 years. It seems to me that is what we had in mind.

I grant it is a very difficult thing to put into language that is appealing to the press and to the people, but that still remains the job, I think, of the government to do it.

I just wondered if some thoughts along that line might not be helpful, because I feel very strongly myself that that is what we are groping for in this struggle in Korea, the first and the most real opportunity to try to make the United Nations have some substance and have some real meaning.

We had that opportunity in Ethiopia and it was turned down by the League of Nations. Wouldn't you say that is a fairly good example?

Secretary Marshall. I think that is a very good example.

Senator Fulbright. If we had done the same thing then as now, or, even better, if we had done the same thing when Hitler moved into the Rhineland and said, "No, you won't"—even if we had to go to war, we might very well have established the principle then we are trying to establish now; is that true?

Secretary Marshall. I think that is so. What we are struggling for is a genuine basis of collective action.

Senator Fulbright. That is right.

Secretary Marshall. To secure the peace.

Senator Fulbright. The trouble we have is that those words, "collective action" and "reason" and "reconciliation of differences" don't sound good and they are not sort of vaguely connected with knights in shining armor and they don't look good in headlines and that is why it is extremely difficult to sell these ideas to the people, it seems to me.

The other approach has a great deal more sex appeal in a political sense, political appeal, than the old-fashioned way.

One other thing. I would take it from that that you do not feel that full-scale war with Russia is inevitable at all.

Secretary Marshall. I do not think it is inevitable. I think it is a very dangerous possibility.

Senator Fulbright. I agree with that.

Secretary Marshall. And I think the degree of danger depends a great deal on how we carry ourselves. One simple factor is that we prepare to meet such an emergency in time to have the deterrent action that we so much hope for.

Omar N. Bradley

TESTIMONY BEFORE THE ARMED SERVICES AND FOREIGN RELATIONS COMMITTEES

General Marshall was followed by General Bradley, Chairman of the Joint Chiefs of Staff. Bradley, who had commanded the US First Army in the campaign that led to the defeat of Nazi Germany, was, like General Eisenhower, considered to be a disciple of General Marshall. He appeared May 15, and made the opening statement printed below.

General Bradley. Before your interrogation on the details of our government's policies in Korea and the Far East, I would like to ask myself this question: What is the great issue at stake in this hearing?

Principally I would say that you are trying to determine the course we should follow as the best road to peace. There are military factors which must be evaluated before a sound decision can be made. At present the issue is obscured in the public mind by many details which do not relate to the task of keeping the peace and making America secure.

The fundamental military issue that has arisen is whether to increase the risk of a global war by taking additional measures that are open to the United States and its allies. We now have a localized conflict in Korea. Some of the military measures under discussion might well place the United States in the position of responsibility for broadening the war and at the same time losing most if not all of our allies.

General MacArthur has stated that there are certain additional measures which can and should be taken, and that by so doing no unacceptable increased risk of global war will result.

The Joint Chiefs of Staff believe that these same measures do increase the risk of global war and that such a risk should not be taken unnecessarily. At the same time we recognize the military advantages that might accrue to the United Nations' position in Korea and to the United States' position in the Far East by these measures. While a field commander very properly estimates his needs from the view-

From *Hearings*, pp. 729–733.

point of operations in his own theater or sphere of action, those responsible for higher direction must necessarily base their actions on broader aspects, and on the needs, actual or prospective, of several theaters. The Joint Chiefs of Staff, in view of their global responsibilities and their perspective with respect to the worldwide strategic situation, are in a better position than is any single theater commander to assess the risk of general war. Moreover, the Joint Chiefs of Staff are best able to judge our own military resources with which to meet that risk.

In order that all may understand the strategy which the Joint Chiefs of Staff believe the United States must pursue, I would like to discuss in broad terms this perspective in which we view our security problems.

As a background to our consideration of global strategy, we must realize that human beings have invented a great variety of techniques designed to influence other nations. Right now, nations are being subjected to persuasion by propaganda and coercion by force of arms. It is my conviction that broad and comprehensive knowledge of the strength, aims, and the policies of nations is basic to understanding the problem of security in a world of tension.

We must understand—as we conduct our foreign affairs and our military affairs—that while power and nationalism prevail, it is up to us to gain strength through cooperative efforts with other nations which have common ideals and objectives with our own. At the same time, we must create and maintain the power essential to persuasion, and to our own security in such a world. We must understand the role and nature, including the limitations, of this power if we are to exercise it wisely.

One of the great power potentials of this world is the United States of America and her allies. The other great power in this world is Soviet Russia and her satellites. As much as we desire peace, we must realize that we have two centers of power supporting opposing ideologies.

From a global viewpoint—and with the security of our nation of prime importance—our military mission is to support a policy of preventing communism from gaining the manpower, the resources, the raw materials, and the industrial capacity essential to world domination. If Soviet Russia ever controls the entire Eurasian land mass, then the Soviet-satellite imperialism may have the broad base upon which to build the military power to rule the world.

Three times in the past five years the Kremlin-inspired imperialism has been thwarted by direct action.

In Berlin, Greece, and Korea, the free nations have opposed Communist aggression with a different type of action. But each time the power of the United States has been called upon and we have become involved. Each incident has cost us money, resources, and some lives.

But in each instance we have prevented the domination of one more area, and the absorption of another source of manpower, raw materials, and resources.

Korea, in spite of the importance of the engagement, must be looked upon with proper perspective. It is just one engagement, just one phase of this battle that we are having with the other power center in the world which opposes us and all we stand for. For five years this "guerrilla diplomacy" has been going on. In each of the actions in which we have participated to oppose this gangster conduct, we have risked World War III. But each time we have used methods short of total war. As costly as Berlin and Greece and Korea may be, they are less expensive than the vast destruction which would be inflicted upon all sides if a total war were to be precipitated.

I am under no illusion that our present strategy of using means short of total war to achieve our ends and oppose communism is a guarantee that a world war will not be thrust upon us. But a policy of patience and determination without provoking a world war, while we improve our military power, is one which we believe we must continue to follow.

As long as we keep the conflict within its present scope, we are holding to a minimum the forces we must commit and tie down.

The strategic alternative, enlargement of the war in Korea to include Red China, would probably delight the Kremlin more than anything else we could do. It would necessarily tie down additional forces, especially our sea power and our air power, while the Soviet Union would not be obliged to put a single man into the conflict.

Under present circumstances, we have recommended against enlarging the war. The course of action often described as a "limited war" with Red China would increase the risk we are taking by engaging too much of our power in an area that is not the critical strategic prize.

Red China is not the powerful nation seeking to dominate the world. Frankly, in the opinion of the Joint Chiefs of Staff, this strategy would involve us in the wrong war, at the wrong place, at the wrong time, and with the wrong enemy.

There are some other considerations which have tended to obscure this main issue. Some critics have not hesitated to state that the policy our government is following, and its included strategy, is not that which has been recommended by the Joint Chiefs of Staff.

Statements have been made that the President, as Commander in Chief, and the Secretary of State and the Secretary of Defense, have a policy all their own, and that the Joint Chiefs of Staff have been overridden.

This is just not so. The Joint Chiefs of Staff have continually given their considered opinion—always from a military viewpoint—concerning our global capabilities and responsibilities and have recommended our present strategy in and for Korea. This has been the course of action which the Secretary of Defense and the Commander in Chief have adopted as far as practicable.

I pointed out earlier that many times the international policy considerations, including the views of our allies, are also considered and in some instances modify the course of action.

In other instances, even after the international considerations and the views of our allies have been considered, the proposed military strategy has not been altered.

Our overall policy has been one of steadfast patience and determination in opposing Communist aggression without provoking unnecessarily a total war.

There are many critics who have become impatient with this strategy and who would like to call for a showdown. From a purely military viewpoint, this is not desirable. We are not in the best military position to seek a showdown, even if it were the nation's desire to forfeit the chances for peace by precipitating a total war.

Undoubtedly, this statement will be misconstrued by some critics who will say, "Why are the Joint Chiefs of Staff advertising the fact that we are not militarily in a position to have a showdown?"

I can assure those critics that with the methods we must pursue in a democracy in order to support a military establishment—including this present investigation of our strategy in the Far East—our capabilities are not unknown to the Communists.

They are apt students of military power, and fully realize that although we are not prepared to deliver any ultimatum, we could hurt them badly if they attacked us or our friends.

They also know that with our potential, and the strength of our allies, in the long run they could not win a war with a United States that is alert, and continuously prepared.

I would not be a proponent of any policy which would ignore the military facts and rush us headlong into a showdown before we are ready. It is true that this policy of armed resistance to aggression, which we pursue while we are getting stronger, often risks a world war. But so far we have taken these risks without disastrous results.

I think our global strategy is paying off and I see no reason to let impatience alter it in the Far East. Certainly the course of action we are pursuing has avoided a total war which could only bring death and destruction to millions of Americans, both in the United States and on the battlefield. Our present course of action has at the same time won us respect and admiration everywhere in the world, both inside and outside the Iron Curtain.

There are also those who deplore the present military situation in Korea and urge us to engage Red China in a larger war to solve this problem. Taking on Red China is not a decisive move, does not guarantee the end of the war in Korea, and may not bring China to her knees. We have only to look back to the five long years when the Japanese, one of the greatest military powers of that time, moved into China and had almost full control of a large part of China, and yet were never able to conclude that war successfully. I would say that from past history one would only jump from a smaller conflict to a larger deadlock at greater expense. My own feeling is to avoid such an engagement if possible because victory in Korea would not be assured and victory over Red China would be many years away. We believe that every effort should be made to settle the present conflict without extending it outside Korea. If this proves to be impossible, then other measures may have to be taken.

In my consideration of this viewpoint, I am going back to the basic objective of the American people—as much peace as we can gain without appeasement.

Some critics of our strategy say if we do not immediately bomb troop concentration points and airfields in Manchuria, it is "appeasement." If we do not immediately set up a blockade of Chinese ports— which to be successful would have to include British and Russian ports in Asia—it is "appeasement." These same critics would say that if we do not provide the logistical support and air and naval assistance to launch Chinese Nationalist troops into China it is "appeasement."

These critics ignore the vital questions:

Will these actions, if taken, actually assure victory in Korea?

Do these actions mean prolongation of the war by bringing Russia into the fight?

Will these actions strip us of our allies in Korea and in other parts of the world?

From a military viewpoint, appeasement occurs when you give up something, which is rightfully free, to an aggressor without putting up a struggle, or making him pay a price. Forsaking Korea—withdrawing from the fight unless we are forced out—would be an appeasement to aggression. Refusing to enlarge the quarrel to the point where our global capabilities are diminished, is certainly not appeasement but is a militarily sound course of action under the present circumstances.

Dean G. Acheson

TESTIMONY BEFORE THE ARMED SERVICES AND FOREIGN RELATIONS COMMITTEES

Except for General A. C. Wedemeyer, who had served under MacArthur and whose testimony was generally sympathetic (see Hearings, pp. 2294–2567), Secretary of State Acheson was the last important witness. The following statement is a portion of his prepared statement read to the Senate committees.

Secretary Acheson.   The attack on Korea was a blow at the foundation of [our program of collective security]. It was a challenge to the whole system of collective security, not only in the Far East, but everywhere in the world. It was a threat to all nations newly arrived at independence. This dagger thrust pinned a warning notice to the wall which said: "Give up or be conquered."

This was a test which would decide whether our collective-security system would survive or would crumble. It would determine whether other nations would be intimidated by this show of force.

The decision to meet force with force in Korea was essential. It was the unanimous view of the political and military advisers of the President that this was the right thing to do. This decision had the full support of the American people because it accorded with the principles by which Americans live.

As a people we condemn aggression of any kind. We reject appeasement of any kind. If we stood with our arms folded while Korea was swallowed up, it would have meant abandoning our principles, and it would have meant the defeat of the collective security system on which our own safety ultimately depends.

What I want to stress here is that it was not only a crucial decision whether or not to meet this aggression; it was no less important how this aggression was to be dealt with.

In the first place, the attack on Korea has been met by collective action. The United States brought the aggression in Korea before the

From *Hearings*, pp. 1714–1720.

United Nations, not only because the Charter requires it, but also because the authority and even the survival of that organization was directly involved.

The response of some members of the United Nations, in terms of their capacities and their other security responsibilities, has been generous and wholehearted.

The total action is admittedly an imperfect one, as might be expected of beginning steps in a collective-security system. But the development of this system requires us to take into consideration the dangers and interests of those associated with us, just as we want them to take into consideration our dangers and interests.

In the second place, our response to the aggression against Korea required a careful estimate of the risks involved in the light of the total world situation.

There was the risk that the conflict might spread into a general war in Asia, a risk that the Chinese Communists might intervene, a risk that the Soviet Union might declare itself in.

We take it for granted that risk of some sort is implicit in any positive policy, and that there is also a risk in doing nothing.

The elements of risk and the means of reducing that risk to us and to the rest of the free world quite properly influenced our policy in Korea.

It has been our purpose to turn back this Communist thrust, and to do it in such a way as to prevent a third world war if we can. This is in accord with one of the most fundamental tenets of our policy— to prevent, insofar as we can do so, another world war.

It is against this basic purpose that the operation in Korea, and the plans for carrying it to a conclusion, need to be considered.

The operation in Korea has been a success. Both the North Koreans and the Chinese Communists declared it to be their purpose to drive the United Nations forces out of Korea and impose Communist rule throughout the entire peninsula. They have been prevented from accomplishing their objective.

It has been charged that the American and allied forces fighting in Korea are engaged in a pointless and inconclusive struggle.

Nothing could be further from the fact. They have been magnificent. Their gallant, determined, and successful fight has checked the

Communist advance and turned it into a retreat. They have adminis-
tered terrible defeats to the Communist forces. In so doing, they
have scored a powerful victory.

Their victory has dealt Communist imperialist aims in Asia a severe set-back.

The alluring prospect for the Communist conspiracy in June 1950
—the prospect of a quick and easy success which would not only
win Korea for the Kremlin but shake the free nations of Asia and
paralyze the defense of Europe—all this has evaporated.

Instead of weakening the rest of the world, they have solidified
it. They have given a powerful impetus to the military preparations
of this country and its associates in and out of the North Atlantic
Treaty Organization.

We have doubled the number of our men under arms, and the
production of materiel has been boosted to a point where it can
begin to have a profound effect on the maintenance of the peace.

The idea of collective security has been put to the test, and has
been sustained. The nations who believe in collective security have
shown that they can stick together and fight together.

New urgency has been given to the negotiation of a peace treaty
with Japan, and of initial security arrangements to build strength in
the Pacific area.

These are some of the results of the attack on Korea, unexpected
by—and I am sure most unwelcome to—the Kremlin.

The objective of our military operation in Korea is to end the aggression, to safeguard against its renewal, and to restore peace.
There is wide agreement on this objective in the domestic discussions of this issue.

Both the Administration and its critics have said that the object
of the courses they propose is to end the aggression and restore
peace. Both are willing—indeed desire—to end the fighting by an
honorable settlement which will end the aggression, provide against
its renewal and restore peace.

Neither will purchase a settlement by allowing the aggressors to
profit by their wrong. Neither believes that the destruction or unconditional surrender of the aggressor is necessary to attain the goal.

General Marshall, General Bradley, and the Joint Chiefs of Staff have given you, in detail, the reasons why they believe that the Chinese Communists will be defeated in Korea and must abandon their purpose.

They report that our forces are in excellent shape, that their morale is high and that they are in good supply position.

They report not only that the mass attacks launched by the enemy have failed to break through the firepower of United Nations forces, but that the offensives of the enemy have been broken and thrown back with enormous enemy casualties.

These defeats in Korea, together with other consequences of this campaign, present grave problems for the Communist authorities in China.

While the manpower resources of China are vast, its supply of trained men is limited. They cannot cover up their casualties. They cannot gloss over the draft of more and more men for military service.

The Chinese Red leaders have betrayed their long-standing pledge of demobilization and the military demand for manpower has, instead, been increased.

Peking has also broken its promises of social and economic improvement. In the great cities, dependent on imported materials, unemployment increases. The regime has not lightened the burdens of the people. It has made them heavier.

All of this is reflected in a sharp increase in repressive measures, and in propaganda to whip up the flagging zeal of their own people.

In the light of all these factors, I believe that the aggression can best be brought to an end with a minimum risk and a minimum loss, by continuing the punishing defeat of the Chinese in Korea. This is being done.

No one can predict when the fighting will stop and when the aggression will end. It is also true that no one could have foretold exactly what would happen when we undertook action to end the Berlin blockade, but we did what we thought was right and the blockade was ended.

No one could have foretold how the aggression in Greece would be terminated, but again we took those measures which our best judgment and sense indicated were the right ones and the aggression ceased.

While the outcome of every course of action in the foreign-policy field cannot be predicted with certainty in advance, it is our responsibility in taking action to apply our best judgment on the basis of the best information at hand.

I think it is fair to say that all of the President's advisers believe the course we are now following gives us the best chance of stopping hostilities and ending the aggression in Korea.

I should like briefly to address myself to the alternative course which was placed before this committee. This course would seek to bring the conflict in Korea to an end by enlarging the sphere of hostilities.

I will not try to review the military considerations involved in this proposed course, since these have been thoroughly discussed by the previous witnesses before your committees.

It is enough to say that it is the judgment of the President's military advisers that the proposed enlargement of our military action would not exercise a prompt and decisive effect in bringing the hostilities to an end. To this judgment there must be added a recognition of the grave risks and other disadvantages of this alternative course.

Against the dubious advantages of spreading the war in an initially limited manner to the mainland of China, there must be measured the risk of a general war with China, the risk of Soviet intervention, and of World War III, as well as the probable effects upon the solidarity of the free-world coalition.

The advocates of this program make two assumptions which require careful examination. They assume that the Soviet Union will not necessarily respond to any action on our part. They also assume that in the buildup of strength relative to the Soviet Union and the Communist sphere, time is not necessarily on our side.

As to Soviet reactions no one can be sure he is forecasting accurately what they would be, but there are certain facts at hand that bear on this question.

We know of Soviet influence in North Korea, of Soviet assistance to the North Koreans and to Communist China, and we know that understandings must have accompanied this assistance. We also know that there is a treaty between the Soviets and the Chinese Communists.

But even if the treaty did not exist, China is the Soviet Union's largest and most important satellite. Russian self-interest in the Far East and the necessity of maintaining prestige in the Communist sphere make it difficult to see how the Soviet Union could ignore a direct attack upon the Chinese mainland.

I cannot accept the assumption that the Soviet Union will go its way regardless of what we do. I do not think that Russian policy is formed that way any more than our own policy is formed that way. This view is certainly not well enough grounded to justify a gamble with the essential security of our nation.

In response to the proposed course of action, there are a number of courses of counteraction open to the Soviets.

They could turn over to the Chinese large numbers of planes with "volunteer" crews for retaliatory action in Korea and outside. They might participate with the Soviet Air Force and the submarine fleet.

The Kremlin could elect to parallel the action taken by Peking and intervene with a half million or more ground-force "volunteers"; or it could go the whole way and launch an all-out war.

Singly, or in combination, these reactions contain explosive possibilities, not only for the Far East, but for the rest of the world as well.

We should also analyze the effect on our allies of our taking steps to initiate the spread of war beyond Korea. It would severely weaken their ties with us and in some instances it might sever them.

They are understandably reluctant to be drawn into a general war in the Far East—one which holds the possibilities of becoming a world war—particularly if it developed out of an American impatience with the progress of the effort to repel aggression, an effort which in their belief offers an honorable and far less catastrophic solution.

If we followed the course proposed, we would be increasing our risks and commitments at the same time that we diminished our strength by reducing the strength and determination of our coalition.

We cannot expect that our collective-security system will long survive if we take steps which unnecessarily and dangerously expose the people who are in the system with us. They would understandably hesitate to be tied to a partner who leads them to a highly dangerous shortcut across a difficult crevasse.

In relation to the total world threat, our safety requires that we strengthen, not weaken, the bonds of our collective-security system.

The power of our coalition to deter an attack depends in part upon the will and the mutual confidence of our partners. If we, by the measures proposed, were to weaken that effect, particularly in the North Atlantic area, we would be jeopardizing the security of an area which is vital to our own national security.

What this adds up to, it seems to me, is that we are being asked to undertake a large risk of general war with China, risk of war with the Soviet Union, and a demonstrable weakening of our collective-security system—all this in return for what?

In return for measures whose effectiveness in bringing the conflict to an early conclusion are judged doubtful by our responsible military authorities.

Before concluding, I should like to deal briefly with the related proposition that we may need to take extreme risks now because time may not be on our side. I believe this is wrong.

The basic premise of our foreign policy is that time is on our side if we make good use of it. That does not necessarily mean that time must bring us to a point where we can match the Soviet Union man-for-man and tank-for-tank.

What it does mean is that we need to use the time we have to build an effective deterrent force. This requires us to create sufficient force-in-being, both in the United States and among our allies, to shield our great potential against the possibility of a quick and easy onslaught, and to ensure that our allies will not suffer occupation and destruction. And back of this shield we need to have the potential that would enable us to win a war.

This is the measure of the force we need; as we approach it, we approach our objective of preventing war.

Can we do this? I believe we can. We and our allies have the capacity to out-produce the Soviet bloc by a staggering margin. There is no doubt about that. Our capacity to produce has been set in motion and is rapidly getting to the point where its output will be vast and its effect significant.

There is also the critical factor of our will. The future belongs to freedom if free men have the will to make time work on their side. I believe the American people and their allies do have the will, the will to work together when their freedom is threatened. This is the ultimate source of our faith and our confidence. A free society can call upon profound resources among its people in behalf of a righteous cause.

[*The Hearings continued through August 17, and concluded with the Democrats on the two committees in support of Truman and the Republicans generally sympathetic to MacArthur. Meanwhile, the war went on. United Nations' forces had moved up north of the 38th Parallel in April, and had held their lines against the Chinese offensive launched on April 22. By the end of May, it was apparent that General Ridgway's army had firepower great enough to more than equal the Chinese advantage in manpower. A UN counteroffensive moved further toward reoccupation of the North Korean capital, Pyongyang. Then, on July 2, Premier Kim Il Sung of North Korea and General Peng Teh-huai, the Chinese commander in Korea, indicated a willingness to begin negotiations.*

Although fighting continued throughout the dreary months of negotiation, the front was more or less stabilized from July 8, 1951, when the talks began, until July 27, 1953, when the truce was finally agreed upon. Korea was divided with the line of demarcation running (west to east) south of the 38th Parallel, and curving north of it about a third of the way across the peninsula.]

II. CIVIL-MILITARY RELATIONS

Walter Millis

TRUMAN AND MACARTHUR

Walter Millis has for thirty years been recognized as a leader among military historians. His study of civil-military relations, written with the assistance of Harvey C. Mansfield and Harold Stein for the Twentieth Century Fund, contains a thorough analysis of the Truman-MacArthur controversy. The selection which is reprinted here focusses on the final break between the President and his military commander in Korea.

The directive of September 15 (issued on the now far distant day of the Inchon landing) had instructed CINCFE[1] that the United States "would not permit itself to become engaged in a general war with Communist China" and, in the event of Chinese intervention, had authorized MacArthur only "to continue military action as long as it offered a reasonable chance of successful resistance." This, if not completely out of date, at least seemed no longer to be controlling in CINCFE's mind. On December 27 Marshall completed a draft directive to meet the new situation. It was discussed among Truman, Acheson, Bradley, Rusk and Marshall during the following day; it was put into final form and dispatched on December 29. . . .

MacArthur, according to Whitney, received this directive "in utter dismay." It declared that Korea was not the place to fight a major war. "Was it, then," in Whitney's words, "a policy that we would meet Communist aggression in Asia only if we could do it without too much trouble?" MacArthur, reading this formal directive from his superiors, made two deductions: first, that the Administration had "completely lost the 'will to win' in Korea"; second, that it was trying to offload upon the general's shoulders its responsibility for the "shameful decision" to evacuate the peninsula. The Commander in Chief Far East sat down late on the night of December 30 to compose an excoriating reply.

. . . What not only Truman but the Joint Chiefs of Staff wanted, and desperately needed, to know was whether MacArthur could and

From *Arms and the State: Civil-Military Elements in National Policy* (New York, 1958), pp. 303–314, 316–317. Reprinted by permission of The Twentieth Century Fund.

[1] Commander in Chief, Far East.—Ed.

would hold on in Korea under the conditions—or "restrictions"—
which had been imposed upon him for what were believed to be the
most compelling reasons of high policy. What they got was not a
"cold, professional" answer to this question; it was in effect an announcement that MacArthur would not play unless both the policy
and the strategy were transformed in accordance with his liking.
Ridgway was in these hours touring the front lines of Eighth Army.
It is not surprising that he was shocked by the state of morale which
he encountered. It was an army of beaten, apprehensive men who had
lost not only their aggressiveness but their alertness. They were "not
patrolling as they should"; they knew nothing about the enemy before
them; they did not know the terrain; they were not preparing rear
lines of defense against the attack which everyone expected to come,
and they did not know what they were fighting for or why they should
be expected to continue.

Ridgway flung himself into the task of infusing a new spirit. When
he met President Syngman Rhee his first words were: "Mr. President,
I am glad to be here. And I've come to stay." It was not the mood in
Tokyo, where they were considering the abandonment of the peninsula and a retreat to "the littoral islands."

Shortly after dark on New Year's Eve (the day after MacArthur's
reply to JCS) the Chinese delivered the expected attack. Despite
Ridgway's efforts, Eighth Army was still spread too thin and was too
dispirited to stem it; on January 2 the hard decision to evacuate
Seoul had to be taken; the UN forces retreated south of the Han into
central Korea, but the prepared lines which Ridgway had urged were
enough to hold against the diminishing enemy attack. The Hungnam
perimeter was abandoned and X Corps rejoined Eighth Army. A
position was reconstituted across the peninsula. It was far south of
the 38th Parallel, but it was also far north of the Pusan beachhead
into which CINCFE had intimated that he must inevitably be driven.
Temporarily the situation had been stabilized. No one knew whether
or how long it could be maintained.

For MacArthur's superiors in Washington, both military and civilian,
his message of December 30 posed a formidable problem. They were
being compelled to deal in these days with issues of rearmament,
of NATO, of global defense and global policy, in which Korea was
only a part, yet into which Korean policy had to be fitted with care if

the whole was to succeed. Yet they had to deal with the Korean aspects through this unusual man, with access to strong popular and political forces, the workings of whose subtle mind they did not easily follow and whose motivations they had been taught by experience to distrust. CINCFE's demand for an all-out war on China (accompanied by the hint that under cover of such a war they might evacuate Korea altogether, thus reducing the American casualties) clearly raised two major questions. One, which was to be endlessly discussed after MacArthur's recall, concerned the danger of bringing on Soviet intervention and a third world war, or at the very least of fragmenting the UN and NATO alliances and leaving us naked to a Soviet-dominated world. The other, which received comparatively little public attention, concerned the effectiveness of MacArthur's strategy, regarded strictly from a military viewpoint.

In his message of December 30 MacArthur had advanced four specific proposals. The first, a naval blockade of China, could not interrupt the main line of Chinese military supply, which was overland from the Soviet Union, and could add little to the embargo which we were already organizing. The second, destruction of China's industrial capacity by air bombardment, could have had only a long-delayed effect upon the operations in Korea. It might ultimately have put so much pressure upon the Mao regime as to lead it to abandon the Korean War and retire behind the Yalu in order to escape further punishment; but all World War II experience with "strategic" and "population" bombing combined to suggest that such a result, if attained at all, could be attained only at the cost of a slaughter of Chinese civilians and a devastation of the country so vast that our people would rebel at the horror while our name would become anathema throughout the world.

It is interesting that when MacArthur returned to lay his program before the Congress and the country, he suppressed this proposal for the destruction of China's "industrial capacity to wage war," doubtless because its real implications were too obvious. On the other hand, in his December 30 message to JCS he wasted no words over the demand for an attack upon the "sanctuary" bases in Manchuria, of which so much was afterward to be made. Doubtless this was because it would be apparent to the experienced military men in JCS that, with his air demonstrably unable to interdict the 200-mile enemy communication line now running from the Yalu to the military frontier, the extension of the air attack across the river, while it could have helped, would hardly have been decisive.

As to the third and fourth points in the MacArthur program, the "use" of Chinese Nationalist troops in Korea had been rejected by everyone on the ground that they would be "ineffective"; while it required a belief in military miracles to imagine that they could create any significant diversion by guerrilla operations in South China. "We are not prolonging this war," as Bradley was later to put it, "just for the fun of it. The only difference is General MacArthur thinks that to do certain additional operations would be decisive, and we do not think they would be decisive. They might help a little bit, but to offset that you must run the risk of opening up World War III." But enmeshed as they were in "security," the Joint Chiefs were never able to get this point of view over clearly to the public. The military-technical aspects of the MacArthur program (if it can be called a "program") were always its most obscure facet.

In Washington, as the new year came in, the public was not yet a factor in the argument, and the Joint Chiefs had no difficulty in appraising the MacArthur recommendations. What they could not clearly judge, through the fluent prose of CINCFE's telegrams, was the extent to which they might be risking the destruction of Eighth Army by following their own policy—which was, essentially, to hang on in Korea as long as possible with the means available in the hope of securing an acceptable cease-fire. They were not on the ground; and the great tradition of independence for the theater commander forbade them from questioning his reports. Their uncertainty about the real position of Eighth Army was MacArthur's greatest weapon against them; and it is hard to doubt that CINCFE at least tried to use it to secure the policies he believed necessary.

On January 9 the Joint Chiefs of Staff, with the approval of the President and the Secretary of State, produced another official directive. CINCFE was told that his proposed retaliatory measures against China could not be permitted, and was again directed to "defend in successive positions" subject to "the safety of his troops and his basic mission of protecting Japan." But it added: "Should it become evident in the judgment of CINCFE that evacuation was essential to avoid severe losses of men and material, CINCFE was at that time to withdraw from Korea to Japan." The reception of this message in Tokyo reflects the curious state of mind now ruling in that proud, defeated and withdrawn headquarters. What they saw in it was not an order but, in Whitney's words, a "booby-trap"! The pro-British if not pro-Communist conspirators in Washington were trying to throw on MacArthur the onus for the Korean debacle and the evacuation which, as a result of it, might become inevitable. "MacArthur refused to be so easily taken in," and on January 10 sent an angry yet subtle reply:

> There is no doubt but that a beachhead line can be held by our existing forces for a limited time in Korea, but this could not be accomplished without losses. . . . The troops are tired from a long and difficult campaign, embittered by the shameful propaganda which has falsely condemned their courage and fighting quality in misunderstood retrograde maneuver, and their morale will become a serious threat to their battle efficiency unless the political basis on which they are asked to trade life for time is quickly delineated, fully understood and so impelling that the hazards of battle are cheerfully accepted.

One cannot help contrasting Ridgway's efforts to restore morale and fighting spirit at the front with this attempt by the theater commander to use the alleged dissatisfactions of his troops to achieve his political ends. CINCFE went on to tell JCS that he was in full agreement with "their" estimate that the limitations imposed on him would eventually render evacuation unavoidable. "In the absence of overriding political considerations, under these conditions the command should be withdrawn from the peninsula just as rapidly as it is feasible to do so." There was a final turn of the screw:

> Under the extraordinary limitations and conditions imposed upon the command in Korea . . . its military position is untenable, but it can hold, if overriding political considerations so dictate, for any length of time up to its complete destruction. Your clarification requested.

This threw Washington into a consternation comparable to that which had been caused nearly a decade before by a similar message from the same officer under similar circumstances. In February 1942, at the height of the defense of Bataan, MacArthur had shocked Washington by supporting a proposal from President Quezon that the Philippines be neutralized and the American troops evacuated. Then, as in 1951, the apparent purpose was to compel the dispatch of reinforcements (which were not yet in existence) and force a reversal of high policy, from the strategy of "Europe first" which had at that time already been adopted to one of "the Far East first." In 1942 MacArthur was told, immediately and emphatically, that "American forces will continue to keep our flag flying in the Philippines so long as there remains any possibility of resistance"; and that put an end to the maneuver. Under the political and psychological conditions of 1951 it was difficult for Washington to be so forthright.

According to Admiral Sherman, the Chief of Naval Operations, "the character of that reply of the 10th January was such as to precipitate an immediate meeting of the Joint Chiefs on the 11th, a further meeting on the 12th; the preparation of a new military directive which was then dispatched, and then the Department of State . . . arranged to send their message. That period of January 9, 10, 11, 12 and 13 was a very difficult one." Washington was not interested in "booby-trapping" General MacArthur. These high military and civilian officials were carrying a tremendous responsibility, trying desperately to reach correct solutions for desperately serious issues of national policy and strategy. At this juncture the Commander in Chief Far East had presented them with the deadliest threat which a military commander—in a democratic society at least—can raise against his military and civil superiors: the threat of the "complete" and useless "destruction" of the armies under his command. That the Joint Chiefs' position was indeed "difficult" is plain. MacArthur's motivations, on the other hand, are more obscure. But whether his real purpose was to force an enlargement of the war or to force an immediate evacuation, one cannot help noting another obvious consequence of his recommendations. Whatever Washington might do, they would have the effect of putting MacArthur in a position in which he would be free of responsibility and free of blame.

Should Washington enlarge the war, this would validate MacArthur's contention that his defeat had been solely due to the inhibitions under which he had suffered; while since this would be a "political" decision which the general had insisted was beyond his "military" competence, any resultant disasters would be the fault of the politicians. Should Washington elect for an immediate evacuation,

that would equally exonerate him of the military reverse and prove
him right in maintaining that Korea could not be held under the
limitations imposed upon him by the politicians. But since he had
expressed his willingness to fight to "destruction" if the politicians
so ordered, he could not be blamed for the evacuation. If Washington
ordered him to stay on the restricted basis, then MacArthur would
be free to wash his hands of the consequences. Whatever disasters
might ensue could not be blamed on him; but neither—as this brilliant
mind only tardily realized—could subsequent successes be laid to
his credit. It may seem invidious to imply that General MacArthur
made so personal and egoistic a calculation of the immense responsibilities of his office; yet we have the faithful Whitney's word for it
that he saw in the January 9 directive only a personal "booby-trap"
and that the January 10 response which caused such alarm in Washington was dictated by a refusal "to be so easily taken in." When
Admiral Sherman was later asked whether there had not been at
this time a "failure of teamwork" between MacArthur and the Joint
Chiefs, his reply, emphatic as it was, must seem an understatement:

> *At this period, possibly better than any other indication* [sic], *the nor-
> mal relationships which are desirable between one echelon of command
> and another had been seriously impaired.*

The crisis produced three documents. The first was another directive, sent on January 11, which repeated the previous instructions, or
"in other words," as Bradley later put it, told him "to stay in Korea."
The second was a JCS "memorandum" dated January 12, on possible
courses to be followed in case we should be forced to back into the
Pusan beachhead or compelled to evacuate. This paper had its source
in the staff studies which JCS had ordered on November 28, a month
and a half before; as finally evolved and approved (after two revi-
sions) it clearly reflected some of the MacArthur ideas. It was submitted to the National Security Council, but a copy went to CINCFE.
The third was a message direct from the President to MacArthur,
sent on January 13. MacArthur had repeatedly insisted that he must
have "political" decisions. "In the absence of overriding political
considerations, . . . the command should be withdrawn," and so on.
It had been intended to explain the political considerations to him in

the military directive, but to the purists in the Pentagon this was a forbidden commingling of the two spheres. After anxious discussion between the President, State and the Joint Chiefs, the "military part" was "pulled out" and sent as a directive; the political part was embodied in Truman's message of January 13, seeking to expound to the general the serious political considerations which underlay his military orders. But no one by that time could have supposed that what MacArthur really wanted was explanations or that he would be materially affected by any given him. The really critical question was no longer CINCFE: it was Eighth Army—its morale, its capabilities, its adequacy as an instrument of the policy not of General MacArthur but of the United States. As Truman's message was dispatched, General Collins was emplaning for another visit to the Far East to find out what was really going on.

It seems not too much to say that with Collins' arrival in the Far East, MacArthur's influence was largely finished. Perhaps this was the real end of that overshadowing career. Collins is represented by MacArthur's supporters as having been under the impression when he landed in Tokyo that evacuation was inevitable. If so, he realized by the time he reached the front in Korea that the peril had been grossly exaggerated. Ridgway had restored Eighth Army to a fighting outfit, while MacArthur had been sitting withdrawn in Tokyo, knowing really very little about the armies he commanded, nursing his personal grievances against an Administration which he detested. From the moment of the retirement in early January into the prepared lines below the Han, Ridgway had started his people on aggressive patrolling. The Chinese at the same time had spent their drive and outrun their communications. Ridgway had felt out the opposition against him, first with platoon and company units, then with battalions and regimental combat teams. On January 25, only ten days after Collins' arrival in the Far East, Ridgway launched a full-scale attack on a two-corps front that "was never stopped until it had driven the enemy back across the Parallel." MacArthur had provided for every contingency save one—the contingency of success.

Belatedly, MacArthur appeared to realize that he was in an untenable position; just as he had realized in the case of his maneuver in the Philippines a decade before. In 1942 he had quickly shifted his stance; he had carried on the great defense of Bataan, and although disaster was inevitable he had emerged from it as the hero of the Pacific war. In 1951 a similar shift was attempted. With the messages from Washington and Collins' arrival it was clear that the MacArthur program of evacuation under cover of an expanded war against China had no future; with the growing success of Eighth Army it was clear that the Washington policy was promising. MacArthur seized upon the President's "political" message of January 13 as his avenue of retreat. As Whitney maintained then and thereafter, this was the "first" indication the Tokyo command had received that Washington intended them to stay in Korea—something which Washington had for weeks been urgently desiring that they should do if possible. Whitney even put an added twist on this contention; during the controversy later in the spring he was quoted in the newspapers:

> General MacArthur's spokesman said today that until January 13 this year, MacArthur believed Washington officials wanted our forces evacuated from Korea and made a scapegoat for some political advantage. Major General Courtney Whitney, MacArthur's aide, said a January 13 message from President Truman was the Government's first clear statement to MacArthur to hold in Korea.

But it was too late by that time. The general could no longer emerge as the hero of policies which he had so persistently obstructed; and the further course of the Korean War passed beyond the influence of the Tokyo headquarters. The controlling factors thenceforth were to be, after the President, State, JCS and Ridgway. . . .

By the middle of March Seoul was being retaken and the armies were again close to the parallel. Our UN allies felt that we should not again invade North Korea without an attempt at a settlement; and State, with the concurrence of Defense, recommended another effort to secure a cease-fire approximately on the parallel. On March 20 General MacArthur was advised that a Presidential announcement was being planned to the effect that the United Nations were prepared to discuss "the conditions of settlement' in Korea. It was explained to CINCFE that this would be done because of the UN belief that a diplomatic effort should be made before another military crossing of the parallel; but that Washington, on the other hand, recognized that the parallel had no military significance and did not want unduly to restrict MacArthur's military operations in the interests of this essentially diplomatic move. State desired MacArthur's recommendations as to how much freedom of military action it should preserve for him over the next few weeks in respect to this artificial boundary. CINCFE replied at once that since he could not clear North Korea in any event with his existing force, his directives required no modification.

A draft for the Presidential statement was thereupon prepared; and it was still being elaborately discussed between State, Defense and the allied representatives in Washington when on March 24 General MacArthur in Tokyo issued his own public demand for a cease-fire. It was very different from that being debated in Washington.

> *Even under the inhibitions which now restrict the activity of the United Nations forces . . . Red China . . . has been shown its complete inability to accomplish by force of arms the conquest of Korea. The enemy, therefore, must now be painfully aware that a decision of the United Nations to depart from its tolerant effort to contain the war to the area of Korea through an expansion of our military operations to its coastal areas and interior bases, would doom Red China to the risk of imminent military collapse. These basic facts being established, there should be no insuperable difficulty in arriving at decisions on the Korean problems if the issues are resolved on their own merits, without being burdened by extraneous matters not directly related to Korea, such as Formosa or China's seat in the United Nations.*
>
> *The Korean nation and its people . . . must not be sacrificed. This is a paramount concern. . . . I stand ready at any time to confer in the field with the commander-in-chief of the enemy forces in the earnest effort to find any military means whereby realization of the political objectives of the United Nations in Korea . . . might be accomplished without further bloodshed.*

Thus adroitly did CINCFE torpedo the Washington political initiative of which he had been privately advised. Unable or unwilling to climb back upon the Washington policy, he was apparently determined to destroy it. With this statement, he transformed what had been intended as an offer to negotiate into what could only come as a demand for surrender, on pain of sanctions which neither Washington nor the UN had any intention of applying and in the interest of an objective (the military unification of Korea) which both Washington and the UN had long since abandoned. Perforce, the draft of the Presidential statement had to be laid aside. In his *Memoirs* the former President recalls the anecdote which Lincoln produced when confronted by a somewhat similar move on the part of General McClellan: ". . . it made me think of the man whose horse kicked up and stuck his foot through the stirrup. He said to the horse: 'If you are going to get on, I will get off.' " Like Lincoln, Truman was in no doubt as to who was going to get on and who would get off. "By this act," he writes, "MacArthur left me no choice—I could no longer tolerate his insubordination."

Richard E. Neustadt

THE EXERCISE OF PRESIDENTIAL POWER

When Richard E. Neustadt's book on presidential power was published in 1960, it came to the attention of John F. Kennedy, who then selected Professor Neustadt as one of his advisors. Neustadt's approach to the Truman-MacArthur controversy is that of a political scientist whose interest is focused on the practical problems of the office of the presidency.

On October 7, 1950 the General Assembly of the United Nations, "recalling that the essential objective was the establishment of a unified independent and democratic Korea," recommended that "all appropriate steps be taken to assure stability" throughout the country, North as well as South. That same day the first non-Korean units of MacArthur's forces crossed the 38th Parallel in pursuit of the enemy so nearly (but not quite) entrapped by the end-run of Inchon three weeks earlier. The General Assembly's words sanctioned this military move, of course, but they did more; they set the "war aim" of the member governments whose troops were under MacArthur's command: a unified, non-Communist Korea. This aim had long been a secondary objective of American foreign policy, pursued by peace-

From *Presidential Power: The Politics of Leadership* (New York, 1960), pp. 123–146. Reprinted by permission of John Wiley & Sons, Inc., Publishers.

ful means. It now became the policy objective of the war. Thus "victory" was now defined for the armed forces and the public of the United States, which never yet—as every school child knew—had failed to "win" a "War."

Three months before, when North Korean armies had invaded South Korea, a less ambitious aim had been envisaged by the authors of American intervention. As Truman, in his *Memoirs,* paraphrases National Security Council minutes of June 29, 1950:

> *I stated categorically that . . . I wanted to take every step necessary to push the North Koreans back behind the 38th Parallel. But I wanted to be sure that we did not become so deeply committed in Korea that we could not take care of such other situations as might develop.*
> *. . . I wanted it clearly understood that our operations were designed to restore peace there and to restore the border.*

The United Nations Resolution of June 27, which both justified and authorized those operations, was drafted in the American State Department. It recommended "such assistance to the Republic of Korea as may be necessary to repel the armed attack and to restore international peace and security in the area." The last phrase was ambiguous, but its inclusion in the draft cannot be said to have reflected any conscious purpose at top departmental levels different from that stated by the President. And in the early weeks of fighting, as our forces were committed and pushed back to the Pusan perimeter, nothing he or Cabinet members said in public contravened the emphasis of his remarks just quoted.

The United Nations resolution of October 7 thus embodied and expressed a real shift in the foreign-policy objective of hostilities, a shift made possible by transformation of the military situation in the last half of September, after Inchon. The new policy objective was no less a war aim of Americans for being an expression of the General Assembly. The United States was in the war as UN agent. In form, not Washington but UN Headquarters at Lake Success was properly the source of such objectives. In fact, the General Assembly's words on this occasion were of Washington's selection. Reportedly, the Secretary of State, Dean Acheson, chose most of them himself. At any rate, the State Department's draft of what became the UN resolution had his personal approval, and the President's. Truman knew its terms before it was proposed at Lake Success. Despite its UN form, the resolution was American in roughly the degree that UN aid to South Korea was American, that is to say in all essentials. Many other governments concurred, of course, the British chief among them. Despite a popular impression to the contrary, this shift of policy objectives was no Washington *diktat.* But the decision was a Washington decision; in that he assented, it was Truman's. . . .

What was Truman's risk? Let me begin by mentioning what it was not. In and of itself, announcement of the new war aim did not *create* a military risk. To be sure, military risks were run by the troop movements that accompanied the announcement (other risks were avoided by abandoning that very poor defense line, the 38th Parallel). But the decision to attempt destruction of the North Korean forces on home grounds preceded the decision on what war aim to announce. The same thing can be said of diplomatic risks. No allies were estranged *by the announcement* of a new war aim. As for potential enemies, it is improbable that their intentions were affected one way or the other. To judge from what the Chinese said, and later did, Peking's concern was with MacArthur's military progress, never mind its foreign-policy objective. Chinese concern was not confined to anything so simple as a buffer zone along the border; an entity called North Korea, not the border, was the stake (perhaps in roughly the same sense that South Korea, under reverse circumstances, was for Washington). Even had the UN promised restoration of an independent North once all resistance ceased—which, naturally, no one proposed—I know of nothing to suggest that Peking would have withheld intervention. The Communist world does not take kindly, it appears, to the dismantling of a member state's facilities for governance: the party and the army. MacArthur's military progress threatened both, no matter what came after. In short, the military risks and diplomatic dangers usually associated with MacArthur's march across the parallel existed independent of the words used in the UN resolution. MacArthur's march was authorized before the words were seen, much less approved, at Lake Success.

Truman's risk when the UN announced its new war aim was of

another sort. The risk was to his own prospective influence in every facet of his work as President. His risk was not the same as Eisenhower's in the Humphrey case. It did bear directly on his Washington relationships or reputation. What he endangered, rather, was that other power source, his prestige with his public outside Washington. . . . What Truman risked was leeway. He gambled with his own ability to get done many things far more important to him than the unification of Korea. His risk was that worst risk for Presidents in public: the teaching of a lesson that rebounds against himself, the rousing of expectancies in conflict with his policies, the risk of action making for confusion not enlightenment. "Korea," as a series of events, was bound to be a foremost "happening" in public consciousness, arousing hopes and fears which could not but affect the look of Truman and his policies. In the degree he needed leeway to accomplish what he wanted, he depended on the lessons that this happening would teach. In the degree he needed national attention, he depended on the focus it provided. Only as Korea could be made to point *his* moral could he foster acquiescence in his regime and his aims. Only by his actions could he influence its teaching. Yet that UN resolution risked imparting to "what happened" the least fortunate of meanings from his point of view: the meaning his opponents compressed into two words, "Truman's War," the bloodletting "he" started, would not "win," and could not stop.

Had the unification of Korea been Truman's dearest object, its announcement as a war aim would have been another matter. But it was among the least of the objectives on his mind. In July and August 1950, in December after Chinese intervention, in his struggles with MacArthur, and thereafter through his last two years of office, his behavior leaves no doubt about the many things he wanted more than that. He wanted to affirm that the UN was not a League of Nations, that aggression would be met with counter-force, that "police actions" were well worth their cost, that the "lesson of the 1930s" had been learned. He wanted to avoid "the wrong war, in the wrong place, at the wrong time," as General Bradley put it—and any "War," if possible. He wanted NATO strengthened fast, both militarily and psychologically. He wanted the United States rearmed without inflation, and prepared, thereafter, to sustain a level of expenditure for military forces and for foreign aid far higher than had seemed achievable before Korea. He also wanted to get on with the Fair Deal, keep Democrats in office, strengthen his congressional support from North and West, and calm the waters stirred by men like Senator McCarthy.

None of these aims *required* unification of Korea (however helpful at sufficiently low cost), and all of them took precedence with Truman. One need but read the "minutes" from Wake Island, where he met MacArthur on October 15, to sense Truman's relative disinterest in Korea save as a symbol of UN success and as a source of seasoned troops for Europe. One need but read between the lines of his address at San Francisco, two days later, to recall that war or no war he retained the hopes for November's congressional election which had brought him "whistle-stopping" West in May, before the war began.

Indeed, Korean unity was so low in Truman's order of priorities that it was off his list within three months of its adoption. It went off London's list on first sight of the Chinese in Korea; Truman was somewhat slower, to his cost. But once the Chinese demonstrated that a widespread war in Asia and a risk of World War III would be the lowest price for unification, he showed firm unwillingness to pay it. By December 1950, as the enemy poured south, his object became merely to hang on. By February 1951, with the lines stabilized and an advance in prospect, he reverted to his aim at the beginning of the war: a restoration of the border and cessation of hostilities. By March, he was preparing to dismiss MacArthur. By June, with the Chinese in full retreat (and with NATO Commander Eisenhower in full cry for troops), Truman was prepared to make a truce on the first strong defense line north of the 38th Parallel, and to dismiss as "real estate"—not his term but the Pentagon's—the territory stretching to the next line north of that, the "waist" of the peninsula where London unsuccessfully had urged a halt some seven months before.

If Truman thus retreated from the war aim of October 1950, rather than pay cash for it in coin of other policies, he did so with the full support of Washington advisers, military, diplomatic, and political alike. And their retreat in chorus was a decorous performance next to the stampede at the UN. Within eight weeks the resolution of October 7 had not only dropped from sight but out of mind and, save for twinges of regret and of embarrassment, seems to have figured further in the thoughts of few, indeed, at Lake Success.

Unfortunately, the new war aim was not so easily expunged from public consciousness in the United States, or from the mind of the commander in the field, General MacArthur. What for Washington and Lake Success was but a passing fancy, taken and abandoned as the war news changed, MacArthur seems to have regarded as the only proper outcome of hostilities, at least of those in which *he* was engaged (scarcely an unreasonable notion for the man who had accepted the surrender of Japan). He had not forced this war aim on his government, but very willingly became its instrument with no sign of the mental reservations hedging its choice by his superiors. When they abandoned it, the consequences of that difference grew severe indeed. . . .

Thus by choosing unification as a war aim the President not only tied Korea's meaning and his prestige to an easy occupation of the North, but he also added something to the likelihood that he would have no benefits to show by way of substitute. The halting of Mac-Arthur short of "victory" might have been troublesome enough, once victory had been defined as unification. Instead, because that was its definition, Truman let MacArthur risk and lose the tangible advantages of ground and of diplomacy gained from five months of fighting. The lessons that Korea taught might not have been as pleasant with a stalemate at the "waist" as with a victory. The actual outcome made those lessons sad, indeed, for Truman and his causes—the sadder since his war aim meant so little in his scheme of things.

These are the terms in which to measure Truman's power risk when he endorsed his State Department's words for the UN. The many things he wanted more than North Korea's conquest called for leeway from his public. To foster public tolerance of him and his aims he needed object lessons that would demonstrate the worth of what he wanted. To make Korea's teaching turn on unification was to risk the opposite result. Korea was the teacher at the center of the stage. To reach and teach his public any President must ride events; he teaches by his doing in the context of events; he teaches as his actions attach meaning to "what happens." The publicizing of a new war aim invited Truman's "students" to attach "wrong" meaning in precisely the degree it should turn costly of accomplishment. Truman gave MacArthur, of all people, the initiative in calculating costs. . . . The greatest risk that Truman ran lay in MacArthur's capability to magnify all other risks.

However, these were not the terms in which the issue came to Truman. The clarifying questions would have been: What should the outcome of this war convey to men outside the Washington community? How may this war aim color what they came to see and feel? Few Presidents, presumably, much less their State Departments, would formulate such questions so precisely; to do so puts an instinct into words. The formulation, though, is not in point. What matters is that nothing of the sort, however, stated or implied, seems to have reached the President. Instead, the issue of a new war aim wore the disguise of military choices; the risks that showed themselves were military risks. The danger in the issue was political, but this was not apparent on its face or in the words of Truman's chief advisers.

How did Truman come to choose a new war aim? The question can be answered only by a chronological account. The story starts in August 1950. In early August after some hesitation, not without some doubts, the President and the Joint Chiefs of Staff approved MacArthur's daring plan to crush the North Koreans: a landing at Inchon, behind them, simultaneous with an offensive at their front on the Pusan perimeter. The date then set (and met) was September 15; as it approached, MacArthur was supremely confident; the White House and the Pentagon were not. But is was clear to Washington that if MacArthur should succeed, even in part, the war would be transformed and he would need some new directives. "What next?" was put to the Departments of State and Defense, and their response eventually became a National Security Council paper, initialled by Truman on September 11. His paraphrase of its conclusion will suggest the hopes and fears—and the uncertainties—involved in the discussions that preceded his approval:

General MacArthur was to conduct . . . military operations either to force the North Koreans behind the 38th Parallel or to destroy their forces [south of it]. If there was no indication or threat of entry of Soviet or Chi-

nese Communist elements in force . . . [he] was to extend his operations north of the parallel and to make plans for the occupation of North Korea . . . . No ground operations were to take place north of the parallel in the event of Soviet or Chinese Communist entry. [Emphasis added.]

The first part of the foregoing was turned into a directive for quick dispatch to MacArthur; the balance was left to await allied consultations and the outcome of Inchon.

MacArthur's purpose, as reported to the Pentagon in August, was destruction of the North Korean forces before they could get behind their border. This he did not manage, as the National Security Council discussions had foreseen he might not do. With this exception (a momentous one), his Inchon operation was a triumph, transforming not the war alone but the emotions felt in Washington and Lake Success. Appetites rose as the troops went forward. On September 26 the UN army from the south made contact with the units from Inchon. On September 28 Seoul was finally liberated. On October 1 some South Korean units crossed the parallel without much opposition.

The North Koreans, though, had crossed ahead of them. The Communist troops were battered, disorganized, but still a force in being. And from no quarter did there come the faintest sign that they were ready to surrender or even to negotiate. On September 21, Senator Knowland of California, gave it as his opinion that to leave them in that state behind the parallel would be "appeasement." For once his views were shared by the Administration and by friendly governments. The border, at the parallel, had proved its insufficiency as a defense line. To break off when it was reached was to invite a new attack across it, when and as the North Koreans chose. Short of pursuing and destroying their field forces, there seemed no effective way to meet that threat. No one around the President proposed to live with it.

Within a week of Inchon all Truman's advisers were agreed upon pursuit, if nothing else turned up to simplify (or complicate) the problem militarily. In consequence, and after some amount of interallied consultation, the Defense and State Departments urged and he approved a second missive to MacArthur; approval seems to have been given on or about September 24; the directive was dispatched September 27. To quote from Truman's *Memoirs:*

. . . [MacArthur] was told that his military objective was "the destruction of the North Korean Armed Forces." In attaining this objective he was authorized to conduct military operations north of the 38th Parallel . . . provided that at the time of such operation there had been no entry into North Korea by major Soviet or Chinese Communist forces, no announcement of an intended entry, and no threat by Russian or Chinese Communists to counter our operations militarily . . . . [Italics added.]

Had Truman (and his Chiefs of Staff) been fully confident of Inchon from the first, or had a measure of success not come so fast thereafter, forethought might have counseled hedging the military objective for MacArthur even further than was done in this second directive. (Within two days of its dispatch he had submitted and gained approval for a plan committing him to moves beyond the waist of the peninsula.) But flat refusal to attempt *some* military exploitation of his sudden, great advantage was not to be expected, in the circumstances, from governments with troops engaged; from Washington and London and the rest it certainly was not forthcoming. There is no evidence that any of the governments with forces under his command were in the least reluctant to pursue the North Koreans.

Strictly speaking, the decision to pursue the North Koreans did not call for UN action; strictly speaking, its approval was already on the books. Destruction of the enemy's armed forces, whether on home grounds or not, was well within the terms of that vague, early-summer phrase: "the restoration of peace and security in the area." But in practice Truman's chief advisers, and the President himself, seem to have taken as a matter of course the need for something more from Lake Success, once it had been decided that MacArthur should go north. In theory Washington might have authority, but the fine print of prior resolutions had been little publicized. Before Inchon, repelling the aggression had meant getting North Koreans out of South Korea in the emphasis of news dispatches generally. Although the Administration might conceive "what next" in terms of how to liquidate the enemy, the press and congressmen and certain UN delegates now posed the issue publicly in terms of the 38th Parallel. To cross or not to cross might seem irrelevant inside the Pentagon and State, but most insiders were aware that on the outside it was being called *the* question.

From the President on down, responsible officials wanted to avoid a look of "going it alone," or putting something over, or relying on fine print, especially when such a look was undeserved. In the circumstances some specific UN sanction seemed to follow logically from the dispatch of new orders to MacArthur. "That is a matter for the UN to decide," said Truman on September 21, when queried at press conference about crossing the parallel; thereafter, UN action was not only logical, it had to happen.

Besides, no one in Washington was now disposed to doubt MacArthur's power to make daring pay. Once he was ordered north it was assumed that he would go there in a hurry. So he did—by October 10 the east coast was in his hands up to Wonsan, just below the waist of the peninsula; on the west, Pyongyang, the North Korean capital, was taken October 19; before the month was out he would control the whole peninsula, and with it the great bulk of North Korea's population ("mainland" Korea to the north and east was mostly barren ground). Foreseeing this in late September both State and Pentagon thought UN guidelines indispensable for occupation of a territory that did not belong to Syngman Rhee. The South Koreans claimed their government, by rights, embraced the North. This belied the UN's declaration of intent, dating from 1947, that a united government should stem from free elections. The issue had been academic for three years; now it would be joined within three weeks, and with it other issues, reconstruction and the like, which went beyond American authority as UN military agent. Psychology aside, these seemed reason enough for something new from Lake Success.

What that something should be does not seem to have taken a great deal of time or long attention from the President's advisers, to say nothing of the President. The desired General Assembly resolution was formally presented by eight UN delegations, *not* including the United States, on the last day of September. Initial drafting must have been completed well before the Joint Chiefs of Staff dispatched their new directive to MacArthur. In line with the instructions given him, what Washington proposed through friends at Lake Success contained no mention of the parallel—Assembly action, in itself, would settle that—and phrased policy objectives briefly and obliquely. . . . The cautions to MacArthur about Russians and Chinese might not embody likelihoods; it was not thought they did. But just in case, there were to be no highly charged, unbreakably committing words upon the record. Instead, the resolution was devoted, mainly, to machinery or intentions for political and economic reconstruction of the country. What I have called a new war aim was conveyed less by the specific words than by the clear assumption underlying all the words: that military action would produce a unified, non-Communist Korea.

Except from UN delegates in Moscow's sphere there was little disposition at Lake Success to argue against prompt endorsement of what Washington proposed. Only the Indians strongly urged delay. Their suggestion was put forward in the interest of a further search for some way to negotiate (which they themselves were not sure how to find). Only the Yugoslavs distinguished sharply between military tactics and policy objectives, while decrying shifts in both. But Tito's delegation, which had chosen to abstain three months before, could not claim much attention from the friends of South Korea. At any rate, the partners in the fighting were agreed, most other delegations willing, votes available, and Washington committed to its own proposal. On October 4 the resolution passed the Political Committee; three days later it went through the General Assembly by a vote of 47 to 5 with 7 abstentions.

It will be clear from this account what face that outcome and its preparations showed to Truman: a tying up of loose ends in his choice of a new target for the troops, a choice which merely set their prior target on new ground. It also will be clear what sort of word he had from his advisers in the circle of the National Security Council and on the day he saw the drafted UN resolution. If other words were heard from other sources, as of course they may have been, they left no traces I can find. In all events, with Acheson and the Joint Chiefs agreed, it is unlikely that he would have listened very hard. Of course, he read five newspapers; no doubt he saw expression of concern about the UN's move. But what the press conveyed were pros and cons couched mostly in the language of a crossing of the parallel. That emphasis, itself, had a significance and held a warning for him. But the language was so academic, from where Truman sat, as to dilute his interest and divert attention. I have no doubt it did. From where he sat the crossing of the parallel had already "occurred," and for good reason, on the day *he* chose to send MacArthur north, two weeks (or more) before the vote at Lake Success.

One difficulty with the press as an adviser to a President is that he has enough to crowd his calendar and mind without attending closely to debate on prospects which for him are past (unless, of course, a trial balloon is up; this was no trial balloon). Not even readers of the *New York Times*—not even its columnists—move in precisely the same time-dimension as the man who sits where Truman did in the days after Inchon.

Had something tangible occurred during those days to emphasize the diplomatic risks of moving north, one can assume that Truman's advisers would have changed their tune, the State Department, Pentagon, and press alike. But unless one took as tangible the casual word of Chinese generals or the phrasing of a Peking speech—which no one in authority inclined to do—nothing of the sort developed in the interval between Inchon and the last stages of UN proceedings. Not until the first week of October did there come the sort of threat presumably envisaged in September's two directives to MacArthur. Then it came from such a source, in such a way, as to invite discounting by Americans.

On October 3 the Indian ambassador to mainland China, K. M. Panikkar, advised his government—which passed the word abroad—that Chou En-lai, the Chinese Foreign Minister, had told him:

> *if the United Nations forces crossed the 38th Parallel China would send in troops to help the North Koreans. However, this action would not be taken if only South Koreans crossed the 38th parallel.*

I quote the paraphrase in Truman's *Memoirs,* where he also sets forth, faithfully, the gist of the appraisal he received from his advisers:

> *. . . the problem . . . was that Mr. Panikkar had in the past played the game of the Chinese Communists. . . . It might . . . be no more than a relay of Communist propaganda. There was also then pending in . . . the General Assembly . . . a clear authorization for the United Nations commander to operate in North Korea. The key vote on the resolution was due the following day, and it appeared quite likely that Chou En-lai's "message" was a bald attempt to blackmail the United Nations. . . .*

Besides, since the directives to MacArthur, Moscow not Peking had been the Pentagon's great worry. Now that the UN was on the march, an intervention by Chinese, alone, seemed relatively easy to withstand and *therefore* most unlikely to occur (an interesting exercise in logic). "They have no air," as Truman was to be told, wrongly, at Wake Island; further comfort was derived from the reflection that their ground attack had not come when it could have been decisive, near Pusan. In Washington no less than at MacArthur's headquarters there was some lack of readiness "to take seriously a country which up until this time had been notorious for its political and military weakness."

Even had Peking appeared more formidable, more in earnest, less a mere blackmailer; even had the British, say, not Panikkar, been chosen to transmit Chou's threat, it is improbable that Truman's chief advisers would have counseled abandoning MacArthur's broad advance or putting off the General Assembly action. It is equally improbable that Truman would have accepted such advice if offered. A threat of intervention *in Korea* could but stress the military need for rapid movement north; only there would troops find strong defense lines. And by that late date, October 3, the UN's pending action had become identified in press accounts as the "clear authorization" Truman later called it. By that time, to proceed without it would have caused immense embarrassment both at home and abroad. Not to proceed at all would have meant overturning every tactical consideration and diplomatic assumption on which policy had rested for three weeks with no more reason than a verbal warning, given second-hand, and such evaluation as could be obtained in one or two days after its receipt. Before Chou's warning, Truman's power risk was called to his attention neither by the terms of what he was deciding nor by what he learned from his associates. When the warning came, he scarcely could have chosen *not* to take the risk, no matter how aware he might have been.

This chronological account explains why Truman acted as he did in making unification the aim of the Korean War. He chose his aim because it seemed to follow from the military movement at virtually no diplomatic risk. With the military opportunity before them and with diplomatic dangers out of sight, the men he leaned on for advice saw little risk of any sort. There is nothing in the record to suggest that he saw more than they did. In June it had been clear to him that restoration of the border was worth fighting for. In August when he sanctioned plans for Inchon he evidently saw no need to take an early stand on what should happen if the enemy escaped destruction south of the border. When the contingency arose, he met it in the way that then appeared most opportune. Chou's warning challenged the perspective of the moment, but the warning was too suspect and arrived too late to affect choices taken ten days earlier. The President incurred his power risk without assessing it, when he made the choices put to him in August and September.

Having incurred the risk before Chou's warning came, why make it worse thereafter? The question arises because Truman spent October adding to his power risk with every choice he made. The new war aim had been announced by the UN in cautious words; Truman promptly and repeatedly restated it himself without equivocation. MacArthur's northward march had been approved with qualifications; Truman promptly waived the major qualification. The President's own course throughout October heightened every danger of "wrong" meaning for Korea if there should be some substance in Chou's warning. And it cannot be said that an alternative approach was urged on Truman by his circle of advisers. Unhappily for him he chose as they advised.

The President's own choices in October consisted of words addressed to MacArthur and of other words addressed to public audiences. On October 8, the second day of general advance past the parallel, Truman approved new instructions to MacArthur in the words proposed by the Joint Chiefs of Staff and endorsed by General Marshall, now the Secretary of Defense, with Acheson's concurrence:

> In light of the possible intervention of Chinese Communist forces in North Korea the following amplification of our directive [of September 25] is forwarded for your guidance:
>
> "Hereafter in the event of open or covert employment anywhere in Korea of major Chinese Communist units, without prior announcement, you should continue the action as long as, in your judgment, action by forces now under your control offers a reasonable chance of success." [Italics added.]

"Success" as thus unqualified could not now be expected to mean anything but enemy destruction for the sake of unification. "Reasonable" now was delegated to the judgment of MacArthur with no other qualifier than a limit on his forces. In the weeks to come he would misjudge with tragic consequences, but it cannot be charged that he exceeded his instructions. Nothing said by anybody at Wake Island on October 15 qualified this delegation to MacArthur; indeed, it was confirmed by the prevailing atmosphere of confidence in him. Nothing said in public on the President's return diluted the commitment to a unified Korea. Rather the Wake Island communiqué, the San Francisco speech, a presidential address to the UN (at its birthday celebration on October 24), all added weight and definiteness to the war aim, publicized it further, promised its achievement cheap, and made it Truman's own. The discretion given to MacArthur in October contributed directly to disaster in November. When disaster came, the White House bore the brunt of popular frustration with the consequences of MacArthur's judgment. Truman's public statements of October contributed to this result.

Why was the President so optimistic in October? His optimism was the product, mainly, of MacArthur's confident assurance at Wake Island. The general had told Truman flatly (as the latter recollects their private conversation), "that if any Chinese were to enter Korea they would face certain disaster, but he did not expect them to try anything that foolish." The President had this to match against Washington estimates that Peking *could* mount an effective intervention but probably *would* do no more than covertly assist the North Koreans. Intervention of the sort suggested by Chou's warning was discounted on all grounds of logic (Washington's) as buttressed by some diplomatic inquiries in other capitals (including Taipei, naturally, but not, of course, Peking). These estimates were scarcely worrisome; they were made less so by the general's reassurance. For Truman and his speech writers MacArthur's word sufficed—and so it seems to have done for the others at Wake Island, the Chairman of the Joint Chiefs of Staff, the State Department's Ambassador-at-Large, the Secretary of the Army, and assorted lesser lights.

Chou's warning of October 3 thus faded out of sight, and everything looked as it had before: a military victory assuring in its train a gratifying policy objective. Perhaps it is more accurate to say that the look of things by mid-October was not as it had been, it was more so. Victory was closer, the war aim was embraced in public by the

President, and privately in government Korean unification grew weightier each day. In White House memoranda and in papers for the National Security Council, in intelligence evaluations, and the like, repeated use of such terms as "the UN objective," "the decision of the UN," "the UN's purpose to unify," soon dulled awareness that the new war aim was nothing but a target of opportunity chosen rather casually (and at first provisionally) by the very men who read these words. The tendency of bureaucratic language to create in private the same images presented to the public never should be underrated. By the middle of October, I would say, in their minds no less than in public, Truman and the rest were thinking of the UN aim not as a mere convenience but as a cause.

When Truman spoke at San Francisco and at Lake Success he had no inkling that the Chinese had begun a massive, hidden move across the Yalu. Two weeks after Wake Island some five Chinese armies were established in the mountainous terrain directly north of the peninsula. Reinforced, by stealth, for four weeks more, that striking force was almost to destroy MacArthur. Even before November 1 it made a mockery of his existing orders. We know that now, but Truman did not know it then. The location of the Chinese striking force remained unknown to the Americans until it struck, November 28.

Truman did learn early in November that the war would not end on the pleasant note his government had sounded. Two weeks after his address at the UN he knew the outcome could not be successful in the way he had defined success. By late October Chinese presence in Korea was confirmed from contacts on the battlefield. In the first week of November MacArthur insisted upon bombing Yalu bridges because troops "pouring" south threatened "ultimate destruction of the [UN] forces . . . ." Before November 10, Truman's advisers had informed him, in effect, that military action limited to present forces, confined to Korea, could not achieve the military target set September 27: destruction of the enemy's armed forces. Everyone agreed that no more troops could be spared for MacArthur and that he should not enlarge the boundaries of the war. But he now faced a new enemy with airpower and troops massed north of the Yalu and with several tens of thousand men already south of it. So Washington believed when UN aircraft were employed against the Yalu bridges.

Washington was wrong about proportions north and south, but it was no secret that the river probably would be a bridge of ice before MacArthur could complete his occupation of North Korea. At the least, negotiation would be necessary to that occupation, necessary to its maintenance and probably to its achievement. At the most, if Peking meant the worst, unification would no longer be a viable objective; Chinese *capabilities* were not in doubt.

Thus within a month of MacArthur's march past the 38th Parallel, it became plain that the policy objective, the war aim, once supposed to follow from the military action, now could only follow from a diplomatic deal with the unrecognized, avowedly hostile claimants to Formosa—or be given up entirely. That these were the alternatives of policy, and that there were no others short of risking general war, was clear from the intelligence available to Washington in the first week of November. As Truman's *Memoirs* show, the policy dilemma was implicitly *accepted* by all parties to a National Security Council discussion on November 9. The President was not among the parties on that day. He got a briefing afterwards, however, and acceded to the views he heard expressed. Truman has recorded Acheson's summation of those views:

> . . . *[Acheson] pointed out that it was agreed that General MacArthur's directive should not now be changed and* he should be free to do what he could in a military way, *but without bombing Manchuria. At the same time, the State Department would seek ways to find out whether negotiations with the Chinese Communists were possible, although one problem was that we lacked any direct contacts with the Peking regime . . . [Italics added.]*

In other words, MacArthur's opportunity, once the *occasion* for a new war aim, now was reduced to "doing what he could" in aid of diplomatic efforts no less dubious than those urged by the Indians six weeks earlier. So far as this had the discussion wandered from assumptions—and from preconditions—voiced in mid-September.

With Washington's assumptions changed, why were MacArthur's orders left unaltered? Why was he still to pursue the objective of September 27 with the discretion of October 8? Why was the man whom Truman had considered firing in August now left the discretion to attempt what Washington no longer thought he could achieve?

The National Security Council discussion of November 9 suggests
an answer. To quote again from Truman's *Memoirs:*

> *General Bradley stated that . . .[if] the Chinese desired only to set up*
> *a buffer area . . . negotiations might be fruitful . . . [but if not] . . . we*
> should be able to hold in the general area of our present positions . . .
> [with] . . . *increasing question of how much pressure we could stand with-*
> *out attacking Manchurian bases.*
>   *. . . Marshall pointed out . . . that our eastern front in Korea was widely*
> *dispersed and thinly spread and that this represented an added risk. . . .*
> *Bradley replied that of course General MacArthur had done this in order*
> to carry out his directive that he was to occupy the whole country and
> hold elections.
>   *. . . Acheson asked . . . if there was any line that was better from a*
> *military point of view than the* present *one, and Bradley replied that . . .*
> *the farther* back *. . . the easier it would be to maintain . . . however, he*
> *realized that* any backward movement . . . might lose us the South Ko-
> reans' will to fight. *[Italics added.]*

In terms of foreign policy, to halt MacArthur or to pull him back
would not have clarified Chinese intentions; neither would it aid the
diplomatic bargaining. In military terms to call a halt seemed over-
cautious, given *policy* objectives and the chance these could be
salvaged by diplomacy. In fact there was no chance, but Truman's
National Security Council advisers did not know that. Instead, they
knew, or rather thought, that Peking very likely wanted only a buffer
zone. They reasoned, it appears, that mainland China was dependent
on the Russians and that more ambitious wants would mean *Russia*
was courting war. As Bradley put it to the National Security Council,
Peking's alternative intentions might be either "to force us into a
war of attrition . . . where we might be in danger of losing if the
Soviets decided to start a global war," or "to drive us completely
off the Korean peninsula . . . [which] would mean World War III
because [the Chinese] would be unable to do it alone, and Soviet
entry would inevitably extend the fighting . . . ." But Moscow, it was
thought, did not want general war; the Chinese, then, would have
to show restraint.

Why these Americans, who had proclaimed *their own* aversion to
world war, should have thought Stalin would assume that *he* risked

general war if Peking acted, I will not endeavor to explain. It is enough to see that this is how they reasoned; thereby they discounted what they knew on November 9. Besides, there was the thing they did not know: that Peking's striking force was on the *south* side of the Yalu.

With Chinese aims misunderstood, with Moscow's risks misread, with this one fact unknown, Truman's advisers focused on the diplomatic prospects as intently as they once had done on military opportunities. While they sought to assess the chances for diplomacy, MacArthur should "do what he could." This was the course they urged upon the President after their meeting of November 9. This was the course he followed. The issue as it reached him wore a diplomatic face which fatally obscured the military risk, a reversal, in effect, of late September's situation. But this time, in contrast with the other, the issue's look cannot be said to have obscured the risk to his own influence. On the contrary, its diplomatic features bore a strong family resemblance to those of his prestige. By then United States prestige, UN prestige, were quite as much committed in the world as his at home. By then his problem in relation to his public had become how best to back away from his October promises without harming the many things that made retreat worthwhile. His problem had become how best to make some outcome short of "victory" teach tolerance for him and for his aims. His problem had become how best to *act* in order to *enlighten*. And with but a change of pronoun this conveys his country's problem in relation to its enemies and its allies.

There is no reason to believe that Truman's chief advisers, or the President, himself, considered his prestige apart from issues of diplomacy. Had they done so in these circumstances it is probable that their course would have been much the same. In essence the considerations were alike on either score. Both counseled a postponement of decision. While it was thought that Peking might negotiate, why halt MacArthur before bargaining began? If the Chinese intended otherwise, there was all the more reason for allowing them to demonstrate, so everyone could see that their aggression, not timidity in Washington, had thwarted the UN and stopped MacArthur. Besides, he had done better at Inchon than his superiors expected; conceiv-

ably he might do so again. Thus ran the logic, it appears, beneath
the surface of discussion in the National Security Council, a logic
quite as good in prestige terms as in those of diplomacy.

This was good logic if Peking's forces were where they were
thought to be and if MacArthur's generalship was as infallible as
Inchon had suggested. In the fifteen days between November 9 and
MacArthur's march into an enemy trap, Washington learned little
more of Chinese dispositions. Indeed, their forward elements now
broke off contact, which encouraged the opinion that their purpose
was defensive and their show of force intended but to emphasize
the border. Meanwhile MacArthur, seeming confident again after his
scare about the Yalu bridges, hurried preparations for a victory
march with scattered forces fanning out to occupy the country. His
troops began to move November 25; within three days the Chinese
struck, not from behind the Yalu but from mountains to the south of
it, between MacArthur's columns and behind them. What then occurred, in military terms, was "one of the major decisive battles of
the present century, followed by the longest retreat in American history." The Chinese did not demonstrate mere power to deny the
UN victory; they demonstrated power to deprive MacArthur of his
whole success since Inchon—a power his deployment placed into
their hands.

It was one thing to leave MacArthur's orders unchanged on November 9; it was quite another to leave them unchanged day by day
thereafter while he prepared and began his victory march. On
November 9 the National Security Council had agreed that directives
to MacArthur should be "kept under review," pending "clarification"
of Peking's intent. In accepting this agreement Truman had postponed a change of orders; he had not intended to decide the issue
for all time. Yet this postponement of decision proved to be one of
the most decisive actions Truman ever took. So far as I can ascertain his National Security Council advisers did not raise with him,
nor he with them, the question of concluding that postponement.
In the two-week interval before MacArthur's march the general,
not the President, became the judge and arbiter of White House
risks. Action in October had heightened Truman's personal risk;
inaction in November heightened every danger, military, diplomatic,
and personal alike. Why, then, did Truman passively await the out-

come of MacArthur's plans for victory? I have explained why orders to the general went unchanged in the second week of November. But why were they not altered in the third week or the fourth?

Poor intelligence, or poor evaluation, may account for MacArthur's conduct, but it does not suffice to explain Washington's behavior in the days before his victory march. Although no one there *knew* where the Chinese were, the Pentagon, at least, included men who could read maps and knew where they *might* be. By mid-November some of these men felt virtually certain of the real Chinese location and were becoming worried lest MacArthur fail to concentrate his forces. Before those forces marched, the worry had touched Truman's chief advisers. In the last days, reportedly, it was intense in Bradley's mind and Marshall's and in Acheson's. The British, whose diplomatic fears had outrun Washington's, kept urging that the troops be stopped and forward columns pulled back to the "waist." The American Joint Chiefs of Staff were not prepared to sacrifice MacArthur's plans on London's say-so, but Pentagon unhappiness about those separate columns grew apace, and he was practically implored to show more caution. When he demurred, as under his instructions he had every right to do, the Chiefs of Staff lacked courage (lacking certainty) to seek their alteration from the President. Despite the worry, no one went to Truman—and that outcome turns on matters more complex than poor intelligence.

No one went to Truman because everyone thought someone else should go. Before November 25 the men who had concluded two weeks earlier that Truman should not change MacArthur's orders were agreed, it seems, in wishing that he would. The diplomatic emphasis of earlier discussion ceased to obscure military risks; when those grew sharp enough, it reinforced them. The logic of November 9 led to an opposite conclusion some days later, in the light of what these men had come to fear. On November 9 the Chairman of the Joint Chiefs, Bradley, had waived military risks in deference to foreign policy; . . . But policy had not envisaged tactical disaster; policy suggested its avoidance at all costs. When worry grew, the military chiefs deferred to State; let Acheson, as guardian of "policy," ask Truman to reverse MacArthur. But Acheson, already under fire from the Capitol, was treading warily between the Pentagon and that inveterate idealist about generals, Harry Truman. In immediate terms the risk was "military"; if it justified reversing the commander in the field, then the Joint Chiefs must make the judgment and tell Truman. So Acheson is said to have insisted, understandably enough, and there the matter rested. On a "military" issue the Chiefs of Staff were loath to balk the victor of Inchon, whose tactics might be better than they seemed 8,000 miles away. As for the Secretary of Defense, he had preceded Acheson in State and had been Army Chief of Staff when Bradley was a subordinate commander. Since his return to government Marshall had leaned over backwards not to meddle with the work of his successors in *their* jobs. He also had leaned over backwards not to revive the old army feud between him and Mac-Arthur. What Acheson and Bradley were not ready to initiate, Marshall evidently felt he could not take upon himself.

For cabinet members and for military chiefs, a decision to go to the President is something like a government's decision to go to war; it is not something done each day on every issue. When the issue is reversal of established plans on grounds of sheer conjecture, men of prudence and responsibility may pause, and no wonder. In this instance, moreover, the plans were MacArthur's, and Truman was a man who liked to deal in the concrete.

The President, meanwhile, had little thought of overriding, on his own, the tactical decisions of a qualified commander. That seems to be the face the issue wore for Truman, personally, just before the win-the-war offensive: "You pick your man, you've got to back him up. That's the only way a military organization can work." If he perceived the policy and power risks beneath this surface, these were outweighed by fidelity to military doctrine. That weighting his advisers did not urge him to reverse. Instead, they all kept up the search for clarification. They still were seeking it on November 28.

III THE KOREAN WAR IN RETROSPECT

Alexander L. George

AMERICAN POLICY-MAKING AND THE NORTH KOREAN AGGRESSION

Richard Neustadt's study concentrates on the shifts in American and United Nations policy after the initial involvement in the Korean War. Alexander L. George focuses on the initial involvement itself, and the reversal of the American strategic plan for the Far East.

The Korean War represented the first American experience with the problem of meeting local Communist aggression by means of limited, if costly, warfare. But despite the revulsion with that experience, and the "new look" at military strategy and foreign policy, it may not be the last. The character of recent weapons development and the passing of our thermonuclear monopoly make it probable that in the future, as in the past, American policy-makers will be forced to consider the alternative of local conflict, with all its problems and risks, in determining how to respond to the threat or actuality of Communist moves in the peripheral areas.

In these circumstances, analyses of American policy-making immediately before and during the Korean War may well illuminate the perspectives and considerations relevant to this difficult and dangerous type of operation. Here, no more can be done than to examine the effect of strategic planning and estimates of Communist intentions and behavior on the decision to commit American forces to the defense of South Korea. This decision and even the crucial decision to commit ground forces to eventual offensive operations against the aggressor, was made within a few days of the North Korean attack. Attention, accordingly, is focused on American policy reactions to the war in the first week or ten days following June 25, 1950.

Judging by contemporary newspaper accounts, the American estimate of Soviet strategic intentions for some time prior to June 25 included two important expectations. First, it was thought that there was no immediate danger of an armed attack upon South Korea, although some form of Communist action elsewhere in the world in

From *World Politics* 7 (January 1955): 209–232. Reprinted with permission of The Rand Corporation.

the coming months was expected. Secondly, it was thought that the Politburo would not engage in overt forms of aggression which involved the risk of a general war for the present and for several years hence.

According to James Reston, the North Korean attack seems to have contradicted an important assumption held at the time by American officials, namely that

> . . . *while the Russians would continue trying to gain their ends by indirect aggression through the Communist parties, they would hesitate to use force, at least until they were at the top of their military strength, some time between 1952 and 1954.*
> . . . *The Korean Communists' attack has forced reconsideration of this theory . . . best guess here is that a speed-up in all military programs will now be ordered.* (New York Times, *June 27, 1950.*)

Similarly, the Alsops reported:

> *[Korea] has knocked the basic assumption underlying American policy into a cocked hat. This assumption was that the Kremlin was not now ready, and would not be ready for some years, to risk a world war. Yet the Kremlin has clearly and consciously risked a world war. This in turn means that Washington has been mistaken about Soviet capabilities and intentions.* (Washington Post, *July 5, 1950.*)

The impressions derived from contemporary newspaper accounts were confirmed to a considerable extent by disclosures at the MacArthur hearings. According to Secretary of State Acheson, the possibility of a North Korean attack had been recognized for some time but was not regarded as imminent. Rather, the general view was that the Communists would continue past efforts to take over South Korea by means short of war. And General Bradley's testimony, despite deletions by the security censor, conveyed the idea that policy-makers had been concerned over the possibility of Communist moves in other areas, and consequently had thought, at least initially, that the North Korean attack meant the Soviets were willing to risk a general war.

Interpretations of the North Korean Attack

If the events of June 25 had knocked the basic assumptions of American policy "into a cocked hat," what motivations and calculations were to be assigned to the North Korean attack? And how were broader Soviet strategic intentions to be interpreted? These questions not only were particularly urgent in the hours and days immediately following the attack, when decisions of crucial importance had to be made; they remained matters of analysis and speculation for months after the invasion of South Korea was launched.

The "Diversionary Move" Interpretation. The fact that American policy-makers had been alerted to the possibility of a series of Communist actions at various points throughout the world, but *not* to the attack against South Korea, may have encouraged some of them to suspect that the North Korean attack was a diversionary one. Thus, Hanson Baldwin wrote:

> *The background of our intelligence reports at the time of the Korean invasion showed that the Communists in many parts of the world were preparing a pattern of conquest for this summer, and Korea was only the the first step. . . .* (New York Times, *July 2.*)

This interpretation may have been held by some important military men—for example, General Omar Bradley. According to Drew Pearson's "inside" account of President Truman's meeting of policy advisers on June 25, General Bradley raised the question whether the North Korean attack was merely a diversion prior to the major Soviet blow, possibly against Iran. (*Washington Post,* June 30, July 3.)

If American policy-makers accepted the diversion interpretation of the North Korean attack, it followed logically that they would be reluctant to commit important American military forces to Korea because of the possibility that those forces might soon be needed elsewhere.

The "Soft-spot Probing" Interpretation. Probably derived from George Kennan's analysis of Soviet behavior was the interpretation of the North Korean attack as a "probing" of a "soft-spot."

The first indication that this thesis was being entertained and would influence policy came in a report on President Truman's attitude as he was leaving Kansas City for Washington on June 25.

> *It was understood that the President . . . planned to be as decisive as possible, within the framework of United States foreign policy. This policy is based on meeting the Soviet Union's moves everywhere possible*

by creating situations of strength. (Anthony Leviero, New York Times, June 26.)

And, it was reported (Albert Friendly, *Washington Post*, June 28), "The State Department consensus is that the Korean attack is another bit of 'feeling out,' of probing for soft spots."

After a month's time in which to consider the question of Soviet intentions, some officials in the United States government said to be experienced in dealing with the Russians, were reported to hold the following views:

They conceded the Russians have, by resorting to armed aggression, consciously adopted a much more risky and defiant policy. . . . But they are still of the opinion that the Russians were trying for a quick and easy victory in Korea and that they were not trying to get us off balance in order to start a major all-out war. (James Reston, New York Times, July 23.)

The "Testing" Interpretation. Many newspaper accounts attributed to American policy-makers the view that the North Korean move was intended to test the will of anti-Communist countries to resist open armed aggression by Communist forces. The implication was that if the anti-Communist forces failed to resist, then further Communist aggressions would quickly follow elsewhere in the world. In this respect, the testing interpretation differed from the "soft-spot probing" thesis, which did not imply such dire consequences if the non-Communist powers failed to resist the Korean aggression.

The unique implications of the testing interpretation stemmed from the fact that certain American policy-makers were disposed to view the North Korean aggression in terms of Hitler's early unopposed aggressions. The naked military character of the North Korean attack and the fact that it involved a sudden, massive employment of official armed forces across a clear-cut territorial boundary appear to have been responsible for calling to mind the historical parallel.

Thus, the *New York Times* correspondent Jay Walz reported on June 26 that sources close to top American policy-makers

. . . were certain that the North Korean attack was being viewed as a test of the countries, including the United States, that are standing up against Communist expansion. In such a light, the march across the

North-South Korean border would appear similar to the attacks that Hitler used to make to feel out the opposition.

The Alsops (*Washington Post*, June 28) quoted one of the men who took part in the crucial policy deliberations at Blair House as saying, "This attack on South Korea is an event like Hitler's re-occupation of the Rhineland."

The "Demonstration" Interpretation. An important addition to some versions of the testing and "soft-spot" interpretations was the hypothesis that the Soviets hoped to make of Korea a demonstration of their own strength and of Allied weakness which would have world-wide repercussions. Thus, the Alsops held that the Soviets hoped by such a demonstration to soften up other areas and weaken the position of anti-Communist leaders in the Far East and Western Europe (*Washington Post*, June 28). Later they added that Korea was only the first in a series of Soviet demonstrations of Russian strength and American weakness designed to lead to the crumbling of the Western will to resist (ibid., July 3).

"Soviet Far East Strategy" Interpretations. Some American policy-makers examined the motivation of the North Korean attack within the strategic context of clashing Far East policies and interests. Here the question of Soviet intentions assumed a more complex character, for such interpretations imputed to the Soviet-inspired North Korean action certain defensive calculations. This stood in marked contrast to interpretations when made the simple assumption of Soviet aggressive expansionist tendencies and which regarded the North Korean attack as a sign of Soviet initiative in Far East affairs.

A leading interpretation along these lines was offered by John Foster Dulles, then in charge of the State Department's preparations for a Japanese peace treaty. His thesis was that the North Korean attack was motivated in part by a desire to block American efforts to make Japan a full member of the free world. The attack was a strategic move to place Japan "between the upper [i.e., Sakhalin] and lower [Korean] jaws of the Russian bear." And, more broadly, the Communists hoped that the Korean invasion would dislocate plans being developed by the United States for positive and constructive policies to check the rising tide of communism in Asia and the Pacific. Thus, the attack had also been ordered because the Communists could not tolerate the "hopeful, attractive Asiatic experiment in democracy" that was under way in South Korea and which they had been unable to destroy by indirect aggression (speech of July 1).

The MacArthur hearings contained very little on the interpretations given the North Korean attack at its inception. The diversion interpretation was clearly implied in General Bradley's remarks, thus confirming the attribution of such views to him by newspapermen at the time. General Bradley was also able to recall, though with some difficulty, that the historical parallel with Hitler's early aggressions was also in "the back of our minds." [Secretary of Defense] Johnson's statement of the reasons for entering the Korean conflict possibly implies the testing and demonstration interpretations.

Problems Raised by these Interpretations

In important respects, these several interpretations of the significance of the North Korean attack did not constitute a clear-cut, unambiguous view of broader Soviet strategic intentions. Their conflicting elements, it may be noted, centered precisely on the questions of major relevance for developing an American policy reaction to the North Korean attack: Did the attack signify Soviet general war intentions or, at least, a greater readiness to risk such a war? Was it part of a plan for a series of Communist aggressions? If so, how rigidly determined was this plan? How important was Korea to the Politburo? What conditions and means would be required to force a Soviet withdrawal from the Korean venture?

The diversion and "soft-spot probing" interpretations assumed different answers to the question of whether the Politburo wanted or was ready to risk a general war. The expectation of a series of Soviet moves, in the diversion interpretation, implied a Soviet willingness to take very great risks. In contrast, the "soft-spot probing" thesis minimized the possibility that the Politburo was bent on general war or that it was consciously taking serious risks of general war.

Both the diversion and the testing interpretations held that Moscow had plans for a whole series of aggressive actions in the coming months. But, in contrast to the diversion hypothesis, the testing theory did not regard the schedule of Communist actions as rigidly determined. Rather, it held that if the free nations reacted firmly to the

North Korean aggression, the USSR would refrain from other moves that had been planned.

The testing interpretation differed significantly from the "soft-spot probing" thesis in implying that if the free world did not oppose the North Korean aggression, Stalin, like Hitler, would be led into further, more dangerous adventures. (The historical parallel with Hitler was an important element of the testing interpretation.) In contrast, Kennan's "soft-spot probing" thesis holds that Soviet leaders are not carried away by local successes into risky adventures.

Most versions of the testing, "soft-spot probing," and demonstration interpretations were *generalized* estimates of Soviet intentions and lacked a specific evaluation of Soviet strategy in the Far East. This omission was serious insofar as it might have led to oversimplification and underestimation of the Soviet conception of its interest in regard to Korea. Was the underlying Soviet intention in this instance no different from that present in any other Soviet probing action? Strategic analyses which placed the North Korean attack in the specific context of Far Eastern developments implied otherwise. They portrayed the Communist move in Korea as a *response* to certain American policies and as an anticipation of a forthcoming American initiative, namely, some sort of arrangement with Japan which would increase her independence and strength. An important implication of such strategic analyses, it would seem, was that the general objective aimed at by the Politburo in the Far East was important enough to rule out a retreat except under considerable pressure.

Thus, the various interpretations noted above not only attributed different intentions to the Soviet move in North Korea, but also contained different implications for American policy efforts to induce a Soviet withdrawal from the Korean venture. However, there was no indication during the MacArthur hearings that policy-makers had been conscious of an important divergence in their interpretations of the North Korean attack.

Reversal of the American Strategic Plan for the Far East

Both contemporary journalistic accounts and the MacArthur hearings amply confirm the extent of American unpreparedness for the contingency which arose on June 25. More serious than the intelligence failure and the resulting tactical surprise was the fact that strategic and foreign-policy planning had not foreseen the course of action which the United States actually took in response to the North Korean aggression. This was most dramatically indicated by the abrupt reversal, after June 25, of the basic American strategic plan for the Far East. At the time of the attack, American strategic planning did not call for employment of US forces for the defense of either Korea or Formosa. Nor, evidently, had the strategic plan foreseen any contingencies which might have to be met by any extension of American military commitments in the Far East. Not only was the decision to commit US forces to aid South Korea taken entirely ad hoc, but the major policy decision of June 27, neutralizing Formosa and giving the impression of "drawing the line," was also an improvisation in strategic planning.

That American strategic planning for this area prior to the North Korean attack had contained important gaps was clearer in some respects from disclosures at the MacArthur hearings than from contemporary press accounts. The full significance of former Secretary of Defense Johnson's statement that there had been no war plan for Korea, however, emerges only when the American policy reaction to the Korean attack is seen in the context of such strategic planning for the Far East as had taken place.

The importance to American security of various areas in the Far East had been carefully considered by the Joint Chiefs of Staff and the civilian policy-makers in the twelve to eighteen months before the attack. Planning decisions as to the use or non-use of US military forces to ensure the defense of these areas had been made in terms of their strategic importance to the security of the United States. From such a standpoint, Korea was clearly not of strategic importance. If South Korea came under military attack, therefore, the United States would not act directly with military force in South Korea's defense, but, rather, the matter would be considered under the United Nations.

Was it foreseen, during the period of strategic planning preceding the North Korean aggression, that it might become desirable or necessary to commit US military forces to the defense of South Korea under the aegis of the United Nations? There is no indication of this either in contemporary newspaper accounts or in the MacArthur hearings. Employment of US forces in the defense of South Korea had been ruled out on the grounds of its low strategic importance to American military security. Evidently no thought was given to the possibility that *other considerations* might require such a commitment. And yet it was precisely these other considerations which became paramount in the days following June 25. It is not without significance that the initial decision of June 26 (announced the following day) to use US air and naval forces to help the South Koreans was taken on the initiative of the State Department. As Louis Johnson recalled, "The military neither recommended it nor opposed it," although they did emphasize the difficulties and limitations" of such an action.

It is true that Secretary of State Acheson, as he recalled at the MacArthur hearings, had intimated in a major policy speech of January 15, 1950, that any attack upon South Korea would be dealt with through the United Nations. But while the obligations of the United States by virtue of its membership in the UN may really have been seen as including the possible use of US military forces as part of UN action on behalf of South Korea, there is no indication that the military implications of such an "obligation" or "commitment" were taken into account in American strategic planning.

During the MacArthur hearings, some of the leading participants in the decision to commit US forces to the defense of South Korea occasionally implied, in attempting to explain this step, that Korea was of political, if not strategic, importance. The clearest intimation that the relationship of the United States to peripheral areas rests upon factors other than their strategic importance to American security was given by Secretary of State Acheson. But the fact that strategic and military planning for Korea had not been based upon this broader conception was not explicitly brought out in the course of the lengthy hearings.

What were the unforeseen considerations which led American policy-makers to reverse strategic plans and commit military forces to the defense of Korea? Clearly, this reversal was not motivated by a sudden discovery of the importance of Korea to American military security. Rather, the decision to oppose the North Koreans was motivated by a fear of the consequences of inaction and was influenced by considerations which stemmed from uncertain interpretations of broader Soviet strategic intentions behind the North Korean attack.

In the first place, by acting in Korea, American leaders hoped to deter the Soviets from launching other local aggressions and, thereby, to make a general war less likely. (Both the diversion and testing interpretations of the North Korean attack appear to have been influential in this respect.) Secondly, American leaders feared that failure to oppose the North Korean aggression would markedly weaken (a) the prestige and position of the United States in the cold war; (b) the United Nations and the principle of collective security; and, therefore, also (c) the forces of opposition to Communist expansion throughout the world. (The demonstration interpretation was particularly relevant in this respect.)

Evaluation of the American Decision

In evaluating the policy decision to employ American forces in the defense of South Korea, three questions can be raised.

Did a tendency to view the North Korean aggression in terms of an historical parallel with Hitler's early aggressions lead American policy-makers to exaggerate some of the negative consequences of not opposing the aggression against South Korea?

Our evidence suggests that in the crisis engendered by the North Korean attack, certain leading American policy-makers (President Truman and perhaps Secretary Acheson as well) took their bearings to some extent from the testing interpretation, which made use of the historical parallel with Hitler. Contemporary newspaper accounts are not sufficiently detailed to enable one to judge precisely in what sense the historical parallel with Hitler's aggressions was perceived. The possibility cannot be excluded, however, that Soviet aggression in Korea was incorrectly viewed by some policy-makers in the image of Hitler. To the extent that this was the case, the testing interpretation of the North Korean attack may have blurred in the minds of policy-makes an important general principle of behavior attributed to the Politburo in Kennan's "The Sources of Soviet Conduct."

The testing hypothesis, as has been noted, implied that nonopposition to the North Korean attack would embolden the Kremlin to proceed with further aggressions, already scheduled, which would surely plunge the world into war. For, just as Hitler's early unopposed successes whetted his appetite and led him later into an imprudent underestimation of his opponent's will to resist, so the Politburo's overt aggression in Korea might set off a similar cycle. This reasoning, however, would be difficult to reconcile with Kennan's thesis, which emphasizes the principle of caution in Soviet behavior. Rather, according to Kennan (and other specialists on Soviet behavior), Soviet leaders would feel themselves under a compulsion in such a contingency—unopposed and easy success in the Korean adventure—to adopt an attitude *exactly opposite* to that anticipated by the "testing-parallel-with-Hitler" hypothesis. They would, in other words, tend to estimate their new advantages soberly and restrain any tendency to be carried away by success into risky adventures.

The testing hypothesis could have validity (assuming the Kennan-Leites thesis to be correct) only insofar as it forecast, in the event of successful Communist aggression in Korea, a weakening of the democracies' will to resist and the emergence thereby of new power vacuums elsewhere in the world. That such consequences were feared by American policy-makers seems clear enough, but it is difficult to disentangle this legitimate concern from the further, more questionable, anxiety that Soviet leaders would become afflicted with the same imprudence which led Hitler to blunder into war.

To the extent that this dubious assumption about Soviet behavior influenced the American policy reaction, it served to strengthen motivation for meeting force with force in Korea. To the extent that the testing interpretation took precedence over the "soft-spot probing" thesis, it led to an exaggeration of the negative consequences of an unopposed Communist success in Korea. The result may have been to leave American policy-makers with a feeling that they had less freedom of action in responding to the North Korean aggression than was actually the case.

The decision to employ US forces to aid South Korea raises a further question: Was there a military alternative to American involvement in a ground war in Korea? Could the United States have accepted the military loss of South Korea and attempted to minimize its demoralizing consequences upon the free world by other means?

The character and development of the Korean War were determined to a considerable extent by the decision to use US ground forces to stem the advancing North Koreans and, eventually, to roll them back. This step was taken on June 30, only several days after the earlier decisions to employ US air and naval forces to assist the South Koreans. Since the question whether US naval and air forces can be employed in local wars without risking involvement of sizable ground forces continues to concern American policy-makers, it is useful to examine the development and background of the key decision of June 30.

In the MacArthur hearings, this decision is represented as having been taken, and its timing determined, solely in response to the necessities of the rapidly deteriorating military situation in Korea. The exact sequence of events leading to the decision, however, is difficult to reconstruct from the piecemeal, fragmentary disclosures made during the hearings. A June 25 directive to General MacArthur authorized him to "take action by air and navy to prevent the Inchon-Kimpo-Seoul area from falling into unfriendly hands," an event which might have interfered with efforts to evacuate American nationals. On June 29, use of army combat and service troops was explicitly authorized "to insure the retention of a port and air base in the general area of Pusan." This authorization, too, appears to have been limited to the purpose of ensuring evacuation.

The idea of using US ground troops in offensive operations against the North Koreans was initiated by General MacArthur on June 30. This was General Bradley's testimony, and it was supported by Louis Johnson. There is some question whether American policy-makers, in immediately accepting General MacArthur's recommendation that US combat troops be used to hold the line, went so far as to approve at this time his recommendation of a buildup for offensive ground action. Johnson stated quite positively that the Defense Department interpreted the Administration's decision of June 30 as accepting General MacArthur's recommendations fully, that is, it constituted a policy decision for eventual ground action to clear South Korea. The directive issued to General MacArthur on June 30, in response to his recommendation, stated (as paraphrased at the hearings) merely that "the limitation on the employment of Army forces imposed on June 29, 1950, was rescinded."

The official statement made public on June 30 by President Truman, it was recalled to Louis Johnson while he was testifying, announced merely that General MacArthur had been authorized "to use certain supporting troops." Johnson, in reply, intimated that for security reasons it had been considered unwise to advertise the plan for a buildup for eventual offensive action.

It appears, then, that ground combat forces were committed initially in order to stem the North Korean advance, which the South Korean forces were unable to do. It was not a question, at this time, of preventing the total defeat of the South Korean Army and an overrunning of the entire Korean peninsula. But the decision to give ground assistance to the South Koreans appears to have been accompanied, at the same time, by a separate decision determining subsequent American military strategy for fighting the Korean War by means of a ground offensive. There is no indication in the materials examined for this study that the possibility of an alternative military strategy was considered at this time, that anyone proposed either that US ground forces not be committed at all, or that they be used only to stabilize a line or hold a bridgehead. Nor is there any indication that the possibility of accepting the military loss of the South Korean peninsula was considered, together with an exploration of alternative political and military policies for minimizing the demoralizing consequences of such a course upon the free world.

Evidently the tendency for an initial employment of US ground forces to take on the character of an irreversible commitment was not foreseen. Despite the traditional military view that sizable US ground forces should not become involved in a war on the Asian continent and a concern lest American troops be needed elsewhere in the world, American policy-makers were to find themselves committing increasingly larger forces to the Korean theater. Disclosures at the MacArthur hearings amply confirm that, when taking the initial decision to employ US ground forces to halt and throw back the North Korean aggressor, American policy-makers did not attempt to calculate and did not foresee the size of the force that would be eventually required for that purpose. Thus, it was not known, when initially small forces were committed, that increasingly larger commitments would become necessary. Otherwise, it might be expected that American leaders would have begun earlier to search for alternative military strategies for fighting a local war in Korea or that they would have considered whether acceptance of the probable military loss of the Korean peninsula was not preferable to fighting a large-scale ground war. In the last analysis, the magnificent forging of a military strategy for defeating the North Koreans was an improvisation. American strategic planning not only had not foreseen military involvement of US forces, but it had, up to this time, not really considered the general question of viable military strategies for limited, local wars.

Finally, it may be asked: To what extent were alternative policies considered for purposes of deterring further Communist aggressions?

As has been noted, the desire to discourage Communist moves elsewhere in the world was evidently an important motive for employing military force in direct opposition to the North Korean invader. Another important move to the same end was the June 27 decision to employ the Seventh Fleet to protect Formosa from invasion and to give increased military aid to Indochina and the Philippines. In time, the Korean attack was to strengthen other American cold war policies as well—such as increased rearmament and mobilization at home and the decision to rearm Germany—but there is no evidence that such steps were considered as *alternative* means of deterring the Soviets in the first few days following the North Korean attack, when the basic policy decision of military intervention was being made. Available materials simply do not indicate whether in these days consideration was given to the possibility of not intervening in Korea and of seeking to deter further Communist aggressions elsewhere by any other policy means.

Objectives and Means in American Policy Calculations

Korea provided an excellent illustration of some of the policy dilemmas which may arise when American leaders are forced to deal with Communist aggression in peripheral areas. Particularly evident was the problem of relating objectives and means in formulating a policy reaction to the North Korean attack. American policy-makers did not share a firm and clear-cut view of Soviet strategic intentions behind the North Korean attack. They were therefore forced to act while remaining uncertain as to some of the possible dangers in the situation. Specifically, this meant that they were being guided by several objectives, the implementation of which was not smoothly integrated. They wished to induce a more or less *immediate retreat* or withdrawal on the part of the Communists from the Korean adventure. They wished to *contain* Communist aggression in Korea. They wished, also, to deter the Soviet Union from launching other local aggressions elsewhere. One might add that, in acting in Korea (containment objective), they hoped to avoid provoking Soviet intervention. There is some reason to believe that the means chosen to implement certain of these objectives (deterrence and avoidance of Soviet intervention) prejudiced to some extent the achievement of a Communist retreat or withdrawal.

American policy-makers appear to have hoped, initially, that limited force commitments on behalf of South Korea might succeed in bringing about an immediate, voluntary withdrawal of the North Korean forces back to the 38th Parallel. As spelled out in the first resolution of the United Nations Security Council on June 25, the objective was to secure a cease-fire and a withdrawal of North Korean troops to the border. Similarly, the American note of June 27 to the Soviet Union contained a request that it "use its influence" with the North Koreans to this end.

What was the basis for the expectation or hope that the initial American policy moves of the first few days might succeed in inducing a withdrawal? Contemporary newspaper accounts give a more detailed picture on this score than do disclosures at the MacArthur hearings. This hopeful expectation was evidently derived from the testing interpretation of the North Korean attack, especially that aspect of it which regarded the Communist move into South Korea as an "asking-of-a-question" type of action. The major American decision of June 27, announcing US air and naval support for the South Koreans and "drawing the line" with respect to Formosa, was regarded as giving the answer to such a question.

> *If this estimate of the situation is correct, the Russians will let the North Koreans fall back to their border, the 38th Parallel, and, in their own propaganda, dismiss the affair as something initiated by the North Koreans, independently and without Russian responsibility. (Albert Friendly, Washington Post, June 28, 1950.)*

Similarly, the Alsop brothers reported the American policy-makers' hopeful expectation:

> *The purpose of President Truman's decision [of June 27] . . . is simply*

to persuade the Kremlin that the United States means what it says. It is hoped that the Kremlin, convinced that the United States means business, will soon call off its puppets. (Washington Post, *June 30, 1950.*)

The Soviets declined to intervene in the Korean situation (Soviet reply of June 29 to the American note), and the advancing North Korean forces did not respond to the suggestion that they return to the 38th Parallel. The initial effort to secure a withdrawal or retreat, therefore, was quite unsuccessful.

Accordingly, within a few days, American leaders evidently accepted the fact that the initial withdrawal objective was no longer within the realm of immediate or easy accomplishment. With the commitment of US ground troops to Korea on June 30, policy calculations began to emphasize direct military pressure as a means of inducing withdrawal. With this development, measures aimed at securing withdrawal began to resemble the more familiar containment strategy. The expectation of a withdrawal now appeared to wait upon the creation of a position of military strength in Korea itself. This more realistic conception of the policy prerequisites for realizing the withdrawal objective was reflected in some newspaper accounts: "The hope persisted [in official quarters] that the Kremlin would keep the conflict localized and would call it off *in the end."* (Ferdinand Kuhn, *Washington Post,* July 1, 1950; italics added.)

What conclusion can be drawn from the failure to induce an immediate withdrawal of North Korean forces to the 38th Parallel? According to the Kennan thesis and similar formulations by other specialists on Soviet affairs, the Politburo withdraws or retreats only in the face of strong, determined resistance, not in response to merely a polite diplomatic request. But this statement of the prerequisites for inducing a Soviet retreat is a general hypothesis. As such, it does not furnish a blueprint for policy calculation and action in any specific situation. The *degree of strength* that will deter the Soviet Union from probing a "soft-spot" and the *degree and manner of resistance* which will induce it to withdraw its tentacles are questions which require contextual analysis. The policy utilization of the retreat hypothesis requires estimates of a more specific character, which this thesis itself does not provide.

It is obvious, of course, that the United States and the United Nations in the first days after the North Korean invasion did not induce a withdrawal to the 38th Parallel. The simplest explanation for this failure is that the amount of pressure exerted was insufficient. The UN cease-fire resolution of June 25, the announcement of US air and naval support on June 27, the announcement that "certain" US ground forces were being sent to the South Korean battlefront— all these measures evidently did not constitute a great enough leverage to induce immediate withdrawal from the Korean venture. The American diplomatic request to the Soviet Union on June 27, it may be remarked, contained no threat of further pressure and must have been quite ineffectual from this standpoint.

It may be useful to consider in some detail the impact of the deneutralization of Formosa, a step taken to localize the conflict (the deterrence objective), upon the simultaneous policy objective of inducing an early withdrawal to the 38th Parallel. One may speculate whether the deneutralization of Formosa at this early stage of the Korean War did not drastically alter the Politburo's estimate of the strategic significance of the Korean conflict and place withdrawal of the North Koreans in an entirely different tactical perspective. If we assume that the Soviets moved into South Korea under the impression that the United States had given up this area and, further, that the Soviets were surprised by the American decision to intervene, then the American policy reversal on Formosa might well have seemed to the Politburo evidence of a calculated plan to invite the North Koreans to attack in order to use it as a justification for putting into effect a far more vigorous Far Eastern policy. Such a Politburo image of devious American policy calculations—moreover, one possibly accompanied by expectations of further "aggressive" steps by the United States in the Far East—would have led Soviet leaders to view their interests in the Korean War in a much broader framework than they had when they ordered the North Koreans to attack. The stakes must have been seen now to be much larger than merely the question of control of South Korea. Faced overnight by what seemed to them an increasingly "aggressive," and potentially dangerous, American policy in the Far East, the Soviets now might well have regarded their main objective in the area as that of deterring this development. The initial policy of advance into a peripheral power vacuum may have been speedily transformed into a major defensive effort to oppose what were regarded as American plans for expansion in the Far East.

If this analysis of the Soviet interpretation of the American policy reaction is correct, then the American objective of inducing an immediate withdrawal to the 38th Parallel was considerably complicated by the means chosen for simultaneously pursuing the broader deterrence objective. Deneutralization of Formosa by the US Seventh Fleet, while undoubtedly a manifestation of strength and determination, and however necessary, probably had little value as pressure to induce an immediate withdrawal from the Korean venture. It may actually have made more difficult the realization of this objective.

The withdrawal objective may also have been prejudiced to some extent by an undue American concern over the Politburo's interest in its prestige. Possibly in line with Kennan's thesis on this point, American policy-makers were most careful to give the Politburo a chance to withdraw graciously. This impression is derived from many contemporary newspaper accounts; there is little on the matter in the MacArthur hearings. Numerous commentators noted the unwillingness of official American spokesmen to charge the Soviet Union with direct responsibility for unleashing the attack. President Truman's early decision not to accuse Moscow of having supplied material aid for the North Korean invasion was designed, according to Arthur Krock (*New York Times,* June 28, 1950), to permit the Soviets an opportunity to disavow responsibility or active interest in the aggression and, further, to accept the American diplomatic invitation to bring about a withdrawal of the North Korean forces. Similarly, in an article entitled "Soviet Face-saving Made Still Possible" (*Washington Post,* June 29, 1950), Ferdinand Kuhn reported that Secretary of State Acheson in his press conference had refused to say a word which would connect Soviet Russia with the North Korean invasion, a caution which President Truman had also observed in his statements of June 26 and 27, and the UN Security Council in its resolutions of June 25 and 27.

The question may be raised whether this marked concern for Soviet prestige may not have been interpreted by the Politburo as one indication (among others) that a total withdrawal from the North Korean venture would *not* be necessary. It is interesting to speculate upon what the Politburo reaction would have been, had the United States and the United Nations held it more directly responsible for the North Korean attack or, at least, for bringing about an immediate

North Korean withdrawal to the 38th Parallel. That the Politburo was ready to do so, if need be, was indeed inferred by some observers from the initial Soviet propaganda explanation for the outbreak of Korean hostilities, namely, that South Korean forces attacked first and were driven off and pursued by North Korean forces. Only several days later, when it may have become clear to the Politburo that a total withdrawal would not be necessary, was the Korean "civil war" theme introduced by Gromyko (*New York Times,* July 4, 1950). This shift in the Soviet line constituted an entirely different legitimization of the North Korean action. The "civil war" thesis was, it may be noted, less conducive to the idea of a Soviet-inspired withdrawal of North Korean forces to the 38th Parallel.

The policy of not implicating the USSR directly may have been motivated by more than an estimate of the importance of the prestige factor in Soviet policy. At the time an American policy reaction to the North Korean attack was being formulated, it will be recalled, some American officials seriously feared that the Politburo might be embarking on a series of aggressions. The nonhostile and "correct" American approach to the USSR might, indeed, have been exaggerated by a conscious or unconscious desire not to provoke the Politburo into further aggressions. And, consequently, American cooperation in Soviet face-saving may have taken an exaggerated form which inadvertently undermined the objective of securing an immediate Communist withdrawal in Korea.

In any event, the Korean case raises anew the question, on which there appears to be some disagreement among specialists on Soviet behavior, of the importance of the prestige factor in Soviet policy calculations. In this and other respects, Korea may point to a more general danger inherent in conflicts over peripheral areas. Local wars may get out of hand as a result of interaction between rival policies based on incorrect estimates of each other's intentions. Unless each side correctly estimates the other's intentions and correctly calculates the impact of its actions upon the opponent's image of its intentions, conflicts in peripheral areas may take a course initially undesired by both sides.

Allen S. Whiting

CHINESE POLICY AND THE KOREAN WAR

The armed intervention by the People's Republic of China transformed both the military and political aspects of the Korean War. Once the Chinese crossed the Yalu, they—rather than the Russians—became the dominant power behind the North Koreans. Allen S. Whiting, an associate of the Rand Corporation, offers the standard Western analysis of the Chinese role in the conflict.

Problems of Chinese Communist Policy

. . . Prior to June 25, Peking probably anticipated a quick and decisive North Korean victory, accompanied or swiftly followed by the invasion of Taiwan. The United States and United Nations moves of June 25–30, however, raised doubts on both points. These doubts, in turn, gave rise to decisions that affected China's domestic development and world posture. An understanding of the various issues confronting the new regime at this time may provide insights into Peking's reactions throughout the critical months of 1950.

Taiwan. The Truman order of June 27 abruptly changed the Taiwan situation. Only six months previously the President had declared that the United States would avoid further involvement in the Chinese civil war. Renewed American political, economic, and military support for Chiang Kai-shek now seemed certain. Instead of ending resistance on Taiwan through subversion and a token invasion, the People's Liberation Army now faced the United States Seventh Fleet in addition to reorganized Chinese Nationalist forces. In the United Nations, Secretary General Trygve Lie had been skillfully attempting to break the East-West deadlock on Chinese Communist representation. Now the Chinese Nationalist delegate seemed secure in his place on the Security Council, unless US policy changed or suffered a setback in Taiwan itself.

The alternatives facing Peking were few, clear-cut, and dismal. It could go forward with its planned invasion. The Seventh Fleet might be unable to meet both the Taiwan and the Korean commitments. Postponement of the Taiwan "liberation" would incur immediate political costs and long-term military risks. Substitution of propaganda for a military attack against the US in the Taiwan Strait would call attention to "new China's" impotence on its very doorstep. Words alone would not remove Chiang Kai-shek and his supporters from either Taiwan or the United Nations. Nor would Nationalist resistance ever again be as weak as in 1950, given the prospect of renewed American training and assistance. Furthermore, with America's supply lines being extended and her military units below full strength, a simultaneous invasion of Taiwan and of South Korea might succeed in overwhelming resistance.

On the other hand, Communist desire to avoid general war, particularly with the US atomic superiority, may have outweighed the above considerations. China's vulnerable coastal concentration of industry and transportation made the risk of US air and sea attack extremely hazardous. Should the invasion fail, the political repercussions would be costly for Peking, especially in the coastal, southern, and inner provinces where Nationalist and anti-Communist guerrilla forces still operated. All such risks had to be seriously examined in the light of miscalculations that had preceded the North Korean attack. International reaction to that attack had proved more serious in its political and military consequences than had been anticipated. A Chinese Communist invasion of Taiwan might be interpreted in the West as proof of a coordinated offensive in Asia by the Soviet bloc. US retaliation against mainland China could inflict heavy damage, and Soviet assistance might be slow in coming over the lengthy, strained transport lines, vulnerable to air and sea interdiction. In China's existing condition, an immediate invasion of Taiwan posed far-reaching hazards to the Moscow-Peking axis.

Korea. In addition to the Taiwan problem, Peking faced the prospect that Pyongyang's victory would be delayed, if not altogether thwarted, by US "intervention." While this may have been primarily of Soviet concern, given Russian ascendancy in North Korea, it affected the People's Republic of China to only a slightly lesser degree. Communism was too recently victorious in China to ignore a setback across the Yalu that might reawaken US-Nationalist activities throughout the mainland. Nor could Peking aspire to Asian leadership so long as it appeared unwilling, or unable, to influence events on its border. Should Syngman Rhee as well as Chiang Kai-shek survive because of US military protection, the rising tide of Communist influence might be reversed from the Philippines to India. Japan would then fall securely into the "imperialist camp."

Thus both strategic and ideological considerations argued for maximum support of North Korea against "American aggression." Yet any Chinese assistance, whether propagandistic or military, entailed serious risks for Peking. Manchuria, China's vital industrial base, lay within easy reach of US bases in Japan. Military aid to Pyongyang might invite damaging retaliation. A lesser level of support, limited to propaganda and diplomatic activity, would probably not affect the outcome of the war. In view of the widening international opposition to the North Korean attack, such support might only jeopardize Peking's efforts to enter the UN. Even inaction carried liabilities for China. At best, stalemate in Korea would increase the likelihood of an American-Japanese-South Korean defense system. At worst, the "imperialist camp" might feel encouraged to counterattack the Sino-Soviet bloc on its vulnerable Asian flank.

Could the Korean War be terminated short of total North Korean victory without engendering enemy hopes of Soviet bloc weakness and schism? Would prolongation of the war eventually sap American willingness to fight far from home in a country only recently identified with US interests? Or would it sooner exhaust North Korean strength, increasing the need for bloc support of Pyongyang? China's resources already faced heavy demands of industrial recovery, agricultural reform, and political consolidation. Participation in the Korean War, particularly against growing US-UN forces, might strain these resources to the breaking point.

Finally, Peking had to weigh these alternatives against the interests of its Soviet ally. In Korea, the initial responsibility clearly lay with Moscow. Soviet membership in the UN gave Moscow a voice in international affairs that China lacked. China could not even resolve the question of Taiwan independently, since only Russian air power could protect the PRC[1] should the United States actively support Chiang Kai-shek. The asymmetry of power within the Sino-Soviet

---

[1] People's Republic of China.—Ed.

alliance gave Mao Tse-tung little leverage for advancing Chinese policy where it ran counter to that of Stalin. Thus, some of the basic decisions may have been Russian, regardless of the degree to which they affected Chinese interests. It is possible to summarize known Russian moves and to infer Soviet decisions from the events immediately within our focus. The present treatment of Soviet strategy in Korea, however, must necesarily be related primarily to the question of Peking's role in that war.

China and the Korean War: The Evidence and Its Analysis. The complex and diverse problems just described confronted Peking simultaneously. Not susceptible to quick and final solution, they remained fluid throughout the summer of 1950. Estimates and tentative decisions made immediately after the initial US commitment in June required re-examination during July, as US-UN resistance increased. Furthermore, objective obstacles to the solution of China's problems may have been accompanied by subjective limits on decision-making, such as rigidity in Moscow or inexperience and insufficient information in Peking. Russian behavior toward allies, Communist or non-Communist, had been characterized by inadequate communication and unilateral decisions. In this context the secrecy surrounding Sino-Soviet communications and decisions presents formidable problems to the analyst.

For the sake of clarity it will be well to consider separately the issues of Taiwan and Korea, although it must be remembered that Peking saw them as connected. An attempt will be made to define periods in the Korean War according to the shifts in Sino-Soviet strategy. Although this somewhat oversimplifies the complex and gradual evolution of policy that actually occurred, it will facilitate an understanding of the changes apparent in Chinese estimates of the situation.

Four types of evidence support the present analysis of evolving Chinese policy. First, the PRC leadership issued official statements, primarily for foreign consumption, as formal messages to the UN, as declarations of Mao Tse-tung and Chou En-lai, and as authorized pronouncements from the Ministry of Foreign Affairs. Second, Chinese Communist communications, designed primarily for domestic audiences, reveal official thinking about developments in Korea and Taiwan. Serious analyses by and for the Communist elite appeared as anonymous commentaries in the authoritative daily newspaper *Jen Min Jib Pao* (People's Daily) and in the weekly journal closely associated with the Ministry of Foreign Affairs, *Shih Chieh Chih Shih* (World Culture). Propagandistic interpretations appeared in newspapers, magazines, and radio broadcasts, all closely controlled by the Chinese Communist Party. Third, contemporary US intelligence reports and subsequent unit histories, with their accounts of Chinese Communist prisoners captured in Korea, enable us to reconstruct PLA[2] troop movements. Finally, PRC diplomatic activity, particularly vis-à-vis India and the UN, offers clues to Sino-Soviet strategy.

None of these sources provides a comprehensive picture of decision-making in Peking, nor is the evidence always subject to one exclusive interpretation. At some points, the four types of data each support incompatible hypotheses. At important junctures, however, they suggest a pattern of policy clearly and consistently enough to constrict the range of reasonable explanation for Chinese Communist actions.

One final analytical caution is necessary. Considerable reliance has been placed upon content analysis, both quantitative and qualitative, for inferring shifts in Chinese Communist estimates, strategy, and tactics. The author fully recognizes the risk in attempting to determine the degree to which propaganda reflects the views of the regime, as distinct from the views it is designed to generate among its audiences. Where public communications suggested changing Chinese estimates, these were checked against actual diplomatic or military behavior, which might be expected to reflect such changes. Clues to changed official views occur in shifts of terminology, and in patterns of news omission and emphasis. Frequently their meaning is ambiguous, and other evidence fails to clarify their significance. To the degree that the gleanings from propaganda are borne out by political behavior, however, one may rely upon content analysis.

Peking's Initial Reactions: Korea and Taiwan

Chinese Communist press treatment of the North Korean attack exhibited several characteristics during the period June 27–July 30,

---

[2] People's Liberation Army.—Ed.

1950. Initial reports of the war appeared belatedly and were quickly relegated to secondary positions in the newspapers. Cautious warning of unfavorable consequences from the entry of US armed forces into Korea accompanied propagandistic assertions of confidence that Pyongyang would ultimately triumph. Throughout this period Peking appeared to avoid any specific and immediate commitment to assist North Korea, but instead placed Taiwan, as the primary Chinese problem, ahead of the neighboring war. At the same time, preparations for invading Taiwan slackened, and PLA redeployment suggested planning for future contingencies in Manchuria or Korea. No actual assistance, however, was furnished DPRK[3] forces, which fought desperately to push UN units from their toehold in South Korea before the buildup around Pusan could secure a base for counteroffensives. For Peking, the period appears to have been one of watchful waiting, permitting evaluation of rapidly moving events and their possible consequences. Active responses to US and UN moves in Korea appear to have been determined in Moscow, while Peking's primary responsibility continued to be Taiwan.

The Outbreak of War and the US-UN Response.   No Peking newspaper reported the war for forty-eight hours following the North Korean attack. The silence may have been politically determined, since at least one Shanghai newspaper, on June 26, carried a front-page story, complete with map, headlined, "Southern Puppet Army Attacks North Korea at Three Points, Public Announcement Warns Puppet Government to Stop Advance or Decisive Steps Will Be Taken." The account told of DPRK "police guards" waging "a severe defensive war."

On June 27 *Jen Min Jih Pao* devoted most of page one to NCNA[4] dispatches from Pyongyang, Kim Il-sung's "call to arms," and background information. Yet its editorial assurance of "the certain victory of the Korean people in their struggle for unity and independence" carried no note of immediate concern for Chinese readers. Syngman Rhee was dismissed as "less expert" than Chiang Kai-shek in military and political affairs. No mention was made of the initial Security Council resolution of the previous day, calling upon the DPRK to withdraw above the 38th Parallel. In this as in subsequent Chinese

[3] Democratic People's Republic of [North] Korea.—Ed.
[4] New China News Agency.

reporting in the UN, a time lag of at least forty-eight hours preceded publication of the news. Some UN events were suppressed even longer, suggesting reliance upon Russian interpretation of these matters.

From June 30 to July 6, Korea disappeared into the back pages of *Jen Min Jih Pao,* except for a story on the Han River crossing and a summarized speech from Pyongyang. This probably reflected uncertainty over the American military impact, rather than lack of interest in the war. Thus, the initial *Shih Chieh Chih Shih* comment predicted, "The complete liberation of South Korea is not far off." Similarly, on July 3rd, *Jen Min Jih Pao* expressed perfunctory confidence in North Korean victory. On July 6, however, the newspaper changed its tone. Its second front-page editorial on the war termed it "the central problems of international relations," and warned that Washington was unlikely to "concede defeat." Citing additional American troops, planes, and ships heading for Korea and US pressure upon other nations to join the action, the paper admitted that these "difficulties" would make Communist victory, although certain, "come not so fast." No alarm was sounded nor was any Chinese commitment to relieve the "difficulties" implied. However, this editorial evidenced the first concern over the possible effects of United States actions.

This concern became increasingly manifest in anonymous military commentaries appearing in *Jen Min Jih Pao* at roughly two-week intervals throughout the summer. Bereft of propagandistic bombast, these commentaries struck a consistently more sober note than did general articles on the war. Thus, on July 13, the military writer noted that "more than forty" UN members "appear to be in the American gang." After adding that some "express only a 'limited type of support,'" he differentiated countries that, like France, India, and Denmark, had refused military assistance, from those that, like Great Britain and Thailand, had offered armed units. Despite the likelihood of increasing UN resistance, he concluded, "The imperialists look strong on the outside but are weak on the inside . . . [being] only 'paper tigers.'"

This mixture of caution and confidence reflected the confusing and fluid situation in Korea. On the battle front, the rapid North Korean advance encouraged optimism, but Sino-Soviet awareness of the impending US-UN buildup introduced a pessimistic note. On the one hand, DPRK troops captured Seoul within three days of crossing the 38th Parallel, forcing the ROK[5] government to flee southward to Taejon. Red armies drove fifty miles in the first week to capture Suwon and Wonju, forty miles the second week to Chonan, and eighteen miles the third week to engulf more than half of South Korea. On the other hand, US troop movements indicated the significance of the rear-guard action of American units, slowing the DPRK advance while stabilizing a toehold at the base of the Korean peninsula.

Meanwhile, US Army and Marine units in Okinawa, Hawaii, and at home were publicly reported mobilizing for air and sea transport to Korea, to arrive in early August. At the front, US artillery increased in numbers and size, moving from 105- to 155-mm. howitzers by mid-July, while the new 3.5-inch bazooka proved its effectiveness against DPRK tanks in the battle for Taejon. In addition to the UN control of the air, intensified bombardment from American naval forces brought Communist coastal lines of communication under heavy attack.

TABLE 1
Chronology of United States Troop Arrivals in Korea, July 1–18, 1950

Date	Unit	Embarked from
July 1–2	One-half battalion combat team from 21st Infantry Regiment, 24th Division	Japan
July 4–9	Remainder of 24th Division	Japan
July 9–12	25th Division	Japan
July 18	1st Cavalry Division	Japan
Total		30,000 troops

Source: Department of the Army, *Korea—1950*, (Washington, D.C., 1952). No figures of unit strength are included, but references support the approximate total of 30,000 troops given in Karig, et al., *Battle Report*, p. 89.

"Prolonged War" in Korea. On July 20 the first major battle between DPRK and US forces ended in the Red capture of Taejon. No note of triumph, however, appeared in Chinese Communist com-

---

[5] Republic of [South] Korea.—Ed.

mentaries. On the contrary, one week later *Jen Min Jih Pao* analyzed the first month of war in sober tones, reporting two additional American divisions en route to Korea, mobilization of fresh American mechanized units, White House demands for emergency defense appropriations, and increased United States pressure for men and material from other UN members. Again the warning sounded: "This doubtless increases the difficulties facing the Korean people." Adjoining columns graphically described the devastation of Korea from US napalm bombings.

Almost simultaneously, *World Culture* introduced a phrase of special significance for its Chinese readers, predicting, inter alia, "A prolonged war of attrition will naturally increase the difficulties of the Korean people but it will increase the difficulties of the American imperialists much more." In 1938 Mao Tse-tung's classic study *On the Protracted War* had mapped the years of struggle from material inferiority to superiority, applicable both to China's war against Japan and to the civil conflict between the Chinese Communist Party and the Kuomintang. To depict Pyongyang's future in these terms suggested serious consideration at higher levels of an eventual stalemate, if not possible defeat, in Korea.

The gradual but persistent change in tone of these authoritative commentaries, moving from unqualified confidence in late June to prediction of "prolonged war" in late July, paralleled growing American confidence that a line could be held near the port of Pusan that would permit a perimeter defense protecting the vital buildup area. Informed US reports predicted that out of this area an eventual UN counter-offensive would be launched in conjunction with amphibious landings behind North Korean lines higher up the peninsula.

Yet nowhere did Peking's statements hint at the necessity for Chinese assistance to North Korea. On July 17 a radio broadcast linked a frank warning against undue optimism with assertions of North Korean self-sufficiency: "The American imperialists will not give up and admit defeat. They will strengthen their aggressive force. . . . The victory of the Korean people will come a little slowly [but] . . . there is no doubt that the Korean people . . . have sufficient strength to defeat imperialist aggression and eventually to attain national liberation." Despite generalized exhortations to render "wholehearted support" to Pyongyang's cause, Chinese Communist propaganda seldom spelled out the implications of such support. Infrequently, it was specified as "moral."

Alternatively, it was argued that by "actively preparing for the liberation of Taiwan, we shall be giving efficient aid to the support of Korea." Rarely was the Korean War depicted in terms of China's immediate interests. In an exceptional article of July 26, 1950, *Jen Min Jih Pao* answered the query of why American armed forces were invading Korea, as follows: "To change it into a gangway of aggression for the United States on the borders of China and the Soviet Union."

Peking's broadcasts, then, gave no indication of Chinese Communist commitment to the Korean War. On the contrary, they and the newspapers stressed Taiwan as the only major responsibility confronting the PLA. This did not preclude secret military movements for future contingencies associated with the war, as we shall see shortly. So far as the Chinese people were concerned, however, the North Korean move, while encountering growing enemy opposition, offered no cause for anxiety or alarm.

Taiwan, India, and the UN. In contrast with the delayed and occasionally diffident treatment of the Korean War, Chinese Communist reaction to the June 27 order placing the US Seventh Fleet in the Taiwan Strait was immediate and authoritative. Within twenty-four hours of the Truman statement, Foreign Minister Chou En-lai denounced the move as "armed aggression against the territory of China in total violation of the United Nations charter."

Denying that the American move came as a "surprise," Chou declared: "All that Truman's statement does is merely to expose his premeditated plan and put it into practice. In fact, the attack by the puppet Korean government . . . at the instigation of the US government was . . . designed to create a pretext for the United States to invade Taiwan, Korea, Viet Nam, and the Philippines." Chou pledged the PRC to "liberate Taiwan" regardless of any "obstructive action the United States imperialists may take." Later the same day, at a governmental meeting in Peking, Mao echoed this pledge.

Several points emerge from the timing and content of the Chou and Mao statements. First, the swiftness of the Chinese reaction to US protection of Taiwan as contrasted with the slow response to the Korean War indicates a division of responsibility between Peking and Moscow. Chinese Communist pronouncements on Taiwan may not have required consultation with the Soviet partner, while those on the UN and Korea may have been subject to Russian review. Peking's first public comment on the Security Council resolution of June 25 came four days later. On June 29 *Jen Min Jih Pao* editorially attacked both this resolution and the Truman announcement on Taiwan of June 27, but made no reference to the second Security Council resolution on Korea, also of June 27. Messages to the UN bore out this pattern. Moscow delayed three days before officially protesting the June 25 resolution. No Chinese Communist protest was sent, perhaps because the issue concerned Korea exclusively. The second Security Council resolution elicited no Soviet response for one week. Then within forty-eight hours of Moscow's cable came a parallel protest from Peking, including, however, greater stress on Taiwan.

Aside from the timing, the content of Chinese references to the UN, both in Chou's statement and in his cable of July 6, raises a second point of interest. On the one hand, Peking employed the UN Charter as an acceptable reference to support its case against American action in Taiwan. On the other hand, Peking waited ten days before protesting the Truman announcement to the UN, and then made no demand for action. In strong, almost insulting, language it charged: "By keeping silent on this act of open aggression, the Security Council and the Secretary General of the United Nations have foregone their functions and duties of upholding world peace and therefore have become pliant instruments to the policy of the United States government."

While loath to dismiss the UN altogether, Peking neither acknowledged its authority in Korea nor demanded that it take measures on Taiwan. In general, this seeming ambivalence resulted from Soviet policy. Moscow remained a member of the UN but boycotted its organs, including the Security Council, in protest against the "illegal" representation of the "Chiang Kai-shek clique." If the Russian absence compounded the "illegality" of resolutions passed in June, Peking could scarcely call for Security Council action in July when the Soviet boycott was still going on.

A more specific dilemma, however, confronted Peking. How could it support Pyongyang against UN opposition and still keep open its chances for admission to the UN? On July 1 this issue arose concretely when the Indian ambassador to Peking, K. M. Panikkar, called upon Vice Foreign Minister Chang Han-fu. Panikkar "put forward tentatively the suggestion that the question [of Korea] could probably be solved by referring it to the Security Council, with China taking her legitimate place, and consequently the Soviets giving up their boycott and returning to their vacant seat."

This secret Indian move raised several problems for Sino-Soviet strategists. Only a short time previously Communist analysis had placed the Nehru government squarely in the camp of "American imperialism," castigating its "formal independence" and "playing at neutralism." Yet Nehru had publicly called for PRC admission to the UN, and Panikkar's proposal hinted that this might come as part of a "package deal" on Korea. What further support for bloc goals might Delhi offer? True, it had moved from abstention to acceptance of the June 27 Security Council resolution authorizing military assistance to the Republic of Korea. Yet an official explanation of this move had expressed "hope that even at this stage it may be possible to put an end to the fighting and settle the dispute by mediation."

Peking's "two-camp" world view denied the possibility of disinterested meditation. Was Nehru finally joining the category, acceptable to China, of "national bourgeoisie opposed to imperialism"?

More than UN admission was at stake for Peking. Indian support on the Taiwan issue would be valuable for applying political pressure against the United States. Should PRC admission to the UN accompany settlement of the Korean War, Washington would have little justification for continuing its Seventh Fleet patrol of the Taiwan Strait. How vital these considerations were for Moscow is open to question. The fact remains that Peking made no response to Panikkar's proposal for ten days. On July 10 its favorable reply finally came, undoubtedly after consultation with its Soviet partner.

This delay in the Sino-Soviet response, paralleled in the handling of UN moves, may have stemmed from uncertainty over both Indian and Korean developments. If Delhi's motives puzzled Communist analysts, so did the import and outcome of US action against Pyongyang. Thus Peking reacted slowly and cautiously to diplomatic as well as military developments. On July 9 *Jen Min Jih Pao* reviewed Indian policy without attacking Nehru but with skeptical reference to "Indian 'neutralism.' " Similarly, it depicted the UN as under "American domination" but cited the Charter as a basis for attacking "American imperialist aggression in Korea and Taiwan."

On July 13, acting upon Peking's favorable response to the Panik-kar proposal, Prime Minister Nehru sent identical letters to Premier Stalin and Secretary of State Acheson. He formally suggested that the PRC be admitted to the Security Council, thereby permitting the Soviet delegate to return, and that the United States, the Soviet Union, and People's Republic of China, "with the help and cooperation of other peace-loving nations," informally explore means to end the Korean War and to reach "a permanent solution of the Korean prob-lem." Stalin's prompt acceptance on July 15 contrasted with the Acheson rejection three days later.

The exchange revealed a new turn in Sino-Soviet strategy. Despite Nehru's public condemnation of North Korean "aggression," he clearly stood outside the "American camp," and to this extent was acceptable to the bloc. It was now possible to embarrass the United States diplomatically, for its prestige in Asia would suffer as long as Washington rejected Indian proposals endorsed by Moscow and Peking. If, on the other hand, Washington accepted these proposals, some goals of the Sino-Soviet bloc might be advanced without com-mitting the bloc in advance to compromise on its other aims.

The following weeks gave increasing evidence of a change in bloc policy that utilized diplomatic means in conjunction with military action in Korea. As July drew to a close, Moscow announced that Jacob Malik would end his seven-month boycott of the Security Council on August 1, when he would assume the President's seat according to regular rotation. In the meantime, Peking smoothed over the harsh image of Indian policy outlined in its earlier analyses. On July 13 *Jen Min Jih Pao* noted that Delhi offered "only a limited 'type of support' " for US moves in Korea. After printing the Stalin note in full along with excerpts from the Acheson reply, the paper praised "the world-wide support for the peaceful proposals of J. Nehru and the reply of J. V. Stalin." Its first editorial comment on the correspon-dence called the Indian move "of tremendous world-wide signifi-cance," despite the US rejection. This "showed to all" the growing strength of "the forces of peace."

By selectively quoting the Indian press, the Congress Party, the British Labour Party, and the American press, *Jen Min Jih Pao* depicted universal endorsement of the Nehru-Stalin exchange and opposition to the Acheson statement. Elsewhere the Indian ambassador was reported to have found Mao Tse-tung deeply concerned over Taiwan while viewing the Korean War as "a distant matter."

The Indian *démarche* is of twofold importance. It brought about the first formal, public involvement of Peking in the Korean War. Admittedly, Peking was a passive bystander compared with Delhi, Moscow, and Washington. Yet the Panikkar-Nehru proposals established an important precedent by linking resolution of the Korean conflict with PRC representation in the Security Council. In a sense this legitimized Peking's interest in the war.

Even more significant, however, the Indian proposal challenged the Communist image of a world neatly divided into two warring camps with no "neutral" nations occupying a third position. Full appreciation of this may not have come immediately in Moscow or Peking. Nevertheless *Jen Min Jih Pao*'s gradual shift from criticism to praise of Nehru suggested at least a tactical modification of the "two camps" approach. Furthermore, Nehru's appeal for "mediation," backed as it was by terms initially acceptable to Sino-Soviet strategy, opened up the possibility of using diplomatic as well as military means for handling the Korean imbroglio. It may have helped to persuade Moscow to end its boycott of the Security Council and to return Malik as President of the Council in August. This will be discussed in more detail below. At present it is enough to emphasize that the Sino-Soviet reaction to the Indian proposals of early July stands as an important benchmark in the development of Chinese Communist policy, not only on Korea but on the broader problem of relations with Asia and the world in general.

Taiwan: Invasion Postponed? The Chou En-lai statement of June 28 carried additional clues to Peking's policy that were borne out by subsequent communications to the elite and to the masses. His relative lack of attention to Korea as compared with Taiwan implied a differentiation of interest that was to characterize Chinese Communist comment on the two problems. This comment emerged initially amidst a previously planned campaign, scheduled for July 1–7, connected with a world-wide Communist movement, the so-called Stockholm Peace Appeal. The subsequent call of the World Federation of Trade Unions (WFTU) for international support of Pyongyang resulted in the formation of Chinese People's Committee for Resistance to United States Invasion of Taiwan and Korea. This committee set aside the week, July 17–24, to "unmask US imperialism" and to "prove that the United States is not only not to be feared but that it can be completely defeated."

Although the WFTU directive concerned Korea, Peking's implementation placed primary emphasis upon Taiwan, in the title of the campaign, in its inaugural manifesto, and in all following statements. No help for Korea was specified in the campaign literature other than "moral support" and "sympathy."

In the campaign title the Chinese term *fan tuei* (resist) connoted only attitudinal opposition. Significantly, this term was later changed during the celebrated "Resist-America, Aid-Korea" campaign that accompanied actual intervention in Korea. In November 1950 it was succeeded by *k'ang yi*, connoting active opposition, exemplified by the war with Japan of 1937–1945 when this term appeared in Yenan's propaganda.

Did this attitudinal response, as contrasted with an active response, apply to Taiwan as well as to Korea? This raises the fourth and final point in Chou's statement on the Truman order to the US Seventh Fleet. While expressing confidence "in driving off the American aggressors and in recovering Taiwan," he did not call for prompt invasion. Chou's remarks came in a propagandistic framework, addressed not only to China but to "all peoples throughout the world who love peace, justice and freedom and especially all the oppressed nations and peoples of the East."

A possible clue to the thinking behind Chou's phraseology occurred in a *World Culture* article on the new strategic situation and Taiwan. An unusually sophisticated analysis, it reviewed US policy on China in the context of domestic Republican-Democratic politics, the State Department "White Paper," and the Truman-Acheson statements of early January 1950. It concluded that until June 27, American support for Chiang Kai-shek had come as a reluctant Democratic concession to win Republican endorsement of aid to Syngman Rhee. The Truman-Acheson preferred policy was depicted as control over Taiwan either through trusteeship or through Taiwanese "independence." The new Seventh Fleet order, however, had changed the entire situation. Now military considerations took priority over political preferences in US policy. The writer drew the lesson soberly and succinctly for his readers: "Before June 27, the problem of liberating Taiwan pitted the strength of the PLA against the Chiang Kai-shek remnants, with the help of the American imperialists occupying a background position. Since June 27, the problem of liberating Taiwan pits the strength of the PLA against the American imperialists, with the Kuomintang bandit remnants moving into the background.

Like Chou, *World Culture* refrained from calling for immediate "smashing" of the American imperialists or for invasion. Instead, it predicted that a US defeat in Korea would discourage further aid to Chiang, unwillingly offered in the first place. This analysis tacitly argued for postponing the Taiwan invasion until after Pyongyang had forced the US out of Korea. By implication, the analysis conceded the futility of attacking Taiwan as long as the threat of American interdiction remained. Further public indication that no immediate invasion was planned came from General Ch'en Yi, commanding the East China Military Area and the Third Field Army, which was assigned to the Taiwan operation. In May General Ch'en had exhorted his troops to train intensively in the removal of anti-invasion obstacles. On July 16 he declared: "While we intensify preparations to liberate Taiwan, we must not neglect our task of national economic recovery." This minor shift of emphasis implied a major change in policy.

PLA Redeployment. Chinese Communist military movements provide additional clues to Peking's strategy on Korea and Taiwan. Between mid-May and mid-July, more than 60,000 troops from General Lin Piao's Fourth Field Army completed redeployment to their home base in northeast China, after their victory in south China and Hainan Island. This placed 180,000 of Peking's best troops within one month's march of the Korean battle front. Yet these troops did not cross the Yalu River, nor did other units join the northeastern concentration until mid-September. Ostensibly this redeployment was routine, like other PLA moves throughout China that were designed to reduce military expenditures by assigning troops to economic construction. At the same time, one should not ignore the possible relationship of this particular move to the defense of Manchuria in the event of reversals in Korea, or to eventual assistance for the DPRK forces.

A similar relationship may be deduced from a simultaneous buildup in Shantung, midway between Shanghai and Mukden. Beginning in late June and early July, approximately 30,000 troops from Ch'en Yi's Third Field Army joined an equal number from the Fourth Field Army in this area. Few of the troops appear to have originated in the Shantung peninsula. Unlike other PLA units, these were not given economic assignments but received further training. This appears to have been a reserve force, positioned for contingencies connected with either Korea or Taiwan. Its location permitted quick land and sea movement to northeast China, should the Korean War take a turn for the worse. In addition, it was readily available for movement through northeast China into Korea, should Peking decide to reinforce Pyong-yang. Finally, the Shantung group could respond quickly to a US-Chinese Nationalist attack on the coastal provinces, or it could return to the Chekiang-Fukien area if the Taiwan invasion were rescheduled. Only a portion of the Third Field Army continued amphibious training during July and August, while a significant element moved up to Shantung.

Thus, the PLA dispositions substantiated the clues in the public media that indicated an indefinite postponement of the invasion of Taiwan. The military moves, too, bear out public statements in suggesting that the Korean War was going contrary to initial calculations. Had a North Korean victory remained certain, albeit delayed by a few weeks, there would have been no reason to withdraw forces positioned opposite Taiwan. The context of the Seventh Fleet's orders gave credence to the *World Culture* analysis linking a US defeat in Korea with a US withdrawal from the Taiwan Strait. In the event of US defeat and withdrawal, the invasion might be rescheduled according to the dictates of weather in the fall of 1950.

By reducing its strength opposite Taiwan, however, the Chinese Communist regime gave evidence of a major reappraisal of strategy affecting both Taiwan and Korea. The troop concentration in Shantung province and the forecast of a "prolonged war" indicated concern over the ultimate consequences of the US moves. Although domestic audiences received little indication that Chinese interests were at stake, propagandistic attention to Taiwan and Korea established an atmosphere in which more threatening developments might be countered by Chinese Communist diplomatic or military moves. The Sino-

Soviet response to Indian proposals for mediation, together with the announcement on July 27 that Soviet Delegate Jacob Malik would assume the Presidency of the Security Council in August, indicated that political measures would be tried first. While the PLA redeployment gave no immediate military support to North Korea, it left Chinese Communist forces favorably situated should military support prove necessary.

* * *

We have already noted the series of PLA shifts which increased forces in northeast China and in Shantung during the summer of 1950, as well as the sudden augmentation of the northeast concentration by 120,000 troops in September-October. We have seen that, following the initial redeployment of late May to mid-July, there was little change in troop dispositions until late September, when entire armies moved northward in a process which was to continue throughout the fall of 1950. . . .

Between mid-October and November 1, from 180,000 to 228,000 crack Fourth Field Army troops crossed into North Korea. Yet more than two-thirds of this force had been in northeast China since July. Its failure to enter Korea until one week after UN units had crossed the 38th Parallel suggests, like so much other evidence, Peking's reluctance to enter the war until all political means had been exhausted. One must also take into account, however, the strategic problems that faced Peking in determining to intervene.

First, of course, was the risk of a US counterblow, perhaps with atomic bombs, against the Chinese mainland. We shall examine later the evidence of Chinese Communist concern with this problem as reflected in semiofficial statements and domestic propaganda. It has been suggested that Peking discounted the prospects of any US air attack against mainland China because of advance assurances through Soviet secret agents that high-level plans in Washington ruled out such a move. No evidence has been found to support such speculation. It is unlikely that Peking would have taken so serious a step as entry into the Korean War on the basis of a foreign agent's report about American intentions, particularly in view of past reversals of US policy both on Taiwan and in Korea. Even were such information in the hands of Sino-Soviet strategists, it was at most only a contributing factor in the decision to intervene, and not a determining one.

Second, Mao Tse-tung's strategic doctrine was based on superiority of numbers, large-scale mobile warfare over vast areas, and guerrilla fighting amidst a friendly populace in home territory. Yet these conditions which had accounted for Mao's successes in the Chinese civil war were largely absent in Korea. So far as comparative strength was concerned, during the first half of November reinforcements swelled the CPV[6] strength in Korea to between 270,000 and 340,000 men. However, they faced approximately 440,000 UN troops of vastly superior firepower. Furthermore, only in the northernmost part of Korea did the battlefield extend over a wide front in mountainous territory, suitable for surprise attack and guerrilla warfare. Much of the lower peninsula was a mere one hundred miles wide, and a mobile strategy was hampered there by UN coastal and air attacks. Regardless of Peking's ideological propinquity to Pyongyang, the CVP moved amidst an alien people in unfamiliar territory. Below the 38th Parallel, the populace would be actively hostile.

Logistical problems posed additional obstacles. Transport lines into Korea were readily pinpointed and vulnerable to enemy air attack. The Yalu River would not freeze over sufficiently for heavy movement before November. Until then, six major bridges provided access to the battle front, the most important of which were twin 3,098-foot-long highway and railroad spans linking Antung and Sinuiju. In August US aircraft had allegedly crossed the international boundary line on several occasions. The Chinese command must therefore have been apprehensive about the interdiction of its communication lines at the Yalu, which might have prevented the massing of "volunteers" during the critical buildup phase. This consideration alone must have restrained China's optimism about her military prospects in Korea.

To be sure, there were favorable factors which Peking may have considered to compensate for these negative conditions. First, Peking may have anticipated no serious resistance from the more than 200,000 Republic of Korea troops which comprised over half of the

---

[6] Chinese People's Volunteers.—Ed.

UN force. Initial engagements were likely to be with South Korean units moving toward the Yalu River well in advance of US troops. The first Chinese Communist blow could be delivered against these isolated ROK detachments, inferior in number and far from reinforcements. Success would signal Peking's entry into the war without, however, provoking as threatening a counterblow as if the defeat were suffered primarily by US forces. It would then be up to Washington to choose between continuing the offensive and going over to the defensive. Meanwhile, Chinese People's Volunteers and Democratic People's Republic of Korea armies would occupy the mountainous area bordering China. Should the bridges be cut, heavy equipment and reinforcements could cross the frozen Yalu at will after early November.

In the period between the mid-October CPV crossings of the Yalu and the great Chinese counteroffensive of November 26, the military situation developed in a way that China could interpret as to her own advantage. A seventy-five-mile gap opened between General Walton Walker's Eighth Army on the western front and General E. M. Almond's X Corps which landed at Wonsan on the eastern front. In addition, American reliance upon motorized transport and armored units left these armies, particularly the X Corps, strung out over long, hazardous mountain roads. Not only was the UN force split in two, but the two parts were atomized. Small units were separated from one another by many miles, and both lateral and feeder communications were inadequate. Thus the overall CPV numerical inferiority was offset by the vulnerability of the UN force to local attacks by superior numbers.

Although this reconstruction of Chinese Communist estimates concerning the prospects of intervention, both before and after the Yalu crossing, is based on purely circumstantial evidence, it is borne out by the manner in which Peking entered the war, gradually and with a belated concern for the secrecy of military movements. We shall consider these movements further in examining CPV behavior after the initial contact with UN forces. At this point, however, we must turn to other precombat military preparations for whatever clues they provide to the question of Chinese Communist intervention.

Preparation for Combat. The way in which Peking prepared its troops for combat indirectly sheds light on its decision to enter the

Korean War. The available evidence concerning re-equipment, training, and political indoctrination, although inconclusive, argues against the probability that Chinese military intervention had been determined upon in advance of the conditional warnings issued by Peking in late August and September.

In contrast with the sudden increases in Soviet equipment delivered to DPRK forces in the spring of 1950, just before the invasion, there is little evidence of Soviet deliveries to the PLA prior to CPV entry into North Korea. None of the Chinese armies engaged in the fighting of October-November had been trained in handling Russian weapons, and the only known piece of Soviet equipment used by them at this time was one type of submachine gun. The overwhelming majority of CPV units entered Korea with the same potpourri of captured Japanese and American weapons that had served them during four years of civil war in China. So widespread was their use of American firearms seized from defeated Chinese Nationalist units, that American troops repeatedly mistook enemy for friendly fire.

During the summer and fall, the detailed attention of the Peking press to the destructiveness of US firepower in Korea, both on the ground and in the air, indicated a realistic appraisal at higher levels of enemy strength. In the absence of extensive deliveries of heavier Soviet artillery and antiaircraft weapons, CPV units might be expected to have undergone intensive training and maneuvers to prepare them to face opposition more formidable than they had met hitherto. Except for isolated units, however, most of the troops continued in economic reconstruction until their assignment to Korea. Additional reinforcements were hastily recruited from farms and schools, and these received little training in military tactics before entering combat.

The political indoctrination of CPV units appears to have varied considerably, depending upon the caliber of officers in charge. In early October one group reportedly learned that they were to fight as "volunteers" in Korea. Many of the soldiers in the initial attacks, however, did not learn of their assignment until they were approaching the Yalu River or, in some cases, until after they had actually crossed into North Korea. Except for the routine application of anti-American propaganda, most troops received little indoctrination to prepare them for fighting US forces in Korea.

It is possible that Peking believed its own propaganda concerning the inevitable superiority of the Communist cause and the quick collapse of UN resistance, and therefore made no serious preparations for combat in terms of re-equipment, training, and political indoctrination. In view of the long military history of virtually the entire Chinese Communist Party elite, however, this seems most unlikely. Whatever illusions may have existed in June about the American "paper tiger," the subsequent course of the war had amply demonstrated US military capability. We have noted the early expectation of a "prolonged war" in the Peking press, and its sober accounts of American mobilization throughout the summer. Having experienced the results of miscalculation in June, and having been deterred from the planned invasion of Taiwan by the US Seventh Fleet, it is highly improbable that Sino-Soviet strategy would have calculated upon an easy victory a few months later. Once the successes garnered through the initial impact of surprise had been realized, pursuit of UN forces would face the problem of logistical operations over difficult terrain against unopposed enemy air attacks of a kind which had repeatedly hampered the DPRK in its summer offensives. In short, the same factors which had confronted Pyongyang with "prolonged war" promised to pose a similar problem for Peking.

If faith in easy victory cannot account for China's piecemeal preparations, the relatively short time between the decision to enter the war and the implementation of that decision may have precluded fuller preparation for combat. If the agreement to commit Chinese Communist armies was not arrived at before late August, and then predicated upon the contingency of a UN invasion of North Korea across the 38th Parallel, logistical difficulties were bound to impede rapid, extensive re-equipping with Soviet weapons. Not only did strained transport facilities limit arms shipments from Russian depots, but the training of PLA units in the handling of Soviet weapons was handicapped by the lack of cadres capable of bridging the linguistic gap between Russians and Chinese.

Similarly, warning to Chinese troops of imminent combat in Korea was apparently not authorized until UN forces had actually crossed the parallel, coincident with Peking's official warnings through the Ministry of Foreign Affairs spokesman and domestic elite journals against "supinely tolerating the savage invasion of neighbors."

Whether for security reasons or because of the constraints imposed by the unwillingness of the regime to commit itself publicly before the determining contingency had occurred, few of the troops redeployed in late September and early October knew of their ultimate assignment. It is also possible that concern for morale may have prevented the authorities from telling the troops they were to fight US forces, particularly since the prolonged fighting against Japanese and Chinese Nationalist armies had undoubtedly left the average soldier with little enthusiasm for a new war.

While positive proof is lacking, the evidence indicates that China made no early plans to commit the PLA to combat in Korea. The military movements, the equipping, training, and indoctrination of troops, diplomatic developments, and shifts in the propaganda line all combine to indicate that the initial decision to take military action, should political moves fail, was made in late August. Implementation of this decision came with the initial war alert of early September, the troop redeployment beginning in mid-September, and the formal warnings from Chou En-lai in late September and early October. Final mobilization, however, was not authorized until after the UN rejection of the warnings and the crossing of the parallel.

Mobilizing the Populace. As we have already noted, Chou En-lai's refusal to tolerate "the savage invasion" of China's neighbor was given public prominence by the Foreign Office statement of October 10 and by subsequent editorials in *Jen Min Jih Pao, World Culture,* and *Study.* This opened the first stage in the mobilization of the Chinese people through the public information media. Its distinguishing characteristics are several. First, the war alert of early September reappeared in a massive propaganda campaign throughout China. Unlike the earlier alert, however, this new material contained frequent, explicit references to defending Korea, as well as to protecting the motherland. Second, despite the renewed militancy of public statements, no specific call for "volunteers" occurred at this time. Finally, the campaign began in the guise of "spontaneous" expressions of opinion, with no formal committee to inspire them and with little front-page attention by *Jen Min Jih Pao.* Not until late October, when the issue was joined at the battle front, did the characteristics of the campaign change. The mobilization of public opinion then entered its second stage.

On October 13 *Kung Jen Jih Pao* declared, "We cannot stand idly by when the American imperialist, a notorious enemy, is now expanding its war of aggression against our neighbor and is attempting to extend the aggressive flames to the border of the country." Professor Ch'ien Tuan-sheng, dean of the College of Social Science at Peking National University, was quoted: "Korea and our country are separated by a river. The safety of the Korean People has been threatened. It means that the safety of the Chinese people is also threatened." Workers in Kwangtung swore "never to be afraid of an antiaggression war to safeguard peace" and pledged themselves to "support the statement made by the spokesman of the Foreign Ministry with actual deeds . . . ever ready to deal the American imperialists a telling blow." Representatives of minority nationalities from Inner Mongolia and elsewhere issued a joint statement, warning: "By spreading the flames of aggressive war to the very borders of China, they [American imperialists] are menacing the security of the whole world, but especially of China. . . . We are determined to strengthen the National Defense Forces and to strike down any imperialist aggressor who dares to flout the will of the Chinese people."

Meanwhile *Jen Min Jih Pao* paid the war scant heed, giving it only occasional front-page coverage throughout October as it had in the latter half of September. New official protests against alleged US overflights of Chinese territory received only perfunctory attention. Several factors may have accounted for this somewhat restrained domestic posture at the very time CPV units were crossing the Yalu. Peking may have tempered its home-front propaganda for security purposes connected with concealing its move into Korea. In addition, it may have wished to test enemy response to CPV intervention, before committing itself to total mobilization. In any event, no news of the "volunteers" appeared at this time. Indeed, none of the propaganda themes went beyond a general alert.

October closed with a significant concatenation of inflammatory messages in the three key journals, *Jen Min Jih Pao, World Culture,* and *Study.* The coincidence in timing with the initial fighting between CPV and ROK forces in Korea was in all probability not an accidental one. The belligerency of these articles, written on the eve of combat, is striking. In its first editorial on the Truman statements of mid-October, which had expressly denied US designs beyond Korea,

Jen Min Jih Pao declared: "The ambitions of the US imperialist bandits will not be satisfied with the attack on Korea. Truman will certainly extend his aggressive war to the borders of China . . . following in the footsteps of the Japanese predecessors who also began with aggression against Korea and then the Northeast and the interior of China. But this aggression will not be tolerated by the Chinese people."

Study echoed this alarm, noting, "The war in Korea has now entered a new phase. . . . Their [the US imperialists'] position . . . gravely threatens the security of our fatherland. China and Korea are separated by one river, with the two countries having over 1,000 li of common front." In addition to this defensive theme, there was new emphasis on neighborly obligations which were said to impel Chinese action, since the Korean people "took an active part in China's revolutions and did not hesitate to shed their blood and sacrifice themselves for our cause.

The most complete statement of the intensified war alert came from *World Culture.* Just as this journal had made the initial prophecy of a "prolonged war" and had been the first to declare, "North Korea's defense is our defense," so now, once again, it signaled a new turn of policy. In its editorial call for "resistance against the American imperialist aggressors," it reintroduced the key term *k'ang yi.* This term, connoting active defense, had not been evident since the campaign of early September. Now it became the hallmark of the formal Resist-America, Aid-Korea movement which lasted from November 1950 to the armistice of July 1953. Its appearance at this time, after the first CPV fighting had occurred in Korea but before Peking or Pyongyang had officially announced the "volunteer" movement, marked the transition from partial to full mobilization of public opinion in the People's Republic of China. The editorial in which it appeared merits quotation:

Can the Chinese people be unconcerned with the barbarous aggression against our neighbor, Korea, or with the threat to our national defense line in the Northeast, or with the repeated violations of our territory, our territorial waters, and air? No, we definitely cannot be unconcerned! It is very clear now that American imperialism is following the beaten path of Japanese imperialism—the wishful thinking of annexing Korea, and then from there invading our Northeast, then north China, east China, and finally the whole of Asia and adjacent areas. . . .

We definitely will not beg for [peace] from the aggressor. . . . Neither are we afraid of the aggressor. The American aggressor is not in the least stronger than the fascist Japanese of yesterday, while the Chinese people are more united and stronger than ever before. . . .

The Chinese people will not tolerate a repetition of the history of 45 years ago. Therefore we must be on the same front as the Korean people to oppose and to end the American imperialist aggression. . . . Rise up in the struggle against the American imperialist aggressors, to aid our heroic Korean brethren, and to defend peace in the Far East.

It is interesting to note that assistance to Korea was still justified by its relevance for China's defense. On occasion, it was presented as repayment for past services rendered by the Korean people. Rarely, however, was it recommended on the basis of proletarian internationalism and socialist solidarity.

For a fuller understanding of the Chinese intervention, we must now examine the second stage of the general mobilization for war that began in late October.

Mobilization: The Second Stage

Between October 26 and November 7 the CPV engaged UN forces, both South Korean and American, along a wide front extending from coast to coast. Through surprise and local superiority in numbers, Chinese Communist units defeated their ROK opponents and forced a general withdrawal of Eighth Army lines. On November 5 MacArthur notified Lake Success that Chinese prisoners of war had revealed "Chinese Communist military units deployed for action against the forces of the United Command." Two days later North Korea officially acknowledged that Chinese "volunteers" had been fighting with DPRK units since October 25. At the same time, all Communist forces suddenly broke contact with UN units along the entire battle line. During the following lull, however, Peking continued to send troops across the Yalu River and moved its domestic propaganda campaign into high gear to mobilize "volunteers" for fighting in Korea.

CPV-UN Engagements. Following the capture of Pyongyang on October 19, UN forces advanced rapidly in an attempt to overrun remnant DPRK units and to end the war before winter hit the mountainous area adjoining China. On the west coast, General Walker's

Eighth Army, including British and Turkish troops and flanked by four ROK divisions, crossed the Ch'ongch'on River and advanced toward the temporary DPRK capital of Sinuiju. It encountered stiffening enemy resistance approximately forty miles below the Yalu. On the east coast, General Almond's X Corps had landed at Wonsan and Iwon, and had joined ROK detachments moving up the coast. Its forces advanced inland toward the Changjin Reservoir and probed north toward the Yalu. Between the two main UN armies, ROK detachments advanced toward the Sino-Korean border. There was no continuous defense line and little direct communication linking the two field headquarters.

On October 26 the first UN troops reached the Yalu River. At the border village of Chosan, near the Suiho hydroelectric basin, a battalion of the Seventh Regiment, Sixth ROK Division, looked across into China, well in advance of its parent unit to the south. That night Chinese Communist troops surrounded the battalion and decimated it in an ambush. On October 27, while this action was still in progress, CPV attacks hit the main body of the Sixth ROK Division, with its companion Seventh and Eighth divisions which extended along the flank of the Eighth Army. As South Korean forces fought their way back to Unsan, forty-five miles below the border, they encountered new ambushes by CPV troops who had infiltrated behind their lines.

On November 1 the US First Cavalry Division rushed reinforcements to the beleaguered ROK troops, only to find itself under surprise CPV attack. Heavy fighting continued for two days with growing losses on the American side. Suddenly the Communist attacks ended, and Chinese forces melted back into the hills whence they had come. Nevertheless, General Walker pulled back the entire Eighth Army line, together with the badly mauled ROK divisions, and established defensive positions along the Ch'ongch'on River. Advance units of the US Twenty-fourth Division, already within fifteen miles of the Yalu, retreated fifty miles down the west coast. The initial battle between American and Chinese troops had ended in victory for the Communist side, its first since the Inchon landing and the Pusan breakout of mid-September.

Meanwhile similar action flared up on the east coast. On the day of the Yalu River ambush, the Twenty-sixth Regiment, Third ROK Division, ran into CPV fire near the Changjin Reservoir, seventy-five miles below the border and an equal distance from the engagements on the west coast. On November 2 the US Seventh Marine Regiment arrived to relieve the ROK troops, and fought a five-day battle with the 124th Chinese Communist Forces Division south of Chinhung-ni. By November 7, Communist casualties forced this division to withdraw, and the engagement ended in victory for the UN forces.

At this point the entire front became quiet. No Communist attacks occurred for two weeks, nor did reconnaissance uncover enemy positions along the prospective line of UN advance. Was Peking prepared to give only token resistance in North Korea? Interrogation of two dozen Chinese prisoners of war, captured before November 5, indicated that at least five regular divisions, estimated at 10,000 men each, had crossed the Yalu. Another 200,000 troops were thought to be concentrated at bridgeheads within two nights' march of the front. Actually, as we have seen, more than 180,000 "volunteers" had already entered Korea by this time, and at least 90,000 more were scheduled to join them within three weeks. Given this impressive force and the signal victories attending surprise attacks in October, why did Peking not commit its full strength to an immediate all-out offensive against the disrupted UN defenses?

It is possible that delay was caused by the need for a greater concentration of force than was available when the initial engagements occurred. There are, however, two other possible explanations. First, the pause in the Communist attacks may have been due to the kind of military considerations that are spelled out in Mao Tse-tung's classic study, *On the Protracted War.* Second, political considerations may have dictated a limited blow followed by a suspension of activity, in order to test and examine the UN response to Chinese Communist intervention. These two explanations are not mutually exclusive, but must be reviewed in more detail to determine their compatibility with other evidence on the motivations behind Peking's entry into the war at this time.

Mao's Strategic Design. Although *On the Protracted War* was written during the Japanese invasion of 1938, the volume was republished in China in 1951, implying that its doctrine was still accepted by the Chinese when the Korean War began. The following excerpts highlight the correlation between the book's contents and CPV strategic behavior during October-November 1950:

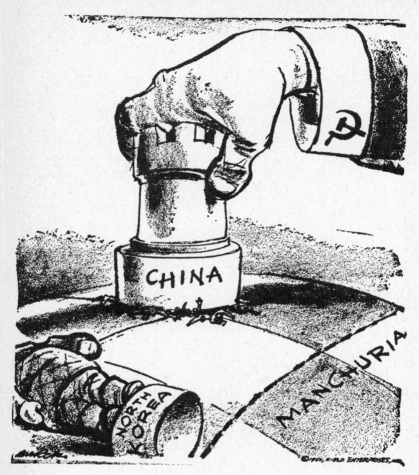

"Your Move!" (*Editorial cartoon by Jacob Burck.   Chicago Sun-Times, 1950*)

The strategy should be that of employing our main forces in a mobile warfare, over an extended, shifting and indefinite front: a strategy depending for success on a high degree of mobility, and featured by swift attack and withdrawal, swift concentration and dispersal. [p. 163]

Adherents of the theory of a quick victory are wrong. They either completely neglect the contrast between strength and weakness and notice only the other contrasts, or they exaggerate China's advantage out of all true proportion and beyond recognition, or with overweening confidence, take the relative strength at one time and one place for that in the whole situation. . . . At any rate, they lack the courage to admit the fact that the enemy is strong while we are weak. [p. 179]

Since the war is a protracted one and the final victory will be China's, we can reasonably imagine that this protracted war will pass through the following three stages. The first stage is one of the enemy's strategic offensive and our strategic defensive. [p. 183]

At the end of the first stage, owing to the insufficiency in his own troops and our firm resistance, the enemy will be forced to fix a point as the terminus of his strategic offensive, halting his strategic offensive on reaching the terminus, he will then enter the stage of retaining the occupied territories. [p. 185]

Because the enemy force, though small, is strong (in equipment and the training of officers and men) while our own force, though big, is weak (only in equipment and the training of officers and men but not in morale), we should, in campaign and battle operations, not only employ a big force to attack from an exterior line a small force on the interior line, but also adopt the aim of quick decision. To achieve quick decision we should generally attack, not an enemy force holding a position, but one on the move. We should have concentrated, beforehand [and] under cover, a big force along the route through which the enemy is sure to pass, suddenly descend on him while he is moving, encircle and attack him before he knows what is happening, and conclude the fighting with all speed. If the battle is well fought, we may annihilate the entire enemy force or the greater part or a part of it. Even if the battle is not well fought, we may still inflict heavy casualties. [p. 209]

We say that it is easy to attack an enemy on the move precisely because he is then not on the alert, that is, he is inadvertent. These two things— creating illusions for the enemy and springing surprise attacks on him —are used to make the enemy face the uncertainties of war while securing for ourselves the greatest possible certainty of gaining superiority, initiative, and victory. [p. 217]

We have always advocated the policy of "luring the enemy to penetrate deep" precisely because this is the most effective military policy for a weak army in strategic defense against a strong army. [p. 224]

These excerpts, omitting references applying only to the Sino-Japanese War, offer an image of combat which parallels the early Chinese tactics in Korea. The Chinese Communist press hinted at the parallel. The term "prolonged war" appeared intermittently throughout the summer of 1950. Even as the "volunteers" staged their initial attacks on UN positions, a *World Culture* writer observed that, "The rugged mountains of North Korea are an ideal graveyard for the imperialist invaders." After describing the advantages for guerrilla warfare now that US troops were advancing inland, he quoted Secretary of Defense George Marshall, "The greatest danger today is lack of reserves in trained manpower." At least in this stage of the war, Mao's strategic doctrine would appear to have been applicable.

Yet this strategic approach was to lose its validity as the Chinese troops moved south. The narrowing of the peninsula below the Sin-anju-Hungnam line precluded any real prospect of mobility, while US air and naval superiority further threatened to limit CPV operations. Does this mean that *On the Protracted War* misled strategists? Or was it seen as operative only for the first stage of hostilities? A third alternative deserves statement, although it cannot be explored without access to materials beyond our reach. Did Peking anticipate a prolonged war in the northern portions of Korea where the strategy would remain operative, and did the precipitate UN withdrawal of December throw its calculations awry? We do not know the answers, although Chinese Communist propaganda explicitly warned the populace to expect a "prolonged struggle" in Korea. Since *On the Protracted War's* first appearance in 1938, however, atomic weapons had entered the picture. To what extent did the atomic bomb affect the calculations of Sino-Soviet strategists in the fall of 1950?

The Atomic Bomb: "A Paper Tiger."   In attempting to reconstruct elite estimates on the consequences of entering the Korean War, we have no direct evidence bearing upon the problem of a US nuclear counterstrike. The Chinese leaders must surely have weighed the probability of an atomic attack, its probable military impact, the accumulative impact of several such attacks upon the economic and political system, and the willingness as well as the capability of Soviet retaliatory power to counter US nuclear blows. In the absence of direct evidence, however, we must infer from scattered, tangential materials the most plausible reconstruction of Chinese Communist thinking on the subject.

That the elite anticipated some risk of US air attack is indicated by the construction of air-raid shelters in Mukden and by air-raid drills in key cities throughout northeast China. In addition, the sudden appearance of MIG fighters along the Yalu River in late October may have been a defensive precaution to interdict bombers en route to military staging areas and industrial centers in Manchuria. On November 1 six to nine MIGs attacked US aircraft along the Yalu River. Throughout the remainder of the month MIG sorties engaged American fighters near the Sino-Korean border. The Russian jets stayed well behind the battle front, and no identification of enemy pilots was possible. However, their skill in maneuver argued against their being Chinese, in terms of the known capabilities of PLA pilots.

We know that the nuclear risk was at least present in the minds of military men in Peking, since General Nieh discussed the matter in September with Ambassador Panikkar. As we shall see from our next review of Chinese Communist propaganda, the regime also expressed awareness of public concern in this area. It issued explicit reassurances in early November on the improbability of a US atomic attack, its impact should it occur, and the probable Soviet response. All of this permits us to conclude that Chinese Communist intervention was decided upon with at least some realization that it might trigger US retaliation through nuclear as well as nonnuclear air attack.

What consequences were anticipated should a US nuclear blow result? Again, we do not know, but several points lead us to suspect that the consequences were not expected to be catastrophic. First, the published remarks, albeit scanty, of Chinese Communist leaders depreciated the strategic significance of atomic bombs. In August 1946 Mao Tse-tung remarked to an American journalist: "The atom bomb is a paper tiger with which the US reactionaries try to terrify the people. It looks terrible, but in fact is not. Of course, the atom bomb is a weapon of mass destruction, but the outcome of war is decided by the people, not by one or two new weapons." It is true that four years had elapsed since Mao spoke these words, but during this time there was no public modification of this disparaging estimate of nuclear power, at least in discussions between Chinese Communist leaders and outsiders. Nieh, in talking with Panikkar, admitted that atomic attacks might kill "a few million people," but added, "After all, China lives on the farms. What can atom bombs do there?"

On the one hand, Nieh's reference to the possible casualties seemed to overstate the case. On the other hand, his dismissal of the consequences was not addressed specifically to the impact upon China's ability to fight in Korea but rather to the likelihood of the US defeating the People's Republic of China on her own ground.

It may be that Soviet strategic estimates led the Chinese Communist analysts to recognize the possibility of a US atomic attack but to underestimate its consequences. If the Chinese Communists relied upon Soviet military publications for information on this matter, they were poorly served. Down to 1950, apparently, little if anything came from this source on the strategic import of nuclear warfare. Chinese strategists may have been informed by their Soviet counterparts that the US supply of atomic bombs was small and the delivery capability weak, making improbable the employment of nuclear power against the Chinese mainland. Soviet development of an atomic bomb in 1949 may have served as some reassurance either that the US could be deterred from an atomic attack by threat of retaliation, or that a US nuclear blow would actually trigger a Soviet nuclear counterblow. Both hypothetical situations were projected in domestic propaganda, as we shall see shortly. We have no information concerning high-level exchanges which may have occurred between Chinese and Soviet planners on this particular aspect of the problem. It is significant, however, that US possession of the atomic bomb does not seem to have compelled reassessment of Mao's strategic doctrine, although the latter was developed in the pre-nuclear age. This does not mean that the Chinese Communist military intervention was undertaken in complete disregard of the possible consequences of a US nuclear strike, but rather that the Chinese accepted a calculated risk, which they felt to be justified by the overriding considerations favoring intervention.

Political Considerations. So long as the US response to Chinese Communist intervention remained uncertain, prudence argued for a cautious approach, lest the enemy be impelled to attack the mainland, perhaps employing his atomic capability. As Mao had warned in 1948:

> *We oppose overestimating the strength of the enemy. . . . But in every particular situation, every specific struggle (no matter whether military,*

*political, economic, or ideological struggle), we must not despise the
enemy. On the contrary, we should take the enemy seriously, concentrate
all our efforts on fighting, and thus we can win victory.*

The chronology is suggestive. On November 5 General MacArthur
dispatched a "special report" to the United Nations, in which he detailed instances of Chinese Communist belligerency in the form of
antiaircraft fire across the Yalu, MIG attacks over the border, and
CPV units in Korea identified by prisoners of war. On November 7
the official DPRK communiqué announced that "volunteer units
formed by the Chinese people participated in operations along with
the People's Armed Forces, under the unified command of the General Headquarters . . . [and] mounted fierce counteroffensives on the
west front on October 25." At this point CPV attacks ceased, and a
lull settled over the battle front.

Disengagement provided Peking with an opportunity to assess the
US and UN reaction to its intervention, to prepare against counter-
blows, and to step up mobilization should the need remain and the
risks be tolerable. By labeling its armies "volunteers" and by limiting
the initial engagements, Peking may have hoped to minimize the US
response and to remain free for political maneuver should the response exceed expectations or should it meet Sino-Soviet goals of
compromise.

On November 11 a Ministry of Foreign Affairs spokesman replied
to the MacArthur report. He admitted that "the Chinese people" were
fighting in Korea, but denied official responsibility for this. His argument merits quotation at length for its relevance to China's problem
of limiting the US response:

*This reasonable expression of the Chinese people's will to assist Korea
and resist American aggression is not without precedent in the history of
the world, and no one can object to it. As is well known, in the eighteenth
century, the progressive people of France, inspired and led by Lafayette,
assisted the American people in their war of independence by similar
voluntary action. Before the Second World War, the democratic people of
all countries of the world, including the British and American people, also
assisted the Spanish people by similar voluntary action in the Spanish
civil war against Franco. All these have been acknowledged throughout
the world as just actions. . . . Since the expression of the Chinese people's
will . . . is so reasonable, so just, so righteous, magnanimous, and so*

flawless, the People's Government of China sees no reason to prevent their voluntary departure for Korea.

Throughout the Spanish civil war, the Non-Intervention Committee, composed chiefly of West European nations, had recognized the fiction of "volunteers" from Germany, Italy, and the Soviet Union. China's contention that her forces in Korea were "volunteers" was not without precedent, and Peking might hope that the analogy with the Spanish civil war would permit a general acceptance of that contention. This device could not be relied upon to deter US military action, but it might discourage or weaken the efforts of America's allies. The "volunteer" approach, the limited initial attack, and the subsequent disengagement, suggest that China intervened in Korea with due consideration of the risks and a determination to minimize them. All the way through, of course, Peking also derived some comfort from the deterrent effect of the Sino-Soviet mutual defense treaty.

If the lull in the ground fighting was intended to test the American response to Chinese intervention, that response was not long in appearing. Until this time the Manchurian sanctuary had been scrupulously observed, and US aircraft had refrained from attacking the Yalu River bridges even at their terminal points in Korea. On November 6–7 MacArthur requested, and the Joint Chiefs of Staff approved, the amending of these restrictions so as to permit attacks on the Korean side of the river. Implementation of this directive gave Peking evidence of the precise degree to which Washington was prepared to modify its strategy in the face of CPV intervention. On the one hand, the US would assume an increased risk of accidental overflight in order to attack entry routes into Korea. On the other hand, it was willing to jeopardize the success of the missions, including the safety of its pilots and planes, rather than attack MIG bases and antiaircraft positions on the Chinese side from which defensive fire protected the crossing points. Hence the waiting period may have served to moderate Peking's fears concerning its sanctuary in the rear. In addition, it may have served as a test of Peking's hopes that the battle front would enter, in accordance with Mao's strategic doctrine, a "second stage" that would find the UN stabilizing its defensive positions along an extended line in North Korea. This would permit a war of attrition close to China's base of supply while ensuring a territorial basis for continuing the official DPRK regime. Thus both political and strategic considerations may have induced Peking to suspend its offensives against the UN lines in November.

Mobilization of the Populace. During this period Chinese Communist communications on the home front dropped the constraints that had characterized the first stage of mobilization. On October 26 the Chinese People's Committee in Defense of World Peace and Against American Aggression was formed in Peking to spearhead the mass propaganda campaign which was to last for the duration of the war. The next day *Jen Min Jih Pao* carried a front-page headline, "American Troops Invading Korea Approach Our Borders." In less than a week every major city in China held public meetings at which thousands pledged to defend the fatherland amidst the "spontaneous demands of volunteers anxious to fight the American imperialists in Korea." On November 2 the Peking press made its first reference to such "volunteers," although a subsequent DPRK communiqué acknowledged their presence at the front since October 25.

At this point all communications media turned to the "Resist-America" theme, with its attendant call for combat in Korea. Despite the battle-front lull, *Jen Min Jih Pao* saturated its pages with war propaganda in its most discursive treatment of the conflict since June 25. The staggering volume of "Resist-America, Aid-Korea" material warrants a separate study in itself. Our principal concern, however, is to determine whether this propaganda reflected the expectations, if not the aims, of the Chinese leaders at the time of the intervention.

Unfortunately, the clues in communications media to the goals and expectations of Peking with respect to military action in Korea are highly ambiguous. Indeed, they are notable more for what they leave unsaid than for what they say. Thus the initial *Jen Min Jih Pao* editorial following CPV action in Korea declared: "The voluntary aid of Chinese patriots . . . will bring the possibility of turning the tide of war, annihilating and repulsing the unconsolidated American troops, and forcing the aggressors to accept a just and peaceful solution of the Korean question." This seemed to argue for a limited use of force to accomplish what political maneuvers had failed to accomplish, namely, a negotiated end to the war along some unspecified line of compromise. Nothing in the article posited the total destruction of UN authority in Korea as the goal of CPV intervention.

Once again it was *World Culture* that provided the most sober estimate of future events. Two articles in successive issues probed the possible consequences of Chinese "volunteer" action. The first, probably written prior to the official DPRK acknowledgment of "volunteer" action, predicted:

> *There are two possibilities. . . . One is that American imperialists will be forced off the Korean peninsula. . . . The second is that after U. S. troops suffer defeat, they [will] continue to increase reinforcements, ceaselessly expending men and material, becoming mired ever deeper and more helplessly. . . . This way American imperialism will have no troops to spare for attacking Indo-China or other places and cannot increase troops in Europe. Its satellites will complain, the antiwar spirit of the U. S. people will increase, and this will prevent the imperialists from starting a large war.*

This was a curious article in the context of mass mobilization. It foresaw the possibility of a "prolonged war," yet its rationale for accepting such a war nowhere touched upon China's immediate interests. Indeed its reference to Europe reflected primarily Soviet interests that were to be served by tying down US forces in Korea. At the very least, the article would seem to have tempered rather than aroused enthusiasm for "volunteering."

One week later a different *World Culture* analyst detailed a wider range of possible consequences from Chinese Communist military action in Korea:

> *It is possible that American imperialists will not dare to carry on all-out war against China, but rather will limit the war to Korea itself, only fighting those Chinese who take part in the Korean war as volunteers. [In this case] the war might go on for a very long time. . . . The Korean people might drive the American imperialists from Korea. . . . The US imperialist troops, after several defeats, might withdraw.*
>
> *The second possibility is that the Americans might . . . ignite World War III.*

The possibility of general war was now explicitly envisaged, albeit with the expressed reassurance of ultimate victory because of Soviet strengths and US weaknesses. The alternative outcome, a "very long war" limited to Korea, was depicted as a "victory" since it would deny the US possession of all Korea and constitute a drain on American resources. The writer explicitly warned that decisive victory might not be attainable "through a knockout blow," thereby raising the prospect of stalemate at the battle front.

So sober a view of future possibilities was perhaps merely preventive medicine to forestall any setbacks in domestic morale that might follow from reverses at the front. Given the previous role of *World Culture*, however, in signaling significant policy developments, it would appear that these estimates reflected at least some of the thinking at higher levels. It is impossible to determine how widely such views may have prevailed within the elite, but taken together with Chinese Communist military and political behavior as a whole, they appear to reflect the genuine doubts and uncertainties of the leaders in determining to intervene.

In this regard, it is significant that throughout its propaganda of November 1950 Peking insisted that the war was likely to be a long one. The guiding directive for the campaign declared: "The patriotic movement of Resist the US, Aid Korea, Protect Our Homes, and Defend Our Country, is possessed of a comparatively prolonged nature . . . to last and wax stronger with time." *Jen Min Jih Pao* warned: "The imperialists have only begun to be battered and they will continue to carry out atrocities. Therefore we must continue to conduct firm counterattacks against them. . . . Forward! March on, under the enemy gunfire and bombs, to final victory!" On the eve of General MacArthur's "win the war" offensive, *Current Affairs Journal* noted: "The enemy has not yet been dealt decisive blows and the American aggressors are prepared for war on a still bigger scale."

This journalistic restraint does not prove conclusively that the goals of intervention were limited or that the elite believed decisive victory to be only a remote possibility. It does suggest, however, Peking's unwillingness to encourage hopes for a quick or total victory. It contrasts markedly with the image of an intervention lightly undertaken in expectation of quick victory, the image which might emerge from a study of equipping, training, and indoctrination alone. In short, hortatory as the appeal to the public was, it nevertheless retained the element of restraint and caution that had marked Peking's more authoritative comment on the Korean War from its inception five months previously.

In addition to conceding the possibility of a prolonged war, Chinese Communist propaganda dealt with the prospect of atomic attacks against the civilian populace. Apart from anti-atomic-bomb material connected with the so-called Stockholm Peace Appeal, a new approach to the nuclear threat appeared at the time of the war alert of late October and early November. A basic directive for "Resist America" propaganda outlined themes to reassure audiences both about the probability of atomic warfare and about the effects of atomic bombs should they be used. "The atomic bomb is now no longer monopolized by the US. The Soviet Union has it too. If the US dares to use the atomic bombs, she naturally will get retaliation, and deservedly." On the other hand, the directive continued:

> *Its military effectiveness, at most, is in large-scale bombing. . . . The atomic bomb itself cannot be the decisive factor in a war. . . . It cannot be employed on the battlefield to destroy directly the fighting power of the opposing army, in order not to annihilate the users themselves. It can only be used against a big and concentrated object like a big armament industry center or huge concentration of troops. Therefore, the more extensive the opponent's territory is and the more scattered the opponents' population is, the less effective will the atom bomb be.*

Jen Min Jih Pao provided graphic eye-witness accounts of the Hiroshima bombing in which survivors denied rumors that sterility was an aftereffect and detailed measures for protection against atomic blasts. Editorials inveighed against fear of the bomb as a military weapon. While this might have reflected the regime's anxiety over public concern about the bomb, rather than its own expectations of atomic attack, it is interesting that Peking did not argue that such an eventuality was out of the question. Its references to Soviet atomic capability, for instance, implied that the latter might deter a US atomic attack but nowhere stated it would guarantee immunity against the threat. In short, the regime appears intentionally to have left open the possibility of a US atomic counterblow to its move into Korea.

To conclude, the first three weeks of November saw Chinese Communist propaganda mobilizing the populace for a prolonged war in Korea. Both the intensity of the campaign and its specific content left little doubt as to the seriousness of the undertaking. Amidst the exhortations to "volunteer" were relatively frank statements of the uncertainties ahead, including the possibilities of atomic attack against China and of World War III. While a quick, total victory in Korea was occasionally envisaged, it received little stress. Seldom was the goal of combat defined beyond the general statement of "achieving a just peace." If the rulers of China entertained a more optimistic or ambitious estimate of the future, they did not reveal it at this time.

Diplomatic Hiatus

It would appear that China considered the die was cast when UN troops crossed the 38th Parallel, and that she then abandoned diplomacy pending a decision on the battle front. It may be more than a coincidence that the Chinese Communist invasion of Tibet began simultaneously with final UN approval of crossing the parallel. The Tibet campaign immediately offended India, which had been important in pleading Peking's cause at Lake Success. Furthermore, the two-month lapse between the Security Council invitation of September 29 and the arrival of Peking's delegate to discuss the Taiwan question on November 24 cannot be wholly attributed to circumstances beyond Peking's control. In part, at least, it suggested a disregard for diplomatic exchanges until military moves had improved the Communist situation in Korea.

Alvin J. Cottrell and James E. Dougherty

THE LESSONS OF KOREA: WAR AND THE POWER OF MAN

By no means does all academic analysis of the Korean War accept the meaningfulness of the term "limited war," nor do all political scientists side with Truman in his conflict with MacArthur. In the following selection Cottrell and Dougherty, two specialists on problems of military policy and national security, raise questions about the political and psychological readiness of the United States to wage "limited wars."

The Korean War represented a crucial turning point in the struggle between the Communists and the Free World. The manner of the American response to the North Korean attack demonstrated to the Communists the West's ability to react swiftly and decisively to an act of outright aggression. But more important still, the Korean War revealed the inadequacy of Western democratic governments to deal with a conflict situation which is protracted and kept indecisive. It was the experience of this war, more than any other single factor, which has given rise, during the last two years, to the debate over the readiness of the United States to wage so-called "limited wars." This debate, insofar as it has centered upon the size and the mobility of American tactical forces on the periphery of the Sino-Soviet bloc, completely misses the crucial point: namely that the problem of waging "limited war" is essentially not one of military power but of political will.

Through the years 1950–1953, the United States was, in terms of sheer military power, the superior contestant. Narrow limits were indeed imposed upon the Korean conflict, but "it was obviously the stronger Power which imposed them and made them stick." It is fair to ask whether the United States, if it had in being all of the elaborate force levels called for by contemporary proponents of the "limited war" doctrine, would even now be able to avoid a repetition of Korea. Since the memory of the Korean War, with all its bitter frustrations,

Reprinted by permission of the publishers from *Orbis* 2 (Spring 1958): 39–60. *Orbis* is the quarterly journal of world affairs published by the Foreign Policy Research Institute of the University of Pennsylvania.

continues to permeate American thinking in the present discussion on weapons policy, a review of United States strategy in that war may serve to remind us that mere possession of the requisite military power does not provide, by itself, an answer to our problems: namely how to meet the intermediate—"limited"—challenges of the Communists.

The Korean War has been the only military conflict directly involving the United States and members of the Communist bloc. The conflict was limited in several ways: The hostilities were confined to a precise geographical area. The nearby territory of Formosa was "neutralized" and the territory north of the Yalu River declared off limits. The war was limited with regard to the nationality of the forces eligible to participate, for the armed forces of the Nationalist Chinese Government, a member of the Security Council which urged UN members to resist the aggression, were not allowed to take part in the action. Furthermore, the war was limited as to weapons employed, types of targets selected and kinds of supplementary operations undertaken. Thus weapons of mass destruction were not used; the rail and supply lines of the Chinese Communists were not hit; and long-range American aerial reconnaissance was ruled out.

It is significant that none of these limitations [was nor] could have been forced upon the United States by the enemy. They all were voluntarily assumed by the United States. The reasons given for accepting these limitations were various, but practically all of them were reducible to fears of one sort or another: fear that the United States would alienate its European allies by prosecuting too vigorously a war in Asia; fear of antagonizing the Asian neutrals if Chiang's forces were utilized; and, above all, fear that the war, if it was not rigidly localized, would become general and global.

The difficulties encountered by the United States during the Korean War sprang in the first instance from a failure to view the struggle against the total strategic background. Probably the Communists themselves did not foresee the full strategic implication of the border crossing on June 24, 1950, and they may not have anticipated the prompt response of the United States and the UN Security Council. The United States entered the war for definite enough a purpose: the defense of a free nation against flagrant Communist aggression. At the outset, the United States and its friends in the United Nations were under no misapprehension as to the fundamental issues, political and moral, raised by the attack on South Korea.

Some of the countries who later assumed a neutralist posture voted in the UN to resist the North Koreans. By October of 1950, when UN forces began their offensive to the Yalu, the General Assembly went beyond the original objective of merely defending South Korea and defined the UN's goal as the establishment of a "unified, independent and democratic government in the sovereign state of Korea." This policy statement was intended and interpreted as an authorization for General MacArthur to move northward to the Yalu River. In the same month, the situation changed ominously when the Chinese Communists began to pour into Korea. Then the Korean War began to assume a different meaning; MacArthur called it an "entirely new war." The West was slow to evaluate the strategic consequences of the conflict with Communist China. Since the war had started over the Korean question, Western diplomats and commentators persisted in regarding it as a war over Korea, in which the additional features of Chinese Communist intervention now had to be taken into account. A mental block obscured the full significance of the fact that the war was now between Communist China and the United States. It took the Communists four months—from June to October 1950—to develop a novel strategy for turning Korea to their own strategic advantage.

Once the Chinese were in the fight, the unity of purpose of the United States and its allies in the UN began to flag. While India began to view Korea as an arena of the Cold War in which she vowed to be neutral, Great Britain "became anxious to minimize her responsibility for sponsoring the decisive resolution" concerning MacArthur's authority to cross the 38th Parallel.

Once it was known that China was the antagonist, what were the decisions to be made by the United States? Some of these decisions, by their very nature, could not even be faced unless the United States formulated for itself a reasonably clear picture of the overall Sino-Soviet strategy in Asia. Policy-making flows from analysis, and analysis hinges on framing the right questions. Several questions had to be asked, and at least hypothetical answers had to be given to them. There is some cause for wondering whether American policy-makers did pose the right questions in October 1950. Why did Communist

China enter the Korean War? Did she come in enthusiastically to defend herself against an American-UN-dominated Korea on her border, or did she come in somewhat reluctantly and fearfully as a result of Soviet cajolery, pressure and promises? Was Mao Tse-tung confident of his estimate of the Korean situation before committing himself? Or did he use the gradual buildup of "volunteer" forces during October to probe his enemy and thus to gauge the Western reaction to his move? Was Stalin prepared to divert sizeable and much-needed resources from the Soviet Union to support the Chinese in the event of large-scale fighting? Were the communists prepared to face atomic conflict? What were the strategic implications of China's move for American interests in Japan, Formosa, Indochina and elsewhere? What did the Communist bloc really stand to gain in Korea? How great and how genuine was the danger that the Korean tinderbox would spark a world conflagration? What was the relation of American objectives in the Far East to American objectives in the NATO community? These and similar questions impinged upon the decisions which had to be made in the fall of 1950, particularly those concerning the role of Chiang's army, the application of an economic and naval blockade to China, going beyond the Yalu and using atomic weapons.

The gravest American error in Korea was the failure to respond decisively during the first few days of the Chinese Communist intervention. Since the United States temporized in the face of Mao Tse-tung's probingly cautious, "unofficial" entry into the war, Mao was able gradually to build up his ground forces in North Korea. The initiative passed out of American hands, and the war became prolonged. The longer the war dragged on, the more often the debate within the United States over the Korean War raised the specter of general war. Whenever it was suggested that the United States take steps to regain the military initiative, the proposals were invariably rejected on the grounds that they involved the danger either of provoking general war or of offending the friends of the United States. The major proposals put forth for regaining the initiative concerned the use of Chiang Kai-shek's Nationalist forces on Formosa, the application of a blockade against China, operations beyond the Yalu River and the introduction of atomic weapons.

There may have been justification for the neutralization of Chiang's forces on Formosa by executive order of June 27, 1950, under which the Seventh Fleet was to protect Formosa and thus restrain Chiang from carrying out air or sea attacks against the mainland. Secretary of State Dean Acheson had argued that if Chinese troops from Taiwan were to join the UN forces in Korea, the Red Chinese might decide to enter the conflict precisely to weaken Chiang's army and thus diminish his capability of defending the island against a potential Communist assault. Another and perhaps the most important reason for the US refusal to permit Chiang's participation was, in a sense, a political one, imposed upon the United States by foreign sentiment and by its own reluctance to offend that sentiment. It was summed up succinctly by W. Averell Harriman in the report which he gave to President Truman on his meeting with General MacArthur in early August 1950:

> He [General MacArthur] did not seem to consider the liability that our support of Chiang on such a move would be to us in the Far East. I explained in great detail why Chiang was a liability and the great danger of a split in the unity of the United Nations on the Chinese-Communist–Formosa policies; the attitude of the British, Nehru and such countries as Norway, who, although stalwart in their determination to resist Russian aggression, did not want to stir up trouble elsewhere.

This decision to hold Chiang "under wraps" should have come in for review and modification as soon as Chinese intervention loomed seriously on the horizon. The argument about noninterference in the Chinese civil war, if it ever had any validity, lost all its effectiveness in October 1950. When intelligence reports were received through Indian and British diplomatic channels concerning an impending Chinese military move into Korea, "intelligence reports" should have immediately been filtered through the same channels to the Communists concerning an impending "deneutralization" of Formosa. Had this been done, Mao may well have reconsidered his policy of introducing "volunteers," who could conceivably have been recalled and publicly "chastised" for unauthorized activities. The pretext of "volunteers" reflected Mao's extreme caution. October and November 1950 were doubtless the critical months in the Korean War, when Mao scanned carefully American responses to his moves and took the measure of the UN's firmness of purpose. The US might at this point have blocked China from entering the war and Mao could have recalled the "volunteers" with a minimum loss of face. General Mac-Arthur, at the time of his dismissal, proposed that restrictions be removed from the deployment of Chiang's forces and that these forces be given substantial American logistical support against China. Regardless of how helpful Chiang's army may have been on the Korean peninsula, it is not mere hindsight to conclude that, had the Chinese Nationalists been poised for action across the Formosa Straits, the Communists would not have felt free to remove sizeable forces from the Fukien area for use in Korea. In his testimony to the Senate on the military situation in the Far East, General MacArthur stated:

> I believe that the minute you took off the inhibitions from the Generalis-simo's forces it would result in relieving the pressure on our front in Korea. I believe that they would have tended to shift the center of gravity of their military mobilization down further south than they are at the present time.

Among the arguments often advanced against accepting Chiang's offer of troops was that the United States might unwittingly commit itself to deploying American ground forces to achieve Chiang's major objective: re-establishing the Nationalist Government on the mainland. This reasoning would have us believe that America could not have controlled the scope of its operations on the Chinese mainland, even though it had demonstrated its ability to impose precise limits on its Korean actions. The US certainly could have supplied Chiang with enough material to allow him to carry out diversionary attacks against the Chinese Communists without running the risk of being drawn into the morass of China. The United States could have reduced or cut off the aid to Chiang if and when his operations conflicted with American strategic objectives. There is no need to conclude that Chiang's ambitions were bound to prevail over American interests. American policy-makers pondered all the possible alternatives before them and assumed fatalistically that, once a decision had been made, all its possible consequences, pleasant and unpleasant, would come to pass by some mysterious process over which they had no control.

The question of invoking economic warfare measures against China raised problems of coalition diplomacy for the United States. There can be little doubt that an intensified application of economic sanctions against Communist China, reinforced by a naval blockade against Communist shipping along the coast of China, would have greatly reduced the strength of the Chinese armies in Korea. Admiral Forrest Sherman, Chief of Naval Operations, made this statement during the Senate hearings:

> *A naval blockade by the United Nations would substantially reduce the war potential of Communist China. . . . China is not capable of taking countermeasures that could appreciably reduce the effectiveness of such a blockade.*
>
> *A naval blockade by the United Nations would be advantageous from a psychological standpoint. It would demonstrate to the Chinese Communists, and to the neighboring Asian peoples, the power of the forces against communism—it would demonstrate the effectiveness of sea power, a power that the Chinese Communists can do little to thwart.*

The general arguments against economic weapons were reducible to one, namely that they could have little effect because of the agricultural character of the Chinese economy and because China would still be able to receive goods from the Soviet bloc. The *Economist* stated its position in this way:

> *It is and should remain the British argument that economic sanctions will do more harm than good. Because the main strategic materials from all sources—oil, for example—are already under embargo, very little of vital importance is going into China from the Western world. A greatly increased effort at control would produce only small additional results, which could have little effect on the slender war potential of Peking. . . . What is more, the strict application of sanctions means sooner or later that an American warship stops on the high seas ships bearing Indian jute to China. . . .*

American allies were firmly opposed to boycott and blockade, because such policies would have hurt their Far East trade, which totals several hundred shiploads per year. Britain, moreover, was concerned over the precarious position of Hongkong. Consequently, the United States was unable to expect its allies to favor General MacArthur's proposal for applying economic sanctions. Nevertheless, the failure to apply sanctions enabled China to protract the conflict without suffering any unusual economic strains. The fact that China was an underdeveloped agrarian nation made her almost totally dependent upon imports for the success of her first five-year plan. Every shipload of goods received in the eastern ports helped to lessen China's need for making demands upon her Soviet ally or the East European satellites. The supply lines from the Soviet Union to Korea, some 4,000 miles in length, were already operating under a heavy strain.

Had the United States been able to persuade all the UN members who had branded China as an aggressor to cut off trade with her, the impact of an embargo upon Communist China's economy and war effort would have proved considerable. Mao was, no doubt, agreeably surprised to see that he was free to make strategic moves in Korea without being forced entirely to rely upon his own meager resources and those of his Soviet ally, who was ill-prepared to increase aid shipments. Central to the Chinese Communist leader's concept of protracted war is the notion of altering the relative power distribution between oneself and the enemy, strengthening the former and weakening the latter by every available means.

There were two principal suggestions for extending operations beyond the Yalu River. The first was to reconnoiter Manchuria and the Chinese coastal areas. As early as July 1950, the Air Force had contemplated flying high-level photo missions over Darien, Port Arthur, Vladivostok and the Kuriles. When President Truman heard about these proposed flights over Soviet-controlled territory, he instructed Secretary of the Air Force Finletter not to allow his Far East commanders "to engage in activities that might give the Soviet Union a pretext to come into open conflict with us." This decision to refrain from sweeping reconnaissance over Soviet areas on the Pacific coast may have been justified at the time, although such restraint precluded our gaining the very intelligence needed to corroborate the Central Intelligence Agency estimate that the USSR did not intend to intervene on a large scale in the Far East. Certainly, official policy on reconnaissance should have undergone review when it became apparent that General MacArthur's post-Inchon offensive would take UN forces into North Korea or, at the very latest, when the State Department learned through Indian and British diplomatic channels that the Chinese Communists had made a definite threat to intervene. Had reconnaissance been conducted, the request for authority to bomb the Yalu bridges could have been made in time to hinder the Communist Chinese buildup of massive ground armies in the Korean peninsula. The continued failure to reconnoiter the area above the

Yalu even after MacArthur reiterated the need for such operations in the spring of 1951 was indefensible.

The second suggestion for going beyond the Yalu related to actual offensive operations in Manchuria, including "hot pursuit" of Communist fighter planes and the bombing of enemy supply routes and industrial centers. It should be made clear that at no time were ground-force operations by American forces north of the Yalu contemplated. Air components alone could have executed whatever additional measures the Chinese intervention made imperative.

The limitations which the United States placed upon itself with respect to the use of air power along the Yalu not only prevented the carrying of the war into Manchuria but, furthermore, prevented the UN forces from holding their line of farthest advance because it deprived them of maximum effective air support. Air Marshal Sir John Slessor wrote as long ago as 1936: "The airplane is not a battlefield weapon—the air striking force is not a rule best employed in the actual zone in which the armies are in contact." Later, Slessor applied this maxim to the military situation which obtained in Korea:

> One of the strongest reasons for my dislike at the time of our advance to the Yalu in 1950 was that to do so would deprive the United Nations armies of the massive support of air power, unless we were prepared to spread the war into Manchuria, which for political reasons we were not prepared to do (whether or not those political reasons were good is irrelevant to this military point). And I am on record as being sure, when our armies were subsequently in retreat toward the 38th parallel, that as soon as they had come back far enough to restore to us the depth in the enemy's rear to enable the air to act freely again, the effect would be to retard and finally to arrest the Communist advance.

The Communists held a unique advantage in being able to use Manchuria as a privileged sanctuary into which their MIGs could retreat after attacking American forces in Korea. On November 13, 1950, the State Department wired instructions to its embassies in six nations to inform the allied governments

> that it may become necessary at an early date to permit UN aircraft to defend themselves in the air space over the Yalu River to the extent of permitting hot pursuit of attacking enemy aircraft up to 2 or 3 minutes' flying time into Manchuria air space.

It is contemplated that UN aircraft would limit themselves to repelling enemy aircraft engaged in offensive missions to Korea.

We believe this would be a minimum reaction to extreme provocation, would not in itself affect adversely the attitude of the enemy toward Korean operations, would serve as a warning, and would add greatly to the morale of UN pilots. . . .

The instructions made it clear that the United States was not seeking the concurrence of the governments concerned. Nonetheless, in the face of the "strongly negative responses" received from those governments, the State and Defense Departments decided that the plans for "hot pursuit" ought to be abandoned. On this issue, too, coalition diplomacy came into conflict with tactical operations which were considered necessary or desirable from a military point of view.

After the United States' allies reacted unfavorably to the "hot pursuit" proposals, it was practically a foregone conclusion that General MacArthur's recommendations for more ambitious operations beyond the Yalu, i.e., bombing Manchuria, would be received with even less enthusiasm in the NATO capitals. General MacArthur frequently stressed the fact that his objective was not to extend the scope of ground operations into China itself, but rather to force China to remove herself from the Korean War by the continued application of added pressure on the Chinese supply lines in Manchuria. Nevertheless, Canada's Lester Pearson publicly expressed doubts that his government could participate in any program in Asia involving commitments on the mainland of China, and the British House of Commons carried on a long discussion about the war on the Chinese mainland if MacArthur's policies were adopted. Secretary of State Acheson testified to the Senate that he deemed it "highly probable" that the Sino-Soviet agreement of 1950 included a Soviet promise to assist China if the Manchurian Railway were subjected to a bombing attack by a foreign power. Secretary Acheson did admit, however, that his views on the risk of direct Russian intervention were based on an analysis of Russian self-interest and treaty obligations, not on specific information from intelligence and diplomatic sources concerning Soviet intentions.

There is no question that of all the proposals advanced for regaining the initiative the suggestion to introduce atomic weapons in Korea was the one fraught with the most serious implications. Despite the fact that by the end of November 1950 approximately 400,000 Chinese had poured into Korea, there were some credible reasons why atomic weapons should not have been used at that time. The American atomic stockpile was then earmarked primarily for use by the Strategic Air Command. The diversion of atomic weapons to Korea might have retarded the buildup of the West's far-flung system of atomic air bases, on which Western deterrent power hinged. Moreover, the technology of tactical atomic weapons and delivery systems had not been developed beyond its earliest stages when the fighting in Korea was at its peak; experiments with low-yield atomic weapons for use against troop concentrations in the immediate battle-zone had scarcely begun. Consequently, Americans and their allies, with the disturbing image of atomic bombs dropped by strategic aircraft on Hiroshima and Nagasaki still vivid in their minds, were unable or unwilling to distinguish between the tactical use of nuclear weapons against enemy armies in the field and their strategic use against urban populations deep in enemy territory.

The West, therefore, cavilled at any suggestion that atomic weapons should or could be used in Korea. In particular the European allies of the United States, more vulnerable to atomic attack than the American Continent, took a less sanguine view of the atomic risks than some American policy-makers. On November 30, 1950, President Truman, perhaps in an effort to bring United States nuclear capability into close support of American diplomacy, hinted at a press conference that the introduction of atomic weapons into the Korean conflict was being discussed. "Naturally, there has been consideration of this subject since the outbreak of the hostilities in Korea, just as there is consideration of the use of all weapons whenever our forces are in combat. Consideration of the use of any weapon is always implicit in the very possession of that weapon." If this guarded reference was intended to frighten the Chinese Communists, the effort backfired. Before the news could have any impact on the strategic thinking of the Chinese Communist leadership, the British Labour Government reacted to this veiled threat with open concern, and Prime Minister Clement Attlee hurried to Washington in order to obtain Mr. Truman's assurance that the Korean War would remain "conventional." Domestic critics voiced misgivings to the effect that, since the atom bomb had become a popular symbol of cataclysmic destruction, its use under any circumstances would set off an uncontrollable chain of events which would propel the world into an unwanted total war. Others argued that, even if global war would not be touched off by atomic warfare in Korea, the peoples of Asia would be even more deeply offended by a new exhibition of "American contempt for Asian lives" than they had been five years earlier at the time of Hiroshima and Nagasaki.

In retrospect, the American decision to forego the actual use of atomic weapons in Korea was the most defensible of all the negative decisions made in Washington. The "atomic question," in a sense, was a false one, for probably it would never have been raised had other conventional alternatives, which were available for dealing with Communist China's aggression, been adopted with vigor and determination. It was one thing, however, to decide that the United States would not bring to bear its most powerful military weapon upon a given conflict situation; it was quite another thing to forfeit the psychological and political value inherent in the possession of the atomic bomb by communicating such a decision baldly to the enemy. The disclosure of our intentions may well have served to reassure our allies or to placate an ill-informed public incited by irresponsible party politicians and segments of the press. But however much the Western public may have wished to ignore the fact, the Korean War was fought in the atomic age, and one of the contestants in this war was an atomic power. Hence atomic weapons had a role to play in the strategy of war, even if they were never actually employed.

Today, when nuclear weapons constitute such an important component of the Western defense establishment, it is essential that we read correctly the lessons of the Korean War with regard to the American decision not to use the atomic bomb. For some Americans, who for the first time had occasion to pass prior judgment upon the potential use of atomic weapons, the problem was a moral one. For others the problem was political, since they conceived of it in terms of Asian sentiments or NATO solidarity. These objections were, at least in the context of the Korean War, more logical than those which sprang from a fear that the use of atomic weapons was certain to touch off World War III. There are weighty reasons for concluding that the Soviet Union was willing to be drawn, in 1950–1951, into a general war with the West neither in Korea nor, as some people feared, in Europe. In either case, the question confronting the Russians was identical: Were they ready for general war? It is clear now that the time was not at all appropriate for the Kremlin to risk large-scale conflict with the West had the latter applied additional pressure upon Communist China. Stalin was in no position to enter the Korean War openly. His Far East air force was not strong enough to stand a contest of attrition and replacement production with the United States. The Soviet Union, moreover, would have encountered serious logistic difficulties in attempting to establish and supply operational bases in North Korea, some 4,000 miles from the locus of Russian industrial power. Had the United States increased military pressure in Korea, one wonders how long the Communist bloc would have attempted to match the West in a war in which technical equipment and material resources (rather than manpower, which was far more expendable for the Communists) were being devoured at a steadily increasing rate. The Soviets, had they attempted to intervene massively against the United States in the Far East or launched an attack against Western Europe, could not have avoided the type of war which has long been the nightmare both of the Tsarist and Bolshevik strategists: a two-front all-out war against a powerful enemy. During World War II, the Kremlin had been at pains to avoid a showdown with the Japanese while holding off the Germans in the West. By contrast, the United States, between 1942 and 1945, was strong enough to take on two powerful enemies on opposite sides of the globe.

Most important of all, Russian atomic stockpiles and strategic delivery capabilities were distinctly inferior to those at the disposal of the US. Communist conflict doctrine prescribes the postponement of the all-out, decisive engagement until overwhelming victory is assured. It is, therefore, unlikely that the Soviet Union would have allowed itself to be drawn into a war beyond its borders under circumstances as unfavorable as those surrounding the Korean War. When asked whether the bombing of Manchurian air bases would bring the Soviets into the conflict and thereby touch off World War III, General Mark Clark replied to the Senate Subcommittee investigating the war: "I do not think you can drag the Soviets into a world war except at a time and place of their own choosing. They have been doing too well in the Cold War."

Despite the limitations which the United States imposed upon itself, it was the consensus of Western observers at the scene that the UN forces were on the verge of breaking through the Communists' lines in June 1951. At this point, the Communists feared that the United States was about to mount a tactical offensive in Korea, supported by the extension of air operations into Manchuria. They switched to a strategy of protracted truce negotiations to prevent being driven out of Korea and to demoralize the West by weakening its will to take up the fight again later. This was the second crucial juncture of the war. Just as the circumspect use of "volunteers" had enabled Mao's forces to enter the war with a minimum risk of provoking a commensurate action by the United States against China, the changeover to truce talks in June 1951 eliminated, for all practical purposes, any further danger that Mao's forces might suffer a serious military reversal. Thus the negotiations provided a perfect alibi for a Chinese withdrawal from the shooting war—with their major units intact and well-trained and with the prestige of having fought the United States to a stalemate. The first American strategic mistake had been the failure to act swiftly in November 1950 to counter the stealthy Chinese entrance into the war; the second major blunder by the United States was the virtual decision to accept the Communist demand for a cessation of hostilities prior to the opening of truce negotiations.

Had the US followed the World War I example of continuing the offensive until the armistice was actually signed, the Korean War might well have ended by mid-summer of 1951 on much more favorable terms for the Free World and for Korea. Instead, the United States gave the Communists an invaluable breathing spell. The precarious military position of the Communists should have been evident from the fact that the first diplomatic overtures for a truce were made by Soviet UN Delegate Yakov Malik in a radio speech on June 23, 1951. The Communists' dilemma did not escape a shrewd observer of the Korean scene: "In retrospect, it is clear that in June 1951 the Chinese Communist forces were in a very difficult position. Surrenders had increased noticeably in the preceding weeks; supply had been disrupted by systematic air attacks; it was not clear that the Chinese Communist forces could rally on any pre-determined line to check the United Nations-ROK forces in their advance. The first effect of the de facto cease-fire which followed the offer to negotiate was to relieve this pressure upon the Chinese Communist armies."

Ironically enough, the Soviet Union, in an effort to camouflage the Communists' eagerness for an armistice, tried vainly to have the proposal for a cease-fire originate in the United States. By raising the possibility of a truce as a political issue within the forum of the United Nations, an international organization dedicated to promoting peace, the Communists obtained a de facto cease-fire in the summer of 1951 even while hostilities, technically speaking, were still in progress. Since the Communists found themselves under no serious military pressure, their delegation to the armistice discussions was able to employ delaying tactics and to postpone agreement indefinitely. Meanwhile, the Communists' bargaining power increased in inverse proportion to the psychological willingness of the United Nations Command to resume large-scale military operations. General Matthew Ridgway had argued vehemently against the acceptance of the Communist proposal: he realized that, once a demarcation line had been agreed upon, the United Nations Command could resume offensive ground operations only at the cost of heavy casualties, perhaps 100,000 or more. Ridgway saw no urgent reason for acceding to the Communist demands. As he pointed out later, in every instance when the United Nations Command had been allowed to stand firm on its proposals, the Communists eventually agreed. He was convinced that the United Nations offensive had reached a critical stage and that the Communist forces, badly shaken by the latest UN military operations, obviously wanted nothing so badly as an immediate suspension of hostilities.

Ridgway, however, was overruled by Washington. On November 17, the United Nations Command delegation submitted to its Communist counterpart a proposal providing for a thirty-day period of grace on the basis of the prevailing line of contact. The Communists accepted the proposal, according to Admiral C. Turner Joy, "with obvious relief." Admiral Joy, when testifying before a Senate subcommittee about the Korean armistice negotiations, added:

I would say that the greatest handicap under which we negotiated was the apparent reluctance or inability, in a number of instances, of Washing-

> *ton to give us firm and minimum positions which would be supported by national policy. In other words, positions which we could carry through to the breaking point of negotiations if necessary.*

Acceptance of the idea that the only appropriate conclusion for a limited conflict is a stalemate was a gross error, into which the West was led by its own self-induced paralysis and by shrewd Chinese bluffing.

It was clear from the beginning of the Korean truce talks that the Communists were determined to exploit the talks for maximum propaganda advantage and for wearing down the UN negotiators by harping endlessly on irrelevant issues. The truce conferences were perfectly coordinated with military operations and with other developments that took place far from the tent at Panmunjom. It is now known, for example, that the chief Communist negotiator, a Soviet native of Korean ancestry named Nam Il, simultaneously took a hand in instigating riots and acts of terrorism in the UN prison compounds in South Korea. Nam Il, the negotiator, inveighed with one tirade after another against the killing of prisoners which Nam Il, the conspirator, had helped to provoke. These riots, aside from their great anti-American propaganda value, were also designed to lend weight to the Communist demand that all prisoners be repatriated regardless of choice. This is merely one illustration of the manner in which the Communists integrate truce talks into their overall strategic framework of protracted conflict.

In the light of the contemporary debate over US military strategy, it is important to review the after-effects of the Korean War. The Chinese Communists used the war as a training school in which the most up-to-date technical weapons were available. Thus Korea helped them transform their ill-equipped revolutionary forces into a modern army. Meanwhile, the "Resist America, Aid Korea" campaign conducted by Peking helped considerably to consolidate the new regime at home and to stiffen the political loyalty of the Chinese people. China won and the United States lost considerable prestige in Asia, for this was the first time in history that an Oriental nation held the technically superior West at bay. The Korean War, moreover, gave tremendous impetus to the international Communist campaigns for propagating pacifism, especially through such devices as

the Stockholm Peace Appeal, and strengthening neutralism throughout the Arab-Asian world. Neutralist India, originally a supporter of
the UN decision to counter North Korean aggression, began to sound
a strident note of hostility against the United States as soon as
Communist China became a contestant; the defense of a small
republic then became, in Indian eyes, a case of American intervention in Asian affairs. When, in mid-1951, the Soviet Union espoused
the role of peacemaker, the Asians seemed to forget entirely that
the war had been instigated by a puppet government armed by the
Soviets. By manifesting a willingness to settle for a draw in Korea,
the West virtually admitted that Communist China's right to intervene
in the peninsula was equal to that of the United Nations.

The United States, by waging the kind of war it did in Korea from
November 1950 on, allowed the strategic initiative to pass into the
hands of an enemy leader who had frequently stressed in his military
writings that an army, once it can be forced into a passive position
or deprived of its freedom of action, is on the road to defeat. Mao
Tse-tung fully realized that the side which enjoys superiority at the
outset of the conflict need not retain the initiative throughout the
campaign:

> In the course of a struggle, a correct or incorrect command may trans-
> form inferiority into superiority or passivity into initiative, and vice
> versa. . . . The inferior and passive side can wrestle the initiative and
> victory from the side possessing superiority and the initiative by securing
> the necessary conditions through active endeavor in accordance with
> actual circumstances.

One of the most suitable means of achieving superiority and seizing
the initiative from the enemy, Mao wrote, is to create illusions in
the mind of the enemy, including the illusion that he is up against
overwhelming strength. Mao applied his superior understanding of
strategic principles in Korea to compensate for the overwhelming
superiority of American technological power. Throughout 575 truce
meetings, the Communist leaders stalled for time. The Chinese Communists built up their military power and international support, while
the United States suffered all the "internal and external contradic-
tions" which Mao had forecast for all his enemies: mounting casualty
lists, consumption of war material, decline of troop morale, discon-

tented public opinion at home and the gradual alienation of world opinion.

The United States imposed upon itself a number of severe limitations in conducting the Korean War. The motivation for these restraints was largely a political one. American policy-makers hoped that, with a war policy of forebearance unprecedented in modern history, the United States would earn the respect both of its new Atlantic allies and the uncommitted peoples. This hope, unfortunately, proved to be an illusory one. The United States built up very little credit either in Europe or in Asia: Americans, in fact, found themselves in the incredible position of having to defend themselves against charges of waging "germ warfare," forestalling the "natural integration" of Formosa with the Chinese Mainland, and preventing the restoration of peace in the Far East by keeping Red China out of the United Nations. While Europeans placed little credence in Communist propaganda, most were inclined to blame the United States for placing too much emphasis on the conflict in Korea. Finally, few people in Europe and Asia believed that the United States deserved any praise for limiting the war—for American political leaders, in their efforts to justify the Korean policy, argued frequently that any extension of the war would lead to general war and risk of Communist retaliation against the United States. American motives, consequently, were taken to be more selfish than altruistic.

The decision to meet Communist aggression in Korea in June 1950 was both courageous and wise. But the United States failed to foresee the future implications of the outcome of the Korean War—that popular political support for all subsequent responses to Communist peripheral attacks would to a large extent hinge upon the success of the first direct encounter between American and Communist forces.

There can be little question but that Secretary of State Acheson was confronted by serious political problems during the course of the Korean War. The United States had scarcely begun to construct a defense of Europe through the North Atlantic Treaty Organization when the Korean War broke out. The Europeans, especially the British, were inclined to dissociate the crisis in the Far East from their security interests and feared that an American emphasis of Asia might slow down the development of the Atlantic Alliance. The

United States, on the other hand, had historically been oriented more towards Asia than Europe, and emerged from World War II as the dominant power in the Pacific. Whereas Great Britain was in the process of reducing her political commitments in Asia, the United States, which had borne the greatest burden among the Western powers in fighting the Axis on both fronts, realized its growing strategic responsibilities in both theaters. This divergence of basic interests in the Western Alliance was aggravated by Mao's entry into the war.

There is no doubt, however, that the success of Communist China was in large measure due to Mao's strategy of delay and attrition. Had the United Nations been able to conclude the war with MacArthur's Inchon offensive, America would have been spared many a diplomatic dilemma. Mao, by entering the Korean War, shored up the faltering regime of North Korea and denied the UN a decision with finality. Then, by switching in June 1951 to "attritional" truce talks which lasted for two years, the Communists were able to camouflage their flagging capabilities and resources and, at the same time, to wear down the American will to resume the kind of energetic initiative needed to bring the war to a successful conclusion.

The American people were increasingly dissatisfied with the conduct of the Korean War, which they found both frustrating and pointless. After the experience, in the twentieth century, of two world wars, both of which had ended in climactic, overwhelming victories, it was difficult for Americans to readjust their thinking to the notion of a war which, for two years, had to be fought out along the "line of scrimmage." What Americans objected to was not the fact that the war was kept limited, or waged at a level lower than that of a general war, but rather the fact that its limitations whittled down the real superiority of the United States. Since American policy-makers had posed a false dilemma—either a protracted stalemate or all-out war—popular opinion within the United States tended to conclude that American conventional forces had been misused in Korea. Perhaps the most serious effect of this was to inhibit the freedom of action of US policy-makers when confronted by subsequent crises in so-called peripheral areas.

The Communists, doubtless realizing to what an extent the Korean War had served as a conditioner of the American mind, were able to parlay their psychological gains in Korea into a swift victory in Indochina. A successful prosecution of the war in Korea by the United States might have either convinced the Chinese Communists that a new adventure in Indochina should not be risked or, failing this, prepared the American people for intervention in Indochina.

In recent years, far too much criticism has been hurled at the Dulles policy of "massive retaliation" on the grounds that it did not prevent the loss of North Vietnam. Such criticism, unfortunately, does not go to the root of the problem. Most of the critics of the declaratory policy of "massive retaliation" imply that statements of this sort are relatively worthless in meeting the intermediate range of Communist military threats and that, first and foremost, the United States needs to increase its tactical force levels to fight limited wars in any part of the globe. Yet the experience of Korea shows clearly that the possession of forces "in being" does not of itself assure an effective defense against Communist aggression.

Morton H. Halperin

THE LIMITING PROCESS IN THE KOREAN WAR

Morton Halperin, who teaches at Harvard University, has served as a consultant to the State Department, the Defense Department, and the Rand Corporation. In this selection, Halperin suggests that each side's interpretation of the other's doctrines and intentions influenced the limitations imposed on the war. The article printed here is part of a larger study, Limited War in the Nuclear Age.

The problems of limiting local war in the nuclear-missile age have been analyzed by a number of military strategists; particular local wars have been examined by historians and political scientists. This essay represents an attempt to fuse the two approaches and to test

Reprinted with permission from the *Political Science Quarterly*, Vol. 78, No. 1, March 1963, pp. 13–39.

the logically derived hypotheses of the strategist against a historical event. Korea was the cataylst which forced policy-makers and strategists to take limited war seriously. An understanding of why and how the war remained limited, in addition to contributing to an evaluation of an important event in the cold war, should be of value in analyzing other local wars, past and future.

Before exploring the pressures for restraint, I will briefly outline the limits which were observed by both sides in terms of geography, kinds of weapons, targets and the participation of particular countries.

Both sides limited ground fighting during the war to the Korean peninsula. The war began with the North Korean invasion of South Korea, and Communist ground troops fought both north and south of the 38th Parallel.

The United Nations forces also restricted their ground and air attacks to the Korean peninsula. One of the major expansions of the war (in terms of the geographical limit) was the crossing of the 38th Parallel by United Nations ground forces and the march up to the Yalu River, the northern border of North Korea. Nevertheless, the war remained restricted to the Korean peninsula.

Perhaps the most dramatic and the most frequently discussed limit in the Korean War was the abstention by both sides from the use of atomic capabilities. It should be recalled that these capabilities were substantially smaller than they are now. Both sides had only fission weapons (and no fusion bombs), and both (but particularly the Soviets) had very small stockpiles. Nevertheless, these weapons were potentially decisive, particularly if they had been used in a geographical area more extensive than the Korean peninsula. They would also have had significant impact on the battle had they been used just in Korea. The failure to use nuclear weapons was the only major weapons limit observed by the United Nations forces. On the other hand, the Communist troops not only failed to use nuclear weapons, but also did not employ submarines.

Only the North Koreans and South Koreans participated in the war with all their available forces. The Communist Chinese sent in a large number of troops, but, as Peking continually stressed, all of them entered the war as "volunteers," for Peking never declared war. Although there is some evidence that some Russian pilots flew planes for the Chinese Communists, Russia did not overtly intervene with military forces, either air, sea, or ground. Nor did any other Communist state send troops to fight in the war. The Russians supplied large quantities of material to both Chinese and North Korean troops and gave them extensive diplomatic support.

On the other side, while a large number of states participated in the defense of South Korea, none of them officially declared war, not even the United States. All contributed troops to a United Nations Command in what was termed by the United States a "police action." But the United Nations did exercise one important restraint on the states involved in the war. It refused the offer of Chiang Kai-shek to send Chinese Nationalist troops into battle. Even after the Chinese Communists came in, the renewed offer of Chinese National troops was rejected.

Even within the confines of North and South Korea, both sides refrained from attacking important military targets within the area of combat. The Communists did not attack any targets in South Korea. As a result, Pusan and Inchon, the two major ports through which the United Nations supplied its forces, and therefore highly important military targets, remained free from air harassment, although attacks on them probably would have seriously hampered the United Nations military effort. Pusan, which frequently operated at night, was well-lit and a virtually perfect military target. Yet neither port was attacked either from the air or with mines. Nor were there air attacks on convoys of trucks or trains carrying supplies or on troops in the field in South Korean territory.

Thus, except for North Korean guerrilla operations behind the lines, there was no interdiction of American logistical lines in United Nations territory or international waters. The United Nations confined its interference with Communist supply movements to North Korea except for bombing the Yalu bridges at the middle.

Moreover, the Communists never challenged America's air supremacy or sought to use air operations for anything but dog fights at a low level against the United Nations planes. In addition, the Communists refrained from attacking American planes on the ground or American airfields in South Korea, Japan and Okinawa. Finally, American naval vessels off the Korean coast, including the carriers basing aircraft that were operating in the combat zone, were not attacked either by Communist submarines or aircraft, but were fired on from shore when in range.

In limiting its operations, it is important to note that the United Nations command did not impose comparable restraints on its forces. For example, attacks were made on armies in the field. Convoys were bombed, and the bridges across the Yalu, the key supply points of the Chinese Communists, were attacked. Nevertheless, the United Nations did impose restrictions on targets within the zone of battle. . . .

Prior to the outbreak of the Korean War, the United States believed that a major objective of the Soviet Union was to expand the area under the control of international communism as far as possible. Thus, in responding to the North Korean attack—which had not been anticipated—American objectives were developed in the framework of the belief that the attack was part of a general plan for expansion and perhaps a prelude to general war. The United States sought to prevent the success of this Communist attempt to expand by the use of force in the belief that allowing the Soviets to succeed in Korea would encourage aggression elsewhere. General Bradley expressed this purpose at the MacArthur hearings in describing Korea as "a preventive limited war aimed at avoiding World War III." President Truman later described his objectives in intervening in the Korean War in similar terms:

> Communism was acting in Korea just as Hitler, Mussolini, and the Japanese had acted ten, fifteen, and twenty years earlier. I felt certain that if South Korea was allowed to fall Communist leaders would be emboldened to override nations closer to our own shores. If the Communists were permitted to force their way into the Republic of Korea without opposition from the free world, no small nation would have the courage to resist threats and aggression by stronger Communist neighbors. If this was allowed to go unchallenged it would mean a third world war, just as similar incidents had brought on the second world war.

The defense of Korea was partly motivated by the feeling that the action was necessary to convince the West Europeans that the United States would come to their aid. The Administration was wary of exposing itself to Soviet aggression in Europe by committing its military power in Korea. During the Korean War, in fact, the major American buildup occurred in Europe and not in the Far East. The

Administration was also aware of the danger of splitting the North Atlantic Treaty Organization alliance in a dispute over Far Eastern policy. A major objective throughout the war was to prevent adverse repercussions in Europe while using the episode to strengthen NATO and build up its military capability. America's NATO allies, particularly the British, applied constant pressure on the United States to prevent expansion of the war and to bring it to a swift conclusion. Following an almost inadvertent reference by President Truman at a press conference to the possibility of using atomic weapons, British Prime Minister Clement Attlee flew to the United States to confer with Truman and to propose the seeking of a cease-fire in Korea to be followed by the admission of Communist China to the United Nations. Partly because the defense effort in Korea was carried on under UN auspices, the United States felt obliged to consult constantly with its allies on policy and was influenced by their continuous efforts to halt the expansion of the war and to bring about its conclusion.

Soviet objectives were more closely related to the situation in the Far East. The Soviets were interested in the capture of South Korea for its own sake and probably expected a relatively quick and easy North Korean victory. In addition, the Soviets probably hoped to prevent Japan's alignment with the Western powers. Whiting has suggested the nature of the Soviet Far Eastern objective:

> In view of the multiple pressures directed at Japanese foreign policy, the Communist leaders may have conceived the Korean War as serving ends beyond the immediate control of the peninsula. Military victories in Taiwan and Korea could be heralded as ushering in the Communist era in Asia, that is demonstrating the impotence of America's "puppets," Chiang Kai-shek and Syngman Rhee. The resultant effect upon Japan might swing opportunistic groups behind existing neutralist opposition in Yoshida and prevent his supporting American policy.

The Chinese objectives in entering the Korean War were also based on general political considerations, but of a defensive nature. According to Whiting, the Chinese also hoped to influence the course of United States—Japanese relations. Moreover, they were worried about the loss of prestige they would suffer if they allowed the Western "imperialists" to march unhindered to their borders. And they were perhaps most concerned with the beneficial effects of United

Nations success in Korea on the many opponents of the Communist
regime still active in China and on Taiwan. Whiting concluded:

> *In sum, it was not the particular problems of safeguarding electric power*
> *supplies in North Korea or the industrial base in Manchuria that aroused*
> *Peking to military action. Instead, the final step seems to have been*
> *prompted in part by general concern over the range of opportunities*
> *within Korea that might be exploited by a determined, powerful enemy*
> *on China's doorstep. At the least, a military response might deter the*
> *enemy from further adventures. At the most, it might succeed in inflicting*
> *sufficient damage to force the enemy to compromise his objectives and to*
> *accede to some of Peking's demands. Contrary to some belief, the*
> *Chinese Communist leadership did not enter the Korean War either full*
> *of self-assertive confidence or for primarily expansionist goals.*

The Chinese apparently entered the war with the aim of saving
at least some of North Korea. Their minimal objective was to preserve
the identity of Communist North Korea rather than its total territorial
integrity.

In an effort to secure the political effects discussed above, American battlefield objectives and war termination conditions underwent
considerable fluctuation during the course of the war. When the
United States first intervened, its objective was simply to restore
peace and the South Korean border. Very early in the war and after
the Chinese intervention, the United States considered a total withdrawal from Korea. Later its battlefield objective expanded to include
the unification of Korea. But in the end, the United States accepted
a truce line which closely approximated the status quo ante. As
Neustadt has pointed out, Truman's original decision to seek the
unification of Korea failed to take into account the political objectives
that the United States was pursuing, and in the end, according to
Neustadt, the recognition of this forced the abandonment of the unification effort.

> *Had the unification of Korea been Truman's dearest objective, its an-*
> *nouncement as a war aim would have been another matter. But it was*
> *among the least of the objectives on his mind. In July and August 1950,*
> *in December after Chinese intervention, in his struggles with MacArthur,*
> *and thereafter through his last two years of office, his behavior leaves*
> *no doubt about the many things he wanted more than that. He wanted to*
> *affirm that the UN was not a League of Nations, that aggression would be*

met with counter-force, that "police actions" were well worth their cost, that the "lesson of the 1930s" had been learned. He wanted to avoid "the wrong war, in the wrong place, at the wrong time" as General Bradley put it—and any "war," if possible. He wanted NATO strengthened fast, both militarily and psychologically. He wanted the United States rearmed without inflation, and prepared, thereafter, to sustain a level of expenditure for military forces and for foreign aid far higher than had seemed achievable before Korea.

Once the Soviets recognized that they could not easily secure their objective of demonstrating American weakness and unwillingness to use force, they seemed to have abandoned the battlefield objective of capturing all of Korea. They may have been willing to accept an end to the war with part or perhaps even all of North Korea in Western hands, and ultimately settled for a virtual restoration of the status quo ante.

The North Korean attack on South Korea suggested the willingness of the Communists to seek a limited objective by a limited use of force. The Soviets probably intended to seize South Korea with the use of North Korean forces and then to halt their military operations. When the United States intervened, they recognized their miscalculation of American intentions, while proceeding on the assumption that American intervention need not lead to world war. The attack upon South Korea, moreover, seems to have been motivated by the Soviet compulsion to fill power vacuums. In view of the specific United States declaration that South Korea was outside its defense perimeter, the Soviets could have reasonably counted on a quick and easy victory by the North Koreans. But, while Communist conduct during the war reflected a doctrine that included the limited use of military force, and limited objectives, neither the Chinese nor the Russians seemed to have any idea of the optimum methods of communicating intentions and capabilities to the other side in the course of such a war.

American doctrine, on the other hand, seems to have been much less hospitable to the limitation of warfare. It would appear that the United States had not foreseen the possibility of Soviet military action in South Korea or any other local area unconnected with a general Soviet military offensive. The result was the American decision not to prepare for the defense of South Korea in view of the low estimate of its value in a general war. Thus, the decision of June of 1950 to defend South Korea was not based on a re-estimate of South Korea's military importance, but on a recognition that something had occurred for which American military doctrine had not been prepared. It is important to note that, in its policy decisions throughout the war, the United States was operating without any general theoretical notions of the nature of limited war in the atomic age, and its decisions were probably affected by the lack of such theory.

Each side's image of the other's doctrines and intentions influenced its decisions. The Soviets clearly underestimated the likelihood of American intervention. In the Soviet view, the American declaration that it would defend South Korea only as part of its United Nations obligations had meant that the United States would not in fact defend South Korea. The Soviets failed to anticipate the partly moral and partly political American reaction to aggression. They were insensitive to the importance that the United States would attach to repelling "illegal" aggression, as opposed to less clear-cut violations of international law. . . .

As [Alexander] George has pointed out, the inclination of American policy-makers toward the "testing" interpretation of Soviet doctrine —in which the Korean attack was equated with Hitler's early expansionist moves—may have reinforced the likelihood that the United States would intervene in Korea. If the "soft-spot probing" interpretation of Soviet conduct had been accepted instead, the United States might have been more prone to cede South Korea while taking steps to prevent the existence of power vacuums elsewhere. It was the belief that successful aggression would embolden the Soviets that made the defense of South Korea seem so crucial.

In an analysis of the limiting process, it is important to say again that the Korean War was fought before the era of intercontinental ballistic missiles and fusion weapons. Thus, while both sides could have expanded the war quickly and decisively, there was not the danger that now exists of a sudden unleashing of nuclear missiles which within an hour could destroy a large part of both the United States and the Soviet Union.

Even without this threat of a mutually devastating strategic exchange, the danger of a world war was nevertheless present, and it is significant that both sides seem to have been determined to avoid its occurrence. Truman has reported that the major American aim in Korea was to prevent a third world war; the United States was determined not to give the Soviets any "excuse" to initiate global war. The Russian decision to remain out of the war seemed to be partly motivated by a fear of igniting a global war. In this situation where neither side could gain a decisive advantage by going first, both sides seemed to recognize that, no matter who started the global war, both would suffer major losses. While the United States could have attacked the Soviet Union with its relatively limited stock-pile of atomic weapons, it could probably not have prevented a Soviet ground attack in Western Europe which might result in Communist domination of the European continent. The Soviets had no capacity to attack the United States and could not have prevented an American attack on the Soviet Union. While both sides avoided forcing the other into starting a global war, neither was preoccupied with the possibility of "pre-emption" by its adversary.

The United States was, however, concerned that the Korean War should not lead it to expend those military capabilities which were considered an important deterrent to general war. Whereas today there is a somewhat clearer distinction between the main forces to deter and fight a general war and forces primarily designed for local war, in Korea the United States was, in fact, using the troops and the material which it felt were necessary to deter general war. At the MacArthur hearings, Air Force General Vandenberg rejected a Senator's suggestion that the United States should commit a major part of the American air force to the Korean War effort. He argued instead that the United States must get a cease-fire

> without endangering that one potential that we have which has kept the peace so far, which is the United States Air Force; which, if utilized in a manner to do what your are suggesting, would [sic], because of attrition and because of the size of the Air Force is such and the size of the air force industry is such that we could not still be that deterrent to [general] war which we are today.

During the Korean War, the Truman Administration continued to pursue its domestic political goals. Despite the war, it was "politics as usual" on both sides of the political fence. The President was busily engaged in promoting his Fair Deal program, consolidating the position of the Democratic Party, strengthening his northern and western liberal support in Congress, and calming the political crises raised by such men as Senator [Joseph] McCarthy. Nor was the Administration immune to criticism from the Republican Party which felt it possible, necessary, and desirable to attack the Administration's conduct, as well as to question the basic concept of limited war.

After the MacArthur hearings, a Republican minority report declared:

> We believe that a policy of victory must be announced to the American people in order to restore unity and confidence. It is too much to expect that our people will accept a limited war. Our policy must be to win. Our strategy must be devised to bring about decisive victory.

These few sentences suggest a number of important assumptions about the nature of wartime politics. The first is the notion that the unity of the American people can be achieved only with a declaration that victory is the goal. A further implication is that, after such a declaration, the method of achieving a battlefield victory becomes a "military" problem, that is, beyond the realm of partisan domestic politics. On the other hand, once the government admits that there are other political considerations that affect and moderate the goal of a strictly military victory, then, according to this Republican statement, it is legitimate to criticize the particular policy adopted. Unity will come only when the country is asked to back an absolute goal. If there is no such goal, then it is the duty of the opposition to examine and critically appraise the war effort.

Congress, as a whole, also felt itself free to criticize. The inquiries into the firing of General MacArthur were striking in that they required the Administration, *during the war,* to justify its conduct and to explain publicly what it hoped to accomplish in the war and how it was conducting the war, as well as to explicate a host of particulars which must have been of as much interest to the Communists as they were to the Senators across the table.

The quotation from the Republican Senators also reflects the then still strong American opposition to limited war. The Senators stated flatly that the American people would not accept the strategy of limited war, and indicated their rejection of the strategy as well. The implication is that during a limited war the American government will be subjected to attacks from the political opposition, from Congress, and from public citizens on two grounds: on the legitimacy of fighting a limited war, and on the particular tactics employed in the war.

The general public seems to have shared the Republican Senators' dissatisfaction with the course of the Korean War, at least in its later stages. On the other hand, the public apparently approved the decision of the Eisenhower Administration to end the war short of victory. The public's disapproval of the Korean campaign probably added to the margin of Eisenhower's victory in 1952; his ending the war enhanced the Republican image as the party of peace and increased the Eisenhower plurality in 1956. On the other hand, at least according to the results of the Michigan Survey Research Center voting studies, the Korean War did not have a major or lasting impact on popular political attitudes.

American political leaders seem to have overestimated the effect of the war on the voting public. Korea is taken as demonstrating—as to some extent it did—that local wars are not popular with the American public. Leading the United States into one or expanding it is likely to be perceived as a political liability; ending one on almost any terms may be a political asset.

All these domestic pressures undoubtedly influenced the manner in which the Truman Administration conducted its Korean operations, both by hampering its freedom of action and by increasing the costs of various actions.

The remainder of this essay will explore several of the major decisions to limit or expand the Korean War and the general nature of the Korean War limiting process.

As was noted above, the most dramatic limit on the Korean War was the failure of either side to use its atomic weapons. According to Brodie, there were four reasons why nuclear weapons were not used by the United States:

1. The Joint Chiefs of Staff and civilian policy-makers continued to feel that the war in Korea was basically a Soviet feint. There was, therefore, a strong case for conserving the then relatively limited stockpile of atomic weapons for the principal war which, they thought, would come in Europe. Their fear was not that the employment of nuclear weapons would lead to an

expansion of the war and a Soviet attack on Europe, but rather that Korea was deliberately designed as a decoy to get us to exhaust our nuclear stockpile and our conventional military resources, so that the Soviets could later attack with impunity in Europe. It was the desire, then, to save resources and not the fear of provoking the enemy that was one of the main causes of the American decision not to use nuclear weapons in Korea.

2. American policy was also affected by the reports of local commanders that there were no suitable targets for nuclear weapons in Korea. While the impact of this view was considerable, it apparently reflected an uninformed attitude about the possible uses of nuclear weapons. Commanders in the field came to think, for example, that atomic bombs were of little use against bridges, a belief which Brodie explained as follows:

This odd idea probably resulted from a misreading of the results at Hiroshima and Nagasaki. Some bridges were indeed badly damaged at those places and some were not, but for the latter it was generally forgotten that a bridge only 270 feet from ground zero at Hiroshima was actually 2,100 feet from the point of explosion, and also that it received its blast effect from above rather than from the side.

Nuclear weapons were still relatively new and had not been extensively tested, and it is probable that commanders in the field were too busy to search out potential targets for nuclear weapons.

3. Our allies, particularly the British, were strongly and emotionally opposed to the use of nuclear weapons in the Korean War. This pressure from our allies strengthened our own anxieties and moral doubts about again using these terrible new weapons.

4. A subsidiary reason for the failure to use nuclear weapons in the Korean War was the fear of the retaliatory employment by the Soviets of the few atomic weapons in their possession against Pusan or Japan, despite the American near-monopoly over these weapons. Brodie doubts, however, if this fear played a conscious part in the relevant decisions.

The United States, then, was concerned with the vulnerability of Europe and with coordinating policy with her allies. It was also determined not to be drawn in by a Soviet feint in Korea. But it is important to note that the first and second factors will not obtain in the future. The American stockpile of tactical nuclear weapons is now so great that military commanders may urge their use precisely because they are a nonscarce military resource, and certainly no argument can be made that they should not be used because they are scarce. Military officers now have a much better understanding of the capabilities of nuclear weapons, which, moreover, now come in much smaller sizes. Thus, it will be clear to military commanders that there would be suitable targets for their use in any conceivable future major limited war. While we can expect continued pressure from our allies against the use of nuclear weapons, it is possible that certain allies might advocate their use in some situations. There will, however, be other international political pressures—for example from the uncommitted or neutral states—against nuclear weapons, and the possibility of a Soviet nuclear response will be a much more important determinant of the decision.

We know much less about the details of the Russian decision not to use atomic weapons in Korea. The Russians seemed determined not to supply any material to the forces fighting in Korea which could clearly be labeled as having been supplied by them after the war began. This would certainly be the case with atomic weapons. In addition, the Soviet stockpile of such weapons was so small that its use in a localized military encounter might have seemed wasteful.

Here again, the limit observed by both sides seems not to have resulted from an attempt—or even an awareness of the need—to bargain with the enemy. However, the Soviets were probably more restrained than the United States by the fear that the initiation of nuclear attacks would be met by a response in kind.

The Chinese Communists seem genuinely to have feared the possibility of the American use of nuclear weapons when they intervened in the Korean War. According to Whiting, the Chinese felt that a nuclear response was a real possibility; intervention was considered risky; and every effort was made to delay it and to minimize its consequences. The extent of this Chinese concern was reflected both in its shelter-building program and in domestic Chinese Communist propaganda. But Peking was reassured by the three-week testing period of relatively small Chinese intervention which revealed that United States aircraft, although authorized to bomb the Korean ends of the Yalu bridges, were forbidden to venture into Chinese territory.

The background of the limit on the use of atomic weapons in the Korean War, then, suggests a failure of both sides to understand what the other side was likely to do and what the other side's fears and goals were. It also suggests that, to a large extent, the determination of limits is based on considerations other than those that result from the battlefield interaction. Some of the other limiting points established in the war reveal the same pattern.

One of the major expansions of the Korean War was the decision of the United Nations Command to cross the 38th Parallel. This decision was based partly on the military consideration that one could not stand by and allow the enemy forces to regroup for renewed attack just beyond the border. It was also made on political grounds. When the battlefield conditions changed in its favor, the United States decided to pursue the unification of Korea by military means. In crossing the parallel the United Nations Command was aware of the risk that it might trigger Chinese Communist intervention, and tried by reassuring statements to prevent it. But, it apparently underestimated the Chinese reaction, and, at the same time, it failed to develop a concurrent strategy which, by retaliatory threats or other sanctions, could succeed in preventing Chinese intervention. As Whiting has suggested, the threat to use atomic weapons on the Chinese mainland, if the Chinese intervened, might have been a much more effective deterrent than the attempt to reassure them that a march to the border did not presage an attack on mainland China. The threat to use atomic weapons would have involved major political costs for the United States, and it is not clear that the American government would have warned of a possible atomic attack, even if it recognized its likely effect. Had it been aware that the fear of greater expansion might have deterred Chinese intervention, an alternative course might have been to threaten to expand the war to China with conventional weapons. But even this was not done. In fact a decision was made that Chinese intervention would not lead to conventional bombing beyond the Yalu. MacArthur reportedly believed that this decision had been leaked to the Chinese.

In choosing, instead, to inform the Chinese of its limited objectives, the United States also considered it important to reassure the Chinese that their hydroelectric plants would not be jeopardized by a march up to the Yalu. But, as Whiting has pointed out:

> *It was widely believed in Western circles that a determining factor in Chinese Communist concern over North Korea was the reliance of Manchurian industry upon power supplies across the border as well as along the Yalu River. This belief prompted explicit reassurances from Western spokesmen, both in Washington and at Lake Success, concerning "China's legitimate interests" near the frontier. Yet we have seen that Peking ignored this issue completely in its domestic as well as its foreign communications. The absence of propaganda about the protection of the hydroelectric installations, despite the need to maximize popular response to mobilization of "volunteers," suggests that this consideration played little if any role in motivating Chinese Communist intervention.*

In its advance through North Korea, then, the United Nations Command was attempting to communicate two points to the Chinese Communists: first, that it was prepared to go up to but not beyond the Yalu, and second, that it was prepared to respect China's legitimate interests in the northern regions of North Korea. It sought, therefore, to establish its limited objectives: that United Nations forces would take all North Korea, that the North Korean government would cease to exist, but that China's legitimate industrial interests would be protected. And it sought to assure the Chinese that the capture of North Korea would not be used as a springboard for an attack into China. It assumed that these were the limits in which the Chinese were interested, and that these would serve to keep the Chinese out of the war. But Chinese interests were different and could only be satisfied by different boundary conditions to the war.

*   *   *

American policy-makers have concluded that once the decision was made to cross the 38th Parallel, nothing could be done to affect the Chinese decision. In fact, the State Department reportedly argued in December of 1950 that the Chinese decision to intervene was made prior to the crossing of the 38th Parallel. In one sense, at least, this conclusion may be wrong: the Chinese position might have been altered by threats to expand the war with the use of atomic weapons against China. Moreover, it is by no means certain that the Chinese were interested in preserving the total territorial integrity of North Korea. It is possible, as Whiting suggests, that an American commitment to advance only part way up the peninsula—that is, to permit the maintenance of the North Korean government in some part of its territory—might have been sufficient to deter the Chinese entrance into the war:

> *Neither before [n]or during the first three months of war [Whiting wrote] did the degree of interest in Pyongyang evinced by Peking warrant acceptance at face value of its concern for a "just" peace, based upon the status quo ante.*
>
> *This is not to say that the Chinese Communist leadership was prepared to accept with equanimity the total defeat of North Korea. As a minimal goal, intervention must have been attempted to preserve an entity identifiable as the DPRK, and to prevent unification of all Korea under UN supervision. The late date of Chinese Communist entry into the war suggests that it was the political importance of the North Korean government, rather than its territorial integrity, that was at stake. Although intervention was officially predicated upon UN crossing of the 38th parallel, no Chinese People's Volunteers and Democratic People's Republic of Korea defense lines were established during the August–October period, not even to protect Pyongyang. To Peking, a "just" Korean peace was not an end in itself but rather a means towards fulfilling other related goals of policy.*

Thus, even after the crossing of the 38th Parallel, Chinese intervention might have been prevented, had the United States acted differently. Although it tried to impose limits on expansion, the United States failed to grasp adequately either the reasons that the Chinese felt intervention was necessary or the threats that might have deterred their intervention. Both sides expanded the war, the United Nations by crossing the 38th Parallel and the Chinese by entering the war. Both sides failed to convey to each other the kind of counteraction to be expected which might have deterred expansion. China attempted to prevent the crossing of the 38th Parallel by declaring her intention to intervene, but this intention, relayed by the Indian Ambassador, was not taken seriously by the United Nations Command. The United Nations sought to prevent the Chinese entrance, not by threatening a further expansion, but by attempting to satisfy the Chinese security interests that, it was assumed, might lead her to enter the war.

Despite these two major acts of expansion which followed closely on each other, the war remained limited, and this fact suggests the fallacy of the proposition that the limitation of a war depends on neither side drastically expanding the war at any point. These were major expansions, but neither seems to have brought the sides close to decisions to initiate global war or to expand very substantially the area or intensity of the local war.

Despite the fact that United States planes taking off from airfields in South Korea and Japan, and from aircraft carriers, consistently bombed targets in North Korea, the Communists engaged in almost no bombing south of the 38th Parallel. This was one of the major asymmetries of the war both from a legalistic point of view and in terms of interfering with the military operations of the enemy. Both sides apparently devoted considerable attention to the question of what targets to attack, and a variety of motives affected the relevant decisions.

The American decision to bomb targets in North Korea was made prior to the commitment of American ground troops in June 1950. A month later permission was given to bomb industrial targets in North Korea, but the use of incendiary bombs was not permitted because of the civil damage that would have resulted. The Air Force was not allowed to bomb the areas close to the Soviet and Chinese borders. Rashin was the single industrial center within the forbidden area and it was the only industrial target in North Korea which was not destroyed by mid-September when an end to industrial bombing was ordered by the Joint Chiefs. With this task completed, the bombing of the North Korean halves of the Yalu bridges was authorized. Because of the restrictions imposed, the operation was only partly successful and came to a halt with the freezing of the Yalu in late November. It was not until June 1952 that attacks on the hydroelectric plants in North Korea were authorized; within two weeks almost 90 percent of the North Korean power capacity was destroyed.

American attacks on targets in North Korea steadily expanded. The attacks were aimed at affecting the immediate military situation. The restraints observed had several motives:

1. to avoid extensive civilian destruction considered undesirable on both humanitarian and propaganda grounds;

2. to avoid a spill-over of the war into China or the Soviet Union—the spill-over into China prior to her entry into the war probably did not have a major impact on Chinese policy, but it did create propaganda and political difficulties;
3. to avoid damaging, in the case of the hydroelectric plants, targets considered vital to the Chinese, so as to avoid their entrance into the war, presumably in retaliation.

The Communists exercised far greater restraint on their air forces. Except for a few night "heckling" attacks from small biplanes in the spring of 1951, no air attacks were made on any targets in South Korea. The Communist restraint was not the result of the absence of inviting military targets. The port of Pusan was an extremely inviting target for bombardment and mining. It was the key to the American logistic effort and frequently was lighted up all night. American logistic convoys and troops in the field also could have been hampered by air attacks. A number of factors seem to have influenced the Communist decision not to respond in kind to United Nations air attacks on North Korea:

1. The Communists may have believed that it would have been very difficult, if not impossible, for the United Nations to continue its operations in Korea if Pusan came under heavy attack. It might also have been obvious that, once the United Nations committed itself to the defense of South Korea, it was no longer in a position where it could afford to accept complete withdrawal. Therefore, if attacks on its logistic lines made impossible its continued conduct of an effective ground war in Korea, the United States might have been forced to engage in strategic strikes against the Chinese, if not the Russian, homeland. If the Communists found this supposition credible, they may have concluded that, once their initial grab for South Korea failed, they could not afford to do anything that would lead to their complete control over South Korea. They may have recognized that American confinement of the war to the Korean peninsula was dependent on her ability to fight there effectively.
2. In order to avoid attacks on Chinese air bases just north of the Yalu, Red airmen were not allowed to attack United Nations positions from these bases. Although the Communists were permitting the United States the sanctuary of bases in Japan

and on aircraft carriers, they apparently were afraid that they would not be granted a similar sanctuary for bombing operations. United States planes managed to keep the North Korean airfields out of commission throughout the war. Thus, given that the Chinese limited the use of their fields to staging operations and to fighter planes, they were incapable of bombing operations.

3. There is some evidence to suggest that Soviet pilots constituted a significant part of the "Chinese" air force during the Korean War. If this is true, the explanation for target restraint may have been the desire to avoid the capture of Soviet airmen. This proof of direct Soviet involvement in the war would at the least have been politically damaging and, from a Soviet point of view, might have created an intolerable risk of American retaliation.

By the end of the war the United States was exercising almost no target restraint in North Korea and the Communists were doing no bombing in South Korea. Each side was guided by a complex series of motives and incentives. However, despite the asymmetry of the actions there is nothing to suggest that either side treated its decisions on targets as being closely related to, affected by, or likely to affect, the opponent's decisions on these questions.

The development of the limiting process in the Korean War seems to have been the work, on the whole, of the civilian decision-makers, at least on the American side, in rejecting or approving requests by the military to engage in military operation which would have the effect of expanding the war. In some cases, particularly on the question of using atomic weapons, the military never made the request, and so, in some sense, no decision was made. On three occasions, General MacArthur was refused his requests: to employ Chinese Nationalist troops, to impose a naval blockade on China and to bomb bases and supply lines in China. But a number of MacArthur's requests for permission to expand the war were approved. These included the commitment of American ground forces, the Inchon offensive, and the crossing of the 38th Parallel.

In deciding whether to go on the offensive in the war, Truman reports that the National Security Council recommended the consideration of three factors: action by the Soviet Union and the Chinese Communists, the views of friendly members of the United Nations and the risk of general war. It is clear that this and other decisions were also influenced by American objectives and doctrine, as well as by domestic political pressures. The balancing of the factors varied from decision to decision, but all played a role in the major decisions to limit or expand the war.

Much less is known about the Communist decision-making process or the factors which influenced their decisions to limit or expand the war. The initial decision to keep the Chinese out of the war seems to have been based largely on domestic conditions in China, particularly the desire of the Chinese to implement their program of economic growth and development, and their desire to avoid military entanglements at a time when they had not yet consolidated their hold over their own country. The reasons for the Russians' abstention from open intervention in the war are less clear. It is apparent that Russia was determined not to do anything that directly labeled her as a participant. She did not publicize the participation of any Russian "volunteers" in the war, nor provide any atomic capability, although she did supply large amounts of conventional military equipment. One likely explanation is the Russian fear that her intervention would lead to total war, and, it should be remembered, the strategic balance at this stage was one that drastically favored the West. The United States had the capability of inflicting great destruction on the Soviet homeland with its stock of atomic weapons, while the Soviets had no capability of directly attacking the United States, although they might have been able to take a large part of Western Europe with ground forces. Thus, the Soviets, aware of their inferior strategic position, were probably determined to keep out of the war and to provide no excuse for a direct American attack on the Soviet Union.

It should be noted that both sides apparently arrived at their decisions to limit the war for different reasons and with minimal attention to the battlefield interaction. In addition, they observed very different limits: that is, both did not abstain from the same actions. What we did in North Korea was quite different from what the Communists did in South Korea, but the Chinese used a much greater percentage of their gross national product than we did. Nevertheless, while we used naval vessels and airplanes to bomb troops and airfields beyond Korea, they did not. The United States engaged in logistical interdiction, the Communists did not. Each side, then, observed its own series of limits and restraints only in some general way related to, and dependent on, the limits of the other side.

At least a few of the limits were symmetrical. Both sides restricted their military operations almost entirely to Korea, and neither used nuclear weapons. There was lack of symmetry in that all the military targets in North Korea were attacked but some in South Korea were not. The United States attacked the Chinese points of entry—the Yalu bridges—but the Chinese did not attack ours—the ports. Both sides observed a number of what Schelling has called "legalistic" limitations. The United Nations carefully observed both the Chinese and Russian borders and tried to avoid crossing them inadvertently. There was symmetry in the absence of official declarations of war. The United Nations troops participated in the war in a "police action" capacity, and none of the countries involved, including the United States, declared war. The Chinese used "volunteers," and the Russians supplied equipment and, presumably, technicians but little manpower for the battle.

In some cases, the limits represented a recognition of the battlefield interaction—if one side did something the other was likely to reciprocate—which would result in expansions of the war benefiting neither side. But the origin of many of the limits observed, and part of the explanation for others, lay not within the dynamics of the war itself, but within the domestic and international context in which the war was fought.

John W. Spanier

TRUMAN VERSUS MACARTHUR: ACHILLES REBOUND

John W. Spanier, professor of political science at the University of Florida, has written several well-known books on international affairs. This selection, taken from the last chapter of his book, The Truman-MacArthur Controversy and the Korean War, *studies that controversy in the light of its implications for our democratic institutions.*

MacArthur's fundamental charge against the Administration was that its restrictions kept him from achieving "victory" in the field. Inherent in this accusation was MacArthur's repudiation of the Administration's basic assumptions, above all the supposition that the Soviet Union might be ready and willing to fight a total war, and that the United States, therefore, must not provide an eager Kremlin with any excuse for attack.

MacArthur contended that the Administration divorced theory from practice. In theory, American foreign policy was based upon the assumption that the United States held sufficient power, above all air-atomic striking power, to deter the Soviet Union from launching an all-out war; in practice, American policy-makers acted upon the assumption that a limited extension of the war would hand the Soviets an excuse for precipitating World War III. On the one hand, the Kremlin was allegedly reluctant to engage in global hostilities with the United States because of America's greater retaliatory strength, inherent primarily in the destruction power of the Strategic Air Command; on the other hand, the Kremlin regarded our purported deterrent power with so little respect that it would deliberately risk total war rather than suffer a limited defeat of Communist China (a limited defeat would preclude the unconditional surrender and overthrow of Peking, and leave it weakened but nevertheless in control of the Chinese mainland).

MacArthur failed to see any consistency between the Administration's rationale of its foreign policy, based upon the atomic impact

Reprinted by permission of the publishers from John W. Spanier, *The Truman-MacArthur Controversy and the Korean War.* Cambridge, Mass.: Harvard University Press, Copyright 1959 by the President and Fellows of Harvard College.

of massive retaliation, and its failure to act upon its own premise. If it were true that the United States held the atomic balance—as he believed and the Administration professed—then his recommendations for air attacks and a naval blockade of Communist China could be safely executed. SAC would continue to deter the Soviet Union and ensure that the limited hostilities, although somewhat extended, would remain confined to the Chinese-Korean theater; our superior strategic air power would provide the umbrella under which this expanded limited war could be fought. It was sheer fantasy, MacArthur charged, to suppose that American air attacks upon Manchuria would provide an eager Kremlin the opportunity to enter the battle. The Soviet Union possessed far inferior retaliatory power (the Russians did not begin to develop their long-range air force until 1954); why should it, therefore, be allowed to handcuff American strength? The United States possessed the superior atomic sanction; why should it not take advantage of this greater power? MacArthur pointed to the paradox that the side with the smaller strategic strength had paralyzed the will to act of the side which possessed the more effective striking force. The Administration's fear to act upon his recommendations to attack across the Yalu and the resultant impasse on the Korean battlefield was not a military stalemate, but a stalemate between the Soviet leaders *militarily incapable* of destroying the center of free-world power and American policy-makers *psychologically reluctant* to exploit the advantage of the very atomic balance which they claimed was the primary safeguard of peace.

If the Russian leaders were really militarily capable of winning a total war and were merely seeking a convenient pretext to launch World War III, they would hardly need the United States to furnish the excuse; they were perfectly capable of manufacturing their own. If they were, however, restrained by American air power, they would rather tolerate a limited defeat of their chief ally than risk suicide. North Korea was no more "worth" the cost of an all-out conflict to the Soviet Union than South Korea had been to the United States; nor was Communist China's position in North Korea "worth" that price as long as American objectives remained confined to the Korean peninsula.

MacArthur also dissented from the Administration's assumption that even if an attack upon Communist China would not precipitate

World War III, this country must not become engaged in a "war of attrition" lest this course would weaken NATO and provoke a Soviet attack. The general denied that the Korean War was a Russian maneuver to draw American strength away from Europe and dissipate it against Chinese manpower, a strategic diversion which must be ended as soon as possible at minimum cost to the central effort to strengthen our total-war deterrent.

Not only was the "real" challenge against the enemy's number-one team in Europe hypothetical, for it was "Russia's policy . . . not to sacrifice its own troops but to use those of friends," but:

> *Mr. Truman failed abysmally to comprehend the Soviet strategy in the latter's continuing and relentless effort to control the world . . . He failed to understand that the global panorama has long encompassed three great areas of potential struggle: In the center, Europe; on the flanks, Asia to the north and Africa to the south. Mr. Truman apparently thought of the center as the area of supreme interest and potential struggle, believing that if it could be held safely all else would fall into place . . .*
>
> *What the Soviets sought were the economic frontiers of the World —Asia to the north, Africa to the south—frontiers which possessed such a mighty reservoir of the world's potential wealth in raw resources. The center represented little in economic advance, the flanks everything. The Soviet strategy was merely to defend in Europe but to advance by way of the flanks; to cause the free world to concentrate its resources at the center to the neglect of the vital ends.*

Korea was, therefore, the right war at the right place at the right time, and above all else, with the right enemy. For Communist China was Soviet Russia's chief ally and most powerful friend in Asia. Therefore, a defeat inflicted upon Communist China, however limited that defeat might be, would affect both Soviet strength in Asia and the global balance of power between the Western and Communist blocs. The defeat of the Chinese Communists in Korea would strengthen the friendship and support of the Asian peoples, particularly the Japanese and Filipinos, for the United States; the loss of American prestige in an acceptance of the stalemate would alienate their sympathies. Conversely, Communist China's status would be recognized as "the military colossus of the East"; America's fear to demonstrate its superior strength would make our friends feel less secure and drive the neutral nations deeper into neutralism; for they would feel more threatened as a result of Peking's unchallenged recognition as a strong and menacing neighbor and therefore look upon the Communist states with a more friendly, if also a more apprehensive, eye. The destruction of Communist China's industrial complex, military depots, and communication network would gravely weaken Sino-Soviet offensive strength in the Far East and deter Moscow and Peking from initiating any further aggressive adventures; confining hostilities to the Korean peninsula and concluding the war on the basis of the status quo would leave Sino-Soviet power intact and encourage it to exploit the West's weakness and lack of determination in other areas. Indeed, if the war in Korea were "lost"—by MacArthur's definition—the Western democracies would have suffered such a first-class political and psychological defeat that the Soviets could not but be emboldened to new efforts to undermine Western Europe. But to drive the Chinese Communists out of Korea in accordance with his strategy, MacArthur asserted, would demonstrate to the Western nations that even the Sino-Soviet alliance shrank from certain risky steps; victory would raise Europe's self-confidence by showing the limits of Communist power and the superior strength of the United States. It is for this reason that MacArthur insisted that Korea was *the* test of NATO and that Europe's first line of defense was not in Germany but in Korea.

His war in Korea was not, therefore, a sideshow; it was at the center of the worldwide struggle. The war, to be sure, contained its risks, but this was inherent in the nature of international politics and the original decision to fight in Korea; the conflict also presented a great opportunity to inflict a limited yet severe defeat upon the Sino-Soviet bloc, demonstrate American determination and power, raise Western resolution and self-assurance, and forestall the disaffection of friendly Asian nations. This opportunity outweighed all the risks, particularly since these risks were minimized by the deterrent power of America's superior atomic air-striking power.

MacArthur also emphasized that an alliance could act decisively only if its members were agreed on the nature of the danger facing them. If they were not animated by such a common realization, they not only did not add to the security of the United States; they detracted from it by restraining the United States from taking the steps necessary to safeguard its interests. The argument that the Administration could not accept his recommendations because it could not afford to isolate itself in the face of the Soviet threat toward Europe, was invalid; it was not the existence of the alliance which would deter the enemy's aggression, but the resolution which bound it together in concrete instances which called for vigorous action. When such determination and will power were lacking, the United States must protect its own interests. The Administration's unwillingness to risk the loss of its allies allowed American policy to be dictated by the weaker members of the alliance. Under these circumstances, the achievement of allied unity became self-defeating; for the price of continued cooperation was the substance of action. In MacArthur's opinion, this price was too high and was paid upon the false assumption that unilateral action by the United States in Asia would undermine NATO, isolate this country, and encourage a Soviet attack in Europe. MacArthur believed that this prejudged the issue because it presumed that the United States was more dependent for its security upon its European allies than they upon the United States.

Since he was unwilling to accept formal unity for inaction or half-hearted effort, MacArthur advised that in order to forestall the disastrous effects he foresaw from an acceptance of a Korean stalemate, the United States "go it alone." European reluctance to become involved in major hostilities in the Far East ought not to prevent the Administration from taking actions which were in America's interest; the Administration could not give global scope to an alliance whose conflict of interests in areas outside of Europe paralyzed it.

The United States was sufficiently strong to fight the Korean War by herself; she had to act unilaterally if necessary, and pursue alone those policies which aimed at the preservation of a favorable balance of power. The United States must not allow this balance to be overturned by subordinating her strategy to allied fears; for in the final analysis, the security of Europe depended upon this country's ability to maintain this equilibrium. After the North Korean invasion, the United States had not first asked its allies whether they would approve of American intervention; the American government had acted in accordance with the dictates of national security. Allied consent had subsequently been extended, but it had not been a precondition for action. The Administration ought now to act upon its own precedent.

Communist China's appearance on the battlefield thus brought into the open the almost total disagreement between the Administration and its Commander in Chief, Far East, a disagreement which had, of course, never lain far below the surface and had irritated the relationship between Washington and Tokyo from the beginning of the war. Since shortly after the outbreak of hostilities, MacArthur had openly advocated that the United States maximize its commitment to Chiang Kai-shek and take a strong stand against Communist China; and his repeated "military" criticisms of the Administration's preoccupation with Europe and alleged neglect of American interests in the Far East were hardly new.

But these frequent and vigorous challenges of Administration policy after China's intervention were, however, incompatible with the President's continuing civilian supremacy and authority as chief diplomat and Commander in Chief to formulate and implement the policies the Chief Executive considered necessary to ensure the nation's self preservation. MacArthur embarrassed the Administration by giving the world the impression that the United States spoke with two voices—one civilian, one military—on foreign policy; he confused our allies and increased their reluctance to follow American policy because they feared that the government could not control him; and his March 24 statement actually forestalled the execution of Presidential policy. This situation was intolerable and left Mr. Truman no choice but to dismiss his field commander. But the price the President paid included, among other things, the adoption of a stronger anti-Mao and pro-Chiang policy along the lines advocated by the "old soldier" who refused to fade away.

The Administration's political weakness and vulnerability in Congress was a further cause for the Truman-MacArthur controversy; the President's lack of strength was particularly noticeable in the Senate. The reason for this was that in early 1950 the leadership of the Republican party in Congress on matters of foreign policy returned from the liberal eastern wing of the party to the traditional and predominantly middle-western conservatives, who constitute the majority of Republicans in Congress. These conservative Republicans rejected "bipartisan" cooperation. They believed that partisanship in foreign policy was politically expedient, "me-tooism" in international affairs, as in domestic affairs, resulted in defeat at the polls. Policies stamped

"Oh Say, Can You See—" (*Editorial cartoon by Jacob Burck. Chicago Sun-Times, 1951*)

with the Administration trade-mark were credited by the electorate to the party in power, and not to the "loyal" opposition which had supported them. In addition, Taft Republicans were convinced that the Democratic party, aided by the "heretical" eastern wing of their own party, were destroying the foundations of the American political and economic system, and that this process could be halted only by the restoration to power of the heirs and custodians of the "true" Republican tradition with its belief in a strong legislature, a balanced budget, and a minimum of government intervention in business. Thus partisanship in foreign policy was also an ideological necessity.

The conservative Republicans focused their criticisms upon the New Dealers. The latter's crimes were many: they had fathered "Socialism" and the Welfare State in America; they had involved the United States in World War II; they had "sold out" China and Eastern Europe at the wartime conferences with Stalin; and they had allowed Communist agents and "sympathizers" to infiltrate the American government. In short, the New Dealers were responsible for altering the traditional libertarian American system, entangling the United States in the complications of the international world, and aiding, either unwittingly or deliberately, the forces of World Communism. This conspiratorial interpretation of American domestic and foreign politics could not have been advanced at a more appropriate moment in American postwar history. Popular frustration with the cold war was widespread.

Republican mid-term election successes appeared to prove to orthodox party strategists that opposition per se was good politics, and that their pre-election estimate that attacks upon foreign policy were politically profitable was correct. As a result, after November 7, 1950, they no longer confined their broadsides to Yalta, Teheran, and Potsdam; Alger Hiss and other cases of espionage; the Administration's "loss" of China and responsibility for the war in Korea; they now attacked the whole scope of American foreign policy, particularly the European policy. General MacArthur's close link to this group, among whom such leaders as Taft, Wherry, Bridges, and Knowland were largely oriented toward Asia, lent it great prestige and strengthened its criticisms.

These attacks had even before June 25, 1950, imposed an increasing inflexibility upon American Far Eastern policy; they had prevented the Administration from initiating its Mao Tse-tung policy and forestalled the complete abandonment of Chiang Kai-shek. The Administration's protection of Formosa after the outbreak of North Korean aggression satisfied the opposition only temporarily. As the war progressed, their assaults became increasingly vociferous in their demands for a stronger anti-Mao and pro-Chiang policy; and their electoral gains, together with Communist China's intervention, added to the pressure exerted upon the Administration to adopt General MacArthur's proposal to extend the war and hit across the Yalu River.

These attacks were not, however, powerful enough to achieve this aim; but they were sufficiently strong to place American diplomacy in a domestic political straightjacket which foreclosed negotiations as a means to end hostilities, brought the Administration to endorse a large-scale military-aid program for Chiang, to announce a rather doubtful enthusiasm for his regime, and even to issue a call for a revolution within Communist China. Thus, in May and June 1951, during the Senate inquiry into MacArthur's dismissal, the extraordinary and ridiculous situation arose in which, on the one hand, the Administration was defending its limitation of the war and its dismissal of General MacArthur for advocating the opposite course, and at the same time renouncing its acceptance of the status quo and the implicit recognition of Peking's existence which this implied, and presenting the key issue as the survival of the Chinese Communist regime itself. Since regimes do not, however, negotiate about their own survival, this issue could only have been settled by the total war with Communist China—and perhaps with the Soviet Union—which the Administration had already rejected as too dangerous a course. Thus, if the government's call for an internal revolt within Communist China had been taken seriously by Peking, it would have committed the United States to an interminable war with no possibility of ending it through negotiations or a cease-fire.

Walter Lippmann subsequently wrote that the situation had been so serious that President Truman

> was not able to make peace, because politically he was too weak at home. He was not able to make war because the risks were too great. This dilemma of Truman's was resolved by the election of Eisenhower . . . President Eisenhower signed an armistice which accepted the partition of Korea and a peace without victory because, being himself the victorious commander in World War II and a Republican, he could not be attacked as an appeaser. President Truman and Secretary Acheson, on the other hand, never seemed able to afford to make peace on the only terms which the Chinese would agree to, on the terms, that is to say, which Eisenhower did agree to. The Democrats were too vulnerable to attack from the politi-

cal followers of General MacArthur and of the then powerful Senator McCarthy, and indeed to attack from the whole right wing of the Republican party.

Thus the separation of powers exaggerated the peculiar American tendency to define foreign policy objectives in abstract and ideological terms; for to gain congressional and popular support for their policies, presidents must oversell their policies. This they do, not by presenting the key issues as enlightened—yet nevertheless, "selfish" national interests, but as the highest moral principles and aims.

Whereas interests can, however, be compromised, principles cannot. Their integrity, indeed their survival, can be guaranteed only by the total destruction of the enemy and the complete elimination of the evil which threatens to contaminate, if not to abolish, them. Anything less than the full application of "righteous power," and the achievement of complete victory, creates an embarrassing discrepancy between expectation and reality, and leaves in its wake widespread disillusionment.

The Administration's political weakness was evident, however, not only in its acceptance of much of its critics' policy and its apparent inability to sign an armistice on or near the 38th Parallel, but also in its failure to take effective measures to restrict MacArthur's discretionary powers. Nowhere was this more vividly demonstrated than in North Korea after the first signs of Chinese Communist intervention. MacArthur believed that boldness and a show of force would convince Peking that Korea's fate had already been settled; any hesitation would be interpreted as weakness and an invitation to full-scale intervention. The Administration proposed that only South Korean troops be sent into the area along the Manchurian frontier and northeastern provinces bordering the Soviet Union; by this means it expected to reassure Peking that American troops would not invade Manchuria. But MacArthur advanced the proper "purely military" considerations which he claimed necessitated his advance to the Yalu, and the government surrendered meekly. The reason it later advanced for its laxness was the American tradition granting generals great latitude in determining the tactical means to gain their objectives. This was primarily a rationalization; American policy-makers could hardly have been blind to the interrelationship of tactical means on the one hand and strategic concepts and political consequences on the other.

A more reasonable explanation would attribute their paralysis to the Administration's fear of being accused of "softness" toward Communism, its uncertainty that MacArthur could not again carry off a "tremendous gamble" as at Inchon, its field commander's heightened prestige since that brilliant victory and Republican mid-term victories.

This is not to say that MacArthur's determination to launch his "end of the war" offensive, or the Administration's failure to stop him, were responsible for Communist China's full-scale intervention. The key decision determining the intervention was probably the crossing of the parallel; this is not, however, to excuse Washington's relaxation of political control as MacArthur advanced into North Korea. In seeking allied support for the crossing of the parallel, the Administration had given assurances that it would direct its military operations in North Korea with circumspection, that it would conduct itself with caution and avoid all acts . . . which might provoke either Russia or China. MacArthur's operations, in the view of the allies, hardly supported this understanding; in their opinion, MacArthur's "belligerent" statements, together with his advance to the Yalu, gave Peking reasonable grounds for suspicion of American intentions and at least a partial justification for its intervention. Consequently, London and Paris refused to sanction an extension of the war beyond the Yalu, and slowed down and later eviscerated the Administration's condemnation of Communist China. This one incident, they believed, had shown both MacArthur's liberal—perhaps more appropriately, unwarranted—interpretation of his orders, and the Administration's inability to exert effective control over him. Thus Truman's domestic weakness was one of the principal causes for the lack of allied confidence and insistence upon restraint.

The intensity of the executive-legislative battle not only allowed MacArthur to inject himself into this conflict and exploit his strong legislative support, but made it incumbent upon the Administration to invoke the Joint Chiefs' public support for its policies. Thus, ironically, the President's main reason for dismissing MacArthur, the necessity to preserve the principle of civilian control of the military, had to rely for its defense almost completely upon General Bradley and his three colleagues. The Joint Chiefs, widely regarded as a strictly professional and disinterested body, could command senatorial attention, for they combined the roles of World War II heroes and technical experts; consequently, they bore the chief burden of explaining to the inquiring senators the relationship of military strategy to political objectives, the respective contribution of Europe and Asia to our national security, and the value and role of allies in American policy. Secretary Acheson, despite the articulate, organized, and persuasive presentation of his testimony, could command no such reception; his Congressional audience received him in a more hostile and skeptical mood.

If the Administration's political vulnerability left the Joint Chiefs little choice but to lend their glamor to the government's policies, it also squandered much of their wartime prestige and reputation for political neutrality. Senator Taft's announcement, shortly after General MacArthur's dismissal, that he no longer possessed any confidence in General Bradley's professional judgment—as if "purely military" evaluations were ever without political implications!—is symptomatic of this change of attitude. Apparently the Senator believed that Bradley's opinions were warped by a purported pro-Democratic bias. Taft's criticism, however, even if it were true—and all the evidence belies it—would hardly be germane; for he is not disputing the fact that military men speak for or against national issues of a highly controversial nature in public, but the fact that General Bradley agreed with the President's policy, and disagreed with his, Senator Taft's, views. His point was not that a criticism of his and former President Hoover's almost exclusive reliance on air and sea power for the defense of the American Gibraltar should have been the task of the military's civilian superiors; his point was that General Bradley had found his strategy wanting. His concern was not, therefore, with the problem that partisan alignment of generals implied for the future of civilian supremacy; he was merely incensed that there were also "Democratic Generals," like the chairman of the Joint Chiefs, not just "Republican Generals," like MacArthur.

Nonetheless, the Senator's hostility to General Bradley does draw attention to the manner in which the separation of powers between the President and Congress draws military leaders into political conflict. The danger in this is not that military officers belong, as Senator Taft seemed to believe, to one or the other of the two principal parties. The real threat lies elsewhere: that the generals' independent judgment lends itself to exploitation by both parties; and that this will

signal, as Walter Lippmann has written, "the beginning of an altogether intolerable thing in a republic: namely a schism within the
armed forces between the generals of the Democratic Party and the
generals of the Republican Party"; and that the result will considerably weaken civilian control and presidential direction of foreign
policy.

*   *   *

Limitations are arrived at by a complex and subtle process of
informal negotiations with the enemy in which the two sides never sit
down at a diplomatic table and formally negotiate these limitations
with one another. Instead, they tacitly agree about these limitations
by mutual example. Thus, the United States will permit China to
possess a "privileged sanctuary" beyond the Yalu River; American
fighters and bombers—let alone troops—do not cross the Korean-
Chinese frontier. Similarly, the Chinese do not attack the allied armies
in the field with fighters or bomb the supply ports. Had the UN forces,
however, bombed the Manchurian supply depots, troop-concentration
points, and roads and railroad tracks leading to Korea, thereby perhaps jeopardizing the ability of the Chinese army to withstand a
sustained UN offensive, the Chinese might have been compelled to
attack the UN forces and South Korean ports from the air. Mutual
self-restraint helps to prevent hostilities from escalating. This is not
to say that a particular limitation can never be changed or, that once
lifted, the war will automatically escalate immediately into total war.
Limitation should be discarded only after careful consideration, only
if absolutely necessary, and only if accompanied by a full knowledge
of the risks involved. The greater the number of limitations that are
lifted, the greater the possibilities of escalation, and the very event
which impels both sides to try and keep the hostilities limited—a total
strategic nuclear war—may be precipitated.

The United Nations' decision to cross the 38th Parallel is an obvious example of the risks undertaken when one side violates a tacit
limitation. In a limited war the political objectives are limited. At the
beginning of the Korean hostilities, the objective was to restore the
status quo. While the objective seemed negative (to prevent South
Korea from falling under Communist domination), it also served certain positive political purposes. It demonstrated America's reliability

to her friends and allies. It also showed the Soviets and Chinese the futility—and risks—of using force to transform the balance of power. The political objective then was to demonstrate American determination to stop the Communists from extending their power by force. Once the United Nations force marched across the 38th Parallel, however, the objective became the total elimination of the North Korean government and the unconditional surrender of its armed forces. But Korean unification under United Nations control would have threatened Chinese security. Thus the invasion precipitated her intervention—just as the attempt to overthrow the South Korean government and the Communist threat to Japanese security precipitated American intervention. The invasion to the north, therefore, escalated the war by removing one of the most important limitations.

The problem of preserving these limitations is a question of "communication." It is precisely because they are not formally negotiated that they must somehow be clearly drawn and "obvious." These limitations may make no sense militarily. In fact, from a military point of view, when the aim is the destruction of the enemy's forces, sanctuaries such as Manchuria or Pusan are roadblocks in the way of a military victory. From the point of view of achieving political objectives, however, these limitations make eminently good sense.

Nothing better-illustrates the conflict between the political objective of limited war and the military objective of victory than the problem of who should control the use of tactical nuclear weapons. Militarily, their use is likely to be advocated because of their greater and more "efficient" killing potential. Politically, however, their use may be disastrous. How many invaded states will wish to be "saved from Communism" by being devastated by such destructive weapons? There will be little left to be saved. The threatened use of tactical nuclear weapons *may* encourage the victims of aggression *not* to call for American help.

More significantly, the distinction between nuclear and nonnuclear weapons is obvious, as apparent as a frontier line and not subject to varying interpretations. But if this distinction were discarded and a new one made, say between tactical and strategic nuclear weapons, just where *would* the line be drawn: at 2 kilotons, 20 kilotons (the yield of the Nagasaki bomb), or 2 megatons? Not using tactical nuclear weapons is a simple recognizable limitation and therefore easy to observe; any other distinction raises more problems than it solves.

A field commander like a MacArthur, whether his motives are political or strictly military, will only endanger these limitations. In pursuing "victory," he will press for the lifting of limitations imposed upon him—limitations that are, in a military sense, admittedly illogical and impediments to victory. But in his cry that "there is no substitute for victory," is the danger of escalation. It is particularly for the MacArthurs, therefore, that Clausewitz wrote:

> *The art of war in its highest point of view becomes a policy, but, of course, a policy which fights battles instead of writing notes. According to this view, it is an unpermissible and even harmful distinction, according to which a great military event or the plan for such an event should admit a* purely military *judgment; indeed, it is an unreasonable procedure to consult professional soldiers on the plan of war, that they may give a* purely military *opinion. . . . For war is an instrument of policy; it must necessarily bear the character of policy; it must measure with policy's measure. The conduct of war, in its great outlines, is, therefore, policy itself, which takes up the sword in place of the pen, but does not on the account cease to think according to its own laws.*

These are wise words to remember in an age in which nuclear bombs have outmoded total war as suicidal and made the world safe only for limited wars.

David Horowitz
CONTAINMENT INTO LIBERATION

The bitter debate between those who thought that the Korean War ought to be limited in scope and those who argued for escalation was—despite this basic disagreement—based on an underlying agreement: all parties to the dispute assumed that North Korea was guilty of unprovoked aggression against South Korea. Even during the war, however, there were voices that

Reprinted by permission of Hill and Wang, a division of Farrar, Straus & Giroux, from *The Free World Colossus* by David Horowitz, pp. 114–140. Copyright © 1965 by David Horowitz.

dissented from this assumption. Spokesmen for the Communist Party and independent radicals such as I. F. Stone argued that the major responsibility for the war rested with the American-sponsored ruler South Korea, Syngman Rhee. This position, generally ignored or scoffed at in the 1950s, has been maintained with varying degrees of eloquence and plausibility in the 1960s by William Appleman Williams, Gabriel Kolko, and others of the so-called "revisionist" school of historians. The revisionists have attempted to show that President Truman's harshly anti-Communist policies forced the Soviet Union into the actions usually cited as proof of Russian hostility, intransigeance, and aggression. Revisionist history has led many students of the entire postwar period to change their notions about the origins of the Cold War. Among the most influential of revisionist histories is David Horowitz's The Free World Colossus, *which sets the Korean War in a very different global context from the one described in the previous selections.*

Korea was occupied in 1945 by the Soviet Union and the United States in accord with their agreements at Cairo, Yalta and Potsdam.[1] By August 10, most of North Korea was in Russian hands. American troops landed in South Korea on September 8, and the United States proposed a demarcation line at the 38th Parallel.[2] Based on the exigencies of a military situation, the choice of the 38th Parallel as a line of demarcation was particularly unfortunate, because Korea's Japanese-built industries lay in the north, while the bulk of her population resided in the south. A disinterested policy would have spurred attempts to remove foreign forces at this early stage, while encouraging unification at once. But at the Moscow Conference in December 1945 (without consulting the Koreans) the Foreign Ministers decided that Korea should be held as a joint trusteeship for five years by the occupying powers.

After forty years of Japanese occupation, Korea was eager and ready in 1945 to reassume the tasks of self-government. A nationwide resistance movement existed which had organized revolutionary committees throughout Korea upon Japan's surrender. Although Com-

[1] W. D. Reeve, *The Republic of Korea,* 1963, p. 23; Reeve was in Korea from 1952–1956, most of the time as advisor to the Prime Minister of the South Korean Government. His book was written under the auspices of the Royal Institute of International Affairs. On the ensuing events, cf. Fleming, pp. 589–660, on which this account draws heavily.

[2] Dean Acheson testified in the *MacArthur Hearings* (Part 3, p. 2104) that the division at the 38th was recommended by the Secretary of War, was approved by the Joint Chiefs of Staff, by the State–Army–Navy–Air Force Coordinating Committee, and by the President.

munists were members of nearly all of these committees (they were the only party with a nationwide membership), the committees themselves contained representatives of all groups. In the important province of Cholla Nam Do, the committee was headed by a pro-American Christian pastor.[3]

A representative assembly of these Committees of Preparation for National Independence was held in Seoul on September 6, and formed a national government with jurisdiction over all of Korea, North and South. "If the People's Republic exhibited radical tendencies, it only reflected with reasonable accuracy the views of the Korean majority."[4] Two days later, the American occupation force, headed by General John R. Hodge, landed, ignored the People's Republic Government which had just been formed, made use instead of Japanese and quisling elements, and on October 5 appointed an Advisory Council which contained many "well-known collaborators."[5]

In these little-known events of the immediate postwar period are buried the seeds of the Korean tragedy. At the other end of the globe, during these years, the wartime alliance was giving way to the cold war, the effect of which in Korea was to preclude the possibility of a unified effort to bind up the nation's wounds.

On October 10, the United States Military Government in Korea (USAMIGIK)[6] proclaimed itself to be the only government in South Korea and called for an end to the pronouncements of "irresponsible political groups." These acts "crystalized a large part of Korean thinking into an anti-American mold" and made the people feel that "the liberators had become the oppressors."[7] When a Congress of the People's Republic met on November 20, 1945, and refused to dissolve itself, General Hodge declared its activities unlawful. On February 14, 1946, a Representative Democratic Council, sponsored by the United States Military Government and headed by the just-

---

[3] E. Grant Meade, *American Military Government in Korea,* 1951, pp. 69–72. Meade was a member of the American Military Government.
[4] Ibid. These radical views included "the call for unification, land reform, the ousting of Japanese collaborators, wide extension of the suffrage, and the formation of co-operatives." Reeve, op. cit., p. 24.
[5] Ibid., pp. 59–62.
[6] It should be noted that not a single member of the USAMIGIK spoke Korean. Alfred Crofts, "Our Falling Ramparts—the Case of Korea," *The Nation,* June 25, 1960, p. 545. Crofts himself was a member of USAMIGIK.
[7] Meade, op. cit.

returned Syngman Rhee (who had spent thirty-seven of his seventy years in the United States),[8] was formed. This council was heavily rightist,[9] based on the landlords, capitalists and other conservative elements, and leading liberals refused to participate.[10]

By May 1946, when the Soviet and American members of the Joint Commission were failing to reach agreement on unification, the jails in the American zone were "filled to the rafters" with opponents of the Rhee regime.[11] The reason for the deadlock between the occupying powers was simple. While the United States had set up its own puppet regime in the South, the Russians had acted to achieve similar control in the North. Instead of ignoring the native Korean Government, however, the Russians took "extreme care" to keep themselves in the background, making sure at the same time that the Communist wings within the government councils would be able to establish their control. A government was formed, headed by Kim Il-Sung, a leading Korean Communist and revolutionist against Japanese rule. In March 1946, Kim's Government carried out a land reform, dividing one-half of the existing land between 725,000 landless peasants; this act promoted a feeling of loyalty for his regime from the start.[12]

In the South, the American Military Government issued a decree two years after the Northern reform under which roughly 700,000 acres of former Japanese holdings were sold to 600,000 tenant families. This reform was so popular that nearly all candidates in the election of May 10, 1948 campaigned for further distribution of privately owned lands. But the Rhee Government delayed a new land reform law repeatedly; meanwhile, tenants were being forced by their landlords to buy the plots they tilled on unfavorable terms or be evicted.[13]

Thus, "the unhappy Koreans, who only wanted to be rid of all

---

[8] Crofts, op. cit. "In mid-October, USAMIGIK welcomed Syngman Rhee, Director of the wartime Korean Commission in Washington. . . . His return attracted little general attention, though from the first he seems to have won the favor of collaborationist groups."
[9] Crofts, "Before the American landings, a political Right, associated in popular thought with colonial rule, could not exist; but shortly afterward we were to foster at least three conservative factions." Cf. also Reeve, p. 25.
[10] George M. McCune, *Korea Today,* 1950, pp. 47–52.
[11] Mark Gayn, *Japan Diary,* 1948, p. 431.
[12] McCune, op. cit., pp. 51–53, 201–207.
[13] Ibid., pp. 133–138.

foreigners, rapidly became two countries with very different social outlooks, both halves of the nation suffering great economic hardship from its artificial division."[14]

On November 14, 1947, in the face of failure by the United States and the Soviet Union to reach agreement on Korean unification, the UN General Assembly created a United Nations Temporary Commission on Korea to expedite its independence. The Soviet Union refused this Commission permission to enter North Korea, and eventually it was decided to hold an election in South Korea alone. This decision was opposed strongly by the Australian and Canadian representatives. It was also opposed by the middle-of-the-road and leftist groups in South Korea on the grounds that a separate election would divide the country permanently, and that, moreover, a free atmosphere did not exist. "Only the Rightists favored the separate election."[15] The Communists and Rightists formed terrorist bands before the elections (to be held on May 10, 1948) and in six weeks prior to the balloting, 589 people were killed. The Rightists won a heavy victory and the UN Commission certified that the results "were a valid expression of the will of the electorate in those parts of Korea which were accessible to the Commission." Not too many parts could have been accessible to the Commission, however, as they had only thirty people to observe the elections. A contrary view holds "that the elections were not in fact a free expression of the Korean will."[16]

On December 12, 1948, the UN General Assembly passed, by 41–6, a resolution declaring the Rhee Government to be "a lawful government having effective control over that part of Korea where the Temporary Commission was able to observe . . .; that this Government is based on elections which were a valid expression of the free will of the electorate of that part of Korea . . . ," and further, "that this is the only such [i.e., lawful and freely elected] Government in Korea." The resolution, it should be noted, did *not* give backing to the Rhee Government's subsequent claim to be the only legitimate government for the *whole* of Korea, but only purported to deal with

[14] Fleming, op. cit., p. 592.
[15] McCune, op. cit., pp. 229–230.
[16] Ibid., p. 592; Reeve, pp. 26–27.

the question of the proper government in that part of Korea open to observation by the Temporary Commission.[17]

Despite its UN sanction, the Rhee Government was so unpopular as to make its ability to survive doubtful.[18] Moreover, the tip of the Korean Peninsula was not strategically vital. These realities led American strategists to place it outside of the United States defensive perimeter, which ran from the Aleutians through Japan to the Philippines. As late as January 1950 Secretary of State Acheson publicly defined this perimeter as excluding Korea, a statement which later evoked heavy Republican criticism as having invited the North Korean invasion.[19]

By 1950, the United States was faced with a considerable dilemma. Operating under the mutually dependent theories of conspiracy and containment, the Truman Administration had found it virtually impossible to "explain" to the satisfaction of the American people the "loss" of China, a situation which the right wing was exploiting to the full. Now, new difficulties loomed. Inevitably, the Chinese Communists would attempt to complete their revolution by destroying the remaining Kuomintang forces which had sought refuge on Formosa.

The United States could choose to intervene in Chinese affairs, to defend Chiang, thus driving the wedge deeper between the new China and American interests (at this time Acheson was farsighted enough to perceive that there were basic areas of conflict between Russia and China which could be exploited).[20] Or it could elect to stand by while the Communists disposed of the hopelessly corrupt and ruthless Nationalist remnants.

Acheson's statements, in January 1950, excluding Formosa as well

[17] Reeve, op. cit., p. 27.
[18] It should be noted that the Franchise Law (passed on June 27, 1947) was restrictive, debarring the large group of illiterates, for example. As a result, the government was dominated by "landlords and members of the old aristocracy" (Reeve, p. 31). Two rebellions broke out in 1948, in Yosu and Cheju Do. "While every allowance must be made for government nervousness in the face of rumors of imminent invasion from the north, the 'near-extinction of civil liberties' which followed the [Yosu] rebellion, as well as such strong-arm methods as the razing of villages on 'a vast scale' after an uprising in Cheju Do in April 1948, gave the regime a fascist stamp." Reeve, p. 32. Cf. also Fleming, p. 592.
[19] Cf., for example, campaign speech by Eisenhower, *Time,* October 6, 1952.
[20] John Spanier also deals with the Republican thrusts at this policy and the resulting inflexibility in the American position.

as Korea from the United States' defense perimeter can be seen as an attempt to justify Chiang's collapse from a strategic point of view. Indeed, on December 23, 1949, the State Department had sent a private circular to diplomats abroad preparing them for the fall of Formosa and for the nonintervention of the United States. The right wing went into action immediately. On January 2, former President Hoover and Senator Taft demanded the use of the navy to defend Chiang and, on January 3, the contents of the confidential circular were leaked to the public from Tokyo.

On January 5, the Administration reaffirmed its stand in a written statement which declared that, "The United States has no predatory designs on Formosa or any other Chinese territory. . . . Nor does it have any intention of utilizing its armed forces to interfere in the present situation. The United States Government will not pursue a course which will lead to involvement in the civil conflict in China.[21] Moreover, Acheson declared that this was not basically a strategic decision but had to do "with the fundamental integrity of the United States and with maintaining in the world the belief that when the United States takes a position it sticks to that position and does not change it by reason of transitory expediency or advantage on its part." Acheson was referring to the fact that the United States had promised at Cairo, Yalta and Potsdam that Formosa would be returned to China, i.e. to the government in control of the mainland.[22]

Within six months the nonintervention policy was reversed—and the solemn wartime pledges to restore Formosa to China were broken. In the face of mounting attack by the Republican and Democratic right wing, Acheson survived by "trading policy for time," as Walter Lippmann observed.

In May, Senator Tom Connally, Chairman of the Senate Foreign Relations Committee, said in an interview that many people "believe that events will transpire which will maneuver around and present an incident which will make us fight. That's what a lot of them are saying: "We've got to battle some time, why not now?"[23] Among those who

[21] Spanier, op. cit., p. 55.
[22] Ibid.
[23] Cited in Fleming, pp. 593–594, cf. also I. F. Stone, *The Hidden History of the Korean War*, 1952, p. 22. Stone's main thesis is that MacArthur, Dulles, Chiang and Rhee provoked the Korean War.

had a clear interest in an incident which would call forth American military intervention were the threatened Chiang and Rhee.

Rhee's stake in a possible involvement of United States military forces in the defense of South Korea was great. On May 30, less than four weeks before fighting broke out, Rhee was decisively defeated in the elections. "The regime was left tottering by lack of confidence, both in Korea and abroad."[24] In the face of a deteriorating political position, both Rhee and his Defense Minister for months had been threatening to invade North Korea, declaring that they were ready to "take Pyongyang within a few days" and "do all the fighting needed."[25] Indeed, according to the syndicated right-wing columnist, Holmes Alexander, Secretary of State Acheson "never was quite sure that Rhee did not provoke the Red attack of 1950."[26] At MacArthur's headquarters on that fateful day, John Gunther reported "one of the important members of the occupation [was] called unexpectedly to the telephone. He came back and whispered, 'A big story has just broken. The South Koreans have attacked North Korea!' "[27]

The United States, recognizing Rhee's unreliability, had taken the precaution to arm the South Korean Army with light weapons for defensive purposes only[28] so as to remove any temptation to invade North Korea. This, however, did not rule out provocation. If the North did initiate hostilities, moreover, it is something less than believable that MacArthur's Military Intelligence was entirely unaware of the imminence of the attack, as is generally reported. (The command in Tokyo is supposed to have been "taken utterly by surprise" as was President Truman and the Administration. And this in turn is cited to explain why no counter-buildup was ordered to protect the [38th] Parallel.) But, MacArthur's intelligence chief, Major-General Charles A. Willoughby, has disparaged this "alleged 'surprise' of the North

[24] *US News and World Report,* July 7, 1950, p. 29. Cited in Fleming, p. 594. Reeve, p. 42: "As the election campaign progressed, there were more and more arrests of candidates and their supporters for violating the National Security Law; nevertheless the results showed that most of the electorate preferred candidates not openly associated with the parties of the old Assembly, for 133 independents were elected out of a total of 210 members . . . the President's supporters . . . fell from 56 to 12."
[25] Fleming, op. cit., p. 654.
[26] Ibid.
[27] John Gunther, *The Riddle of MacArthur,* 1951, p. 166.
[28] Department of State, *US Policy in the Korean Crisis,* pp. 21–2.

Korean invasion," saying that "the entire North Korean Army had been alerted for weeks and was in position along the 38th Parallel!"[29] According to John Gunther, the attack was launched from four points and consisted of 70,000 men and 70 tanks, which he considered must have taken a month to six weeks to organize. Thus many agonizing questions about the triggering of this war will have to await a time when further evidence becomes accessible.

If the relative availability of data makes it possible to gain insight into the dynamics of the situation in Washington and the Far East prior to the outbreak of the war, the scarcity of parallel information makes it exceedingly difficult to know the factors at work on the other side of the dividing line. Yet hindsight, and the inevitably wider perspective that distance brings to the view of a once tense political situation, casts serious doubt on the basic Western thesis that the North Korean invasion was directed by the Kremlin as part of a general plan of remorseless expansion.

First, the objective hardly required a major military move because, as Acheson acknowledged subsequently, "the Communists had far from exhausted the potentialities for obtaining their objectives through guerilla and psychological warfare, political pressure and intimidation."[30] This was amply demonstrated by the result of the May election and the approaching demise of the Rhee regime.

Kremlin strategy was also known to be conservative at this time and to be highly sceptical of "adventuristic" moves, a factor which would have been especially important considering the fluid situation in the South. In fact the Communists lost four concrete advantages as a result of the war's outbreak, including "a favorable rearming ratio; the neutrality of certain people; the element of surprise; and the imminent recognition of Red Chinese delegates by the United Nations."[31] Indeed, the thesis of Kremlin direction cannot be squared with the fact that the Soviet Union opted to boycott the UN at precisely that time in protest against Taiwan's presence on the Security Council. If the Kremlin had planned the invasion, it is difficult to understand why they did not postpone the attack for one month until the Russian delegate would have been chairman of the Security

---

[29] Cited in Fleming, p. 599.
[30] Cited in Fleming, p. 599; *MacArthur Hearings* (Part 3), pp. 1990–1991.
[31] Wilbur W. Hitchcock, "North Korea Jumps the Gun," *Current History* (March 1951).

Council and could have frustrated any proposed moves until the North Koreans had defeated the ill-equipped South Korean Army.[32]

Nor was the North Korean Army adequately equipped to carry out an invasion in September 1950 as Joseph Alsop reported from Korea. The United States did not possess air control over the battlefield. There had been many occasions when "even two enemy intruder fighters, attacking the interminable lines of our transport moving over the appalling Korea roads in broad daylight would have been enough to produce a twenty-four hour tangle" and we would "have lost our foothold in Korea." But no enemy planes ever came because the Russians were not "prepared to play the game at all."[33] Even Soviet propaganda was caught napping by the attack. Communist papers were scooped on the outbreak and had no ready story of explanation, an unlikely pass had the invasion been carefully planned.

A former member of the United States Military Government in Korea, analyzing these and other facts inconsistent with the Western thesis, concluded that the attack on South Korea was ordered by Kim Il-Sung of North Korea, not only without instructions from Moscow, but without its knowledge. The immediate event triggering Kim's decision may have been the fact that three envoys sent to Seoul on June 11 to discuss unification had been arrested, and probably shot. A new Russian arms shipment had recently arrived, Rhee had been repudiated at the polls and a bumper rice crop was waiting in the South for the first time since World War II.[34]

Whatever the war's origin, it is very clear that there were elements of genuine civil conflict in the Korean situation which gave it a dynamic of its own. This is borne out by the fact that within weeks of the outbreak of fighting,

> . . . three-fourths of South Korea was overrun. The invaders' Russian tanks could easily have been stopped in the hills by a resolute defense; . . . Communist doctrine had little appeal to a population familiar with the grim reports of Northern refugees. But millions of South Koreans welcomed the prospect of unification, even on Communist terms. They had

[32] Ibid., summarized in Fleming, pp. 606–608.
[33] New York *Herald Tribune,* September 29, 1950. Cf. Walter Lippmann, New York *Herald Tribune,* October 5, 1950, for similar views.
[34] Hitchcock, op. cit.; cf. also Fleming's discussion of this article and other points, pp. 604–608. Cf. Spanier, op. cit., p. 15 et seq., especially p. 29, for official American estimates.

suffered police brutality, intellectual repression and political purge. Few felt much incentive to fight for profiteers or to die for Syngman Rhee. Only 10 percent of the Seoul population abandoned the city; many troops deserted, and a number of public figures, including Kimm Kiu Sic, joined the North.[35]

When the fighting broke out, a cable was sent by the UN Temporary Commission on Korea to the UN's Secretary General declaring that what looked like a full-scale war was in progress, but assessing no blame for the origin of the fighting, even quoting the North Korean radio claim that the South Koreans had invaded during the night and were being pursued south. The report suggested a meeting of the Security Council.[36] With this cable (and no other) before it, the Security Council adopted a United States resolution condemning the armed attack on the Republic of Korea, demanding an immediate withdrawal of North Korean forces to the 38th Parallel and calling on all members to render every assistance to the UN in the execution of this resolution.[37] The question of responsibility for the war was thus "answered," with few facts, by the West's built-in majority in the Security Council, and the juridical groundwork for the subsequent "police action" laid.

On June 27, President Truman ordered "United States Air and Sea forces to give the Korean government troops cover and support."[38] He also commanded the Seventh Fleet to interpose itself between Formosa and China (reversing the policy of nonintervention in the Chinese Civil War) and increased military assistance to the Philippines and to the French troops seeking to maintain their colonial dominance over the rebelling Vietnamese. On the same day, the United States called upon the Security Council to invoke sanctions

[35] Crofts, op. cit. Kimm Kiu Sic, along with Kim Koo, Lyuh Woon Hyeung and Rhee, was one of the leading figures in South Korea's political life. American-educated, he had formed a party in opposition to the left of center Republic of Lyuh Woon Hyeung. Kim Koo, "the most distinguished of the returning émigrés" whose government-in-exile had kept 35,000 troops in the field with the Chinese Nationalist Army, sought peaceful unification with the North until he was assassinated in the South in 1949. Lyuh Woon Hyeung was assassinated in the South in 1947.
[36] Fleming, op. cit., p. 601; Spanier, op. cit., pp. 35–36.
[37] Spanier, p. 39. The countries taking part in the police action were Australia, Belgium, Canada, France, Greece, Turkey, the Netherlands, New Zealand, the Union of South Africa, the United Kingdom, Thailand, the Philippines, Colombia and Ethiopia.
[38] State Department, *White Paper,* op. cit., pp. 21–22.

against North Korea; the Council responded by recommending "such assistance to the Republic of Korea as may be necessary to repel the armed attack and to restore peace and security in the area."[39] This resolution passed, attaining just the necessary seven votes (of eleven) required by the Charter. Yugoslavia voted "no" because she thought the Council did not have enough information, while Egypt and India abstained.

That haste with which these steps were taken was somewhat extraordinary since, as Fleming notes, "up to this time enforcement of the United Nations Charter had not been a compelling motive in Washington."

The UN was brushed aside in Greece, and independent action taken to defeat the Communist guerillas. In Indonesia the United States had brought strong moral pressure to bear on the Netherlands in the Security Council, but no troops and planes were sent to fight the Dutch when they defied a UN cease-fire order. Nor did the United States mobilize the UN to save the infant Israeli Republic when five Arab states invaded Palestine in 1948 to overturn by force the partition plan adopted by the UN General Assembly. Defiance of the UN could not have been more flagrant, but the United States moved no troops and planes to save the victims of Hitler's hate who had gathered in Israel and who appeared to be on the point of being destroyed by the armies of UN members converging on them from all sides. In the end Israel was saved by her own heroic fighting, with arms obtained largely from Communist Czechoslovakia. The US gave no armed support to Israel as the ward of UN.[40]

In any case the UN condemned the North Koreans but never heard their side of the story. To be sure, the Security Council was correct in ordering the withdrawal of the invading North Korean troops from South Korean soil, and in taking steps to force them to do so when they disregarded the order. But after the status quo had been restored, it was incumbent upon the UN to hear both litigants in the dispute to render judgement as an international organization and court. Unfortunately, by the time the status quo had been restored and the North Korean armies were returned to North Korean territory, the UN action was firmly under the control of forces unleashed by America's Cold War crusade.

[39] Security Council, Official Records, 5th year, Doc. 5/1501. Cf. Fleming, p. 601.
[40] Fleming, op. cit., pp. 603–604.

On July 12, 1950, with the North Korean forces racing southward towards Pusan, the House of Representatives applauded Congressmen who urged that the cities of the North Koreans be atom-bombed unless they withdrew in a week's time.[41] On July 31, General MacArthur visited Chiang Kai-shek on Formosa to confer on the defense of the island. Upon his return to Tokyo MacArthur praised Chiang whose "indomitable determination to resist Communist domination arouses my sincere admiration. His determination parallels the common interests and purpose of Americans, that all people in the Pacific should be free—not slaves."[42]

The determination to emancipate the slaves on the other side of the 38th Parallel (and in MacArthur's mind there seems never to have been a doubt that China itself would have to be liberated—soon) led to the key decision in the Korean War, what Fleming has charitably called "the cardinal error in our foreign policy to date [1960]." This was the decision to "liberate" North Korea.

On September 15, MacArthur had landed the marines at Inchon, from where they began to break the North Korean offensive, until on September 30, with the enemy in full retreat, they reached the 38th Parallel. On October 1, MacArthur issued an ultimatum to the North Koreans to lay down their arms and cease hostilities "under such military supervision as I may direct."[43]

As Dean Acheson had recently observed, the "one difference which is just about impossible to negotiate is someone's desire to eliminate your existence altogether." MacArthur's call for North Korea's unconditional surrender merely ensured the continuation of hostilities.[44] Indeed, MacArthur's troops were already preparing to set foot upon North Korean soil.

MacArthur's invasion of North Korea had been fully authorized more than two weeks earlier (on September 11) by President Truman. On September 26, the Joint Chiefs informed MacArthur that his "military objective is the destruction of the North Korean armed forces"—a more ambitious objective than restoration of the status

---

[41] Cited in Fleming, p. 609; New York *Herald Tribune,* July 13, 1950, along with a number of other cries for "a showdown" with Russia.
[42] Spanier, op. cit., p. 71.
[43] Fleming, p. 615.
[44] Cf. Spanier, op. cit., p. 91.

quo ante—and in pursuit of this authorized him to "conduct military operations north of the 38th Parallel."[45]

On September 30, United States Ambassador Warren Austin presented the United States' position to the UN. "The aggressor's forces should not be permitted to have refuge behind an imaginary line. . . . The artificial barrier which has divided North and South Korea has no basis for existence in law or in reason."[46]

On October 1, South Korean forces under MacArthur's command crossed the 38th Parallel and advanced rapidly to points deep in North Korean territory.[47] Six days later, a full month after President Truman had authorized such action, the UN General Assembly approved an American-British resolution which sanctioned, but did not mandate, the northward invasion. The UN invasion of North Korea was, of course, a travesty of basic UN principles.

> It meant that the United Nations were no longer concerned only to repel the invasion and clear South Korea of the enemy. They were now committed to war against the North Koreans, to the invasion of North Korean territory. And they were carrying out this undertaking without first hearing the North Korean case. They were abandoning the principle of attempting to settle the dispute by peaceful means, and were now resorting to force. They were now participants in the dispute, allies of one of the parties to the dispute.[48]

If the UN attempt to unify divided Korea by force at this time was unjustifiable as well as inappropriate because of the character of that body, the United States' role similarly lacks justification. For to seek, as the United States did, to unify Korea by force, was to do exactly what the North Koreans were judged to be so wrong in attempting to do. As President Eisenhower said to Syngman Rhee, in June 1953, to dissuade the latter from breaking the imminent truce: "It was indeed

---

[45] Courtney Whitney, *MacArthur: His Rendezvous with History,* 1956, p. 397. Cited in Spanier, p. 95.
[46] Spanier, op. cit., p. 88. The barrier had been proposed, of course, by the United States. . . .
[47] UN Documents, S/1840, S/1843. Cited in Fleming, p. 617, and Spanier, p. 100.
[48] Ingram, p. 196. The United States contention that there was only one Korea, that North Korea did not exist, that the 38th Parallel was an "artificial barrier" having "no basis for existence in law or reason" cannot be squared, of course, with the original UN resolution calling for the North Koreans to withdraw behind the barrier.

a crime that [North Korea] invoked violence to unite Korea. But I urge that your country not embark upon a similar course. . . ."[49] Thus, in 1953, Eisenhower unwittingly underscored the culpability of United States' actions two years before.

In any case, had the United States-controlled UN forces stopped at the 38th Parallel, the UN's chief objective, as expressed in its June 27 resolution, would have been accomplished, and the principle of collective security would have been dramatically and effectively defended. As it was, *four-fifths* of all American casualties occurred *after* the original UN aim of re-establishing the status quo had been achieved. Assuming similar proportions for North Korean, Chinese and United Nations casualties, the attempt to "liberate" North Korea, a project clearly beyond the jurisdiction of a United Nations organization, resulted in 4 million casualties.[50] Korea itself lay in ruins from end to end, its fields awaste, its industrial centers smashed by American bombs, its villages burned, its people deeply scarred and once again left under the heel of military occupation and dictatorship, the nation more hopelessly divided than before.

This was the terrible price paid for a military operation justified by the United States in terms of preventing "future attacks." ("The aggressor's forces should not be permitted to have refuge behind an imaginary line because that would recreate the threat to the peace of Korea and the world.")[51] The same doctrine was invoked to justify the attempt to drive the North Koreans beyond the Yalu, even after their armies had been smashed;[52] and the same reasoning underlay MacArthur's proposed strategy to bomb Manchuria. Indeed, the same reasoning would have justified a campaign to eliminate threats to the peace all the way to Moscow. Containment, which was, after all, a military and not a diplomatic doctrine, could never be satisfied until it had passed into liberation. The best defense, under a military definition of reality, is always an offense. For the military objective is the elimination of the opponent, not the establishment of a modus vivendi with him.

---

[49] *Time,* June 29, 1953, p. 19.
[50] Fleming, p. 656. A significantly smaller, but equally appalling estimate is given in R. Leckie, *The Korean War,* 1962: 2,415,601 total casualties, exclusive of North Korean civilians.
[51] Spanier, op. cit., p. 88. Statement of Warren Austin, US delegate to the UN.
[52] Ibid., p. 123.

That the crossing of the parallel had dubious legality, was clear from the actions of American leaders themselves. On September 30, when United States forces had reached the 38th Parallel, MacArthur wired Secretary of Defense Marshall that he intended to issue a directive to the Eighth Army to liberate the North under the June 27 UN resolution. Marshall cabled back: "We desire that you proceed with your operations without any further explanation or announcement and let action determine the matter. Our government desires to avoid having to make an issue of the 38th Parallel until we have accomplished our mission."[53] This message reportedly caused even MacArthur to "raise his eyebrows . . . MacArthur could appreciate the President's natural inclination to present the other United Nations governments with a fait accompli."[54]

The strategy was eminently successful. South Korean troops crossed the frontier on October 1, and on October 7 the General Assembly provided, perforce, and necessary sanction. India and six other Afro-Asian nations abstained because it "would impair faith in the United Nations if we were to authorize the unification of Korea by force against North Korea after [resisting] North Korea's attempt to unify Korea by force against South Korea."[55] The United States resolution to sanction action in the North was carried 47–5, a dubious victory since the United States had in its pocket the votes of the South American bloc representing 40 percent of the Assembly, the West-European powers heavily dependent on the United States financially, and such other US dependencies as Turkey, Thailand, Formosa and the Philippines.

If moral and legal considerations were negligible factors in the United States' decision to cross the parallel, power considerations were more seriously weighed. The main question, of course, was whether China would enter the war.

Dean Acheson thought they would not. "Now I give the people in Peking credit for being intelligent enough to see what is happening to them," he said on September 10. "Why they should want to further their own dismemberment and destruction by getting at cross-

---

[53] Ibid., p. 100; Whitney, p. 399.
[54] Whitney, op. cit., p. 399. Spanier thinks this "fait accompli" was actually the work of some "leading Western powers" including Britain. Cf., op. cit., p. 100.
[55] *Time,* June 29, 1953.

purposes with all the free nations of the world who are inherently their friends and have always been friends of the Chinese as against this imperialism coming down from the Soviet Union I cannot see. And since there is nothing in it for them, I don't see why they should yield to what is undoubtedly pressure from the Communist movement to get into the Korean War."⁵⁶ Despite the rapid accumulation of intelligence reports indicating Chinese preparations, Acheson maintained this posture of naive incredulity.

In fact, even after the Chinese had entered the war, Acheson declared that "no possible shred of evidence could have existed in the minds of the Chinese Communist authorities about the intentions of the forces of the United Nations. Repeatedly, and from the very beginning of the action, it had been made clear that the sole mission of the United Nations forces was to repel the aggressors and to restore to the people of Korea their independence."⁵⁷ In other words, the Chinese were to trust these friendly armies to liberate Korea right up to their border and stop there, and to protect Chinese interests in the Yalu dam and power complexes which supplied China's industrial heartland with electrical power. That the Chinese remained unconvinced seems hardly surprising.

Of course "assurance after assurance was offered to Peking"⁵⁸ after US–UN forces had crossed the 38th Parallel to the effect that China's interests would be respected. But the Chinese could cite impressive chapter-and-verse to justify little faith in such promises. On January 5, 1950, for example, President Truman had declared in a written statement that "The United States has no predatory designs on Formosa. . . . Nor does it have any intention of utilizing its armed forces to interfere in the present situation." Six months later, he interposed the Seventh Fleet between Formosa and the mainland and began a military and economic aid program to Chiang's Army. On July 10, 1950, Acheson himself said that the United States was fighting in Korea "solely for the purpose of restoring the Republic of Korea *to its status prior to the invasion from the North.*"⁵⁹ Three months later, the United States was doing precisely what Acheson had de-

---

⁵⁶ Spanier, op. cit., p. 99.
⁵⁷ Ibid., p. 97.
⁵⁸ Ibid., p. 120.
⁵⁹ Spanier, op. cit., pp. 88–89, State Department *Bulletin* 23 (July 10, 1960): 46. Emphasis added.

clared it would not do, that is, seeking by force to alter the previous status quo.

On October 23 (a month before China entered the war), a spokesman for the United States First Corps announced that "foreign troops would be halted forty miles south of the Yalu." Forty-eight hours later, the plan was denied by the Eighth Army in Korea and MacArthur's headquarters, which felt that such action would "establish a new '38th Parallel.' . . . It would also offer a North Korean Government a segment of territory where it might freely reorganize for new blows against the Korean Republic."[60]

Thus, it did not require that the Chinese leaders be paranoid to interpret United States' actions in terms of classic aggression. And indeed, on November 28, a Chinese spokesman at the United Nations made this charge, saying that the Chinese people "know fully well that the United States Government has taken this series of aggressive actions with the purpose of realizing its fanatical devotion of dominating Asia and the world. One of the master-planners of Japanese aggression, Tanaka, once said: 'to conquer the world, one must first conquer Asia; to conquer Asia, one must first conquer China; to conquer China, one must first conquer Korea and Taiwan.' . . . American Imperialism . . . plagiarizes Tanaka's memorandum, and follows the beaten path of Japan's imperialist aggressors!"[61]

In terms of MacArthur's actions, at least, the accusation was not so far-fetched. The Supreme Commander had declared in Seoul, Korea, in August 1948:

This barrier [the 38th Parallel] must and will be torn down. Nothing shall prevent the ultimate unity of your people as free men of a free nation. . . . The manner in which those issues are resolved will determine in large measure not only the unity and well-being of your people, but also the future stability of the continent of Asia.[62]

This could only mean the destruction of Communist power. "The lands touching the Pacific" MacArthur had declared earlier "with their billions of inhabitants will determine the course of history for the next ten thousand years!"

---

[60] Spanier, op. cit., p. 123. "Headquarters did not explain how an almost totally defeated enemy would rebuild his army for such a strike."
[61] Spanier, op. cit., pp. 86–87.
[62] John Gunther, op. cit., p. 169; cited in Fleming, p. 595.

Eventually, MacArthur had to be relieved of his post to prevent him from spreading the war to China by enlisting the forces of Chiang Kai-shek and bombing Manchuria. Upon his return home, he was given a demonstration of popular support never before witnessed in the United States.

At the beginning of October, as United Nations armies invaded North Korea, the Chinese leaders warned publicly that China would not "supinely tolerate the destruction of its neighbor." But the US-led advance continued relentlessly. In the last half of October, 250,000 Chinese troops were reported massing along the Korean frontier. By the end of October, the first Chinese "volunteers" had been taken prisoner.[63]

On November 5, after a Chinese strike which sent a United Nations army into retreat,[64] MacArthur still contended that the Chinese probably would not officially enter the war.[65] Even in his last fatal attack which brought the Chinese in "with both feet" he felt that his boldness would convince Peking that Korea's fate had already been settled, particularly since he had publicly announced that the "new and nerve-shattering experiences" of a modern army's fire power and low-level strafing had demoralized the Chinese Communist forces.[66] MacArthur operated at this time—and throughout the war—on this thesis which he had expressed with utmost candor: ". . . it is in the pattern of the Oriental psychology to respect and follow aggressive, resolute and dynamic leadership."[67]

After the November 5 setback at the hands of the Chinese forces, "abrupt calm" developed on the battlefront, and a series of diplomatic moves began. Britain strongly urged the United States to permit the Chinese to occupy a buffer zone; Churchill supported the endeavor.[68] Meanwhile, the Chinese were scheduled to arrive at the United Nations in New York. On November 22, "well-informed

---

[63] At the MacArthur Hearings, General Collins, Chairman of the Joint Chiefs of Staff, declared that intelligence concerning the Chinese intention to intervene during this period was "voluminous." Cf. Fleming, p. 616 n. Also Spanier, pp. 114–115.
[64] Spanier, op. cit., pp. 118–119.
[65] Ibid., p. 121. The Chinese were claiming at this point that their troops were volunteers.
[66] Ibid., p. 122.
[67] Cited in Fleming, p. 612: *New York Times,* August 29, 1950.
[68] Cited in Fleming, p. 621: *New York Times,* November 14, 1950; New York *Herald Tribune,* November 16, 17, 1950.

sources" in Washington indicated that agreement on a plan for a buffer strip along the Manchurian border was near and awaited "primary approval of its military details by General of the Army, Douglas MacArthur." Final agreement was expected momentarily.[69]

Then, on November 24, *the day the representative of the Chinese Communist Government arrived in New York* to participate in the United Nations Security Council debate, MacArthur launched a 100,000-man offensive towards the Yalu River. "He launched it knowing there were at least 100,000 men facing him in front and 40,000 guerillas behind him. He also knew that the size of his assaulting force was inadequate for a frontal attack; he therefore split his attacking army in two [the wings were so far apart and liaison between them was so difficult that it was established through Tokyo instead],[70] thereby creating an attractive and fatal vacuum in the middle of his line."[71]

In the light of this, MacArthur's move could have had only one objective: to prevent a peace settlement and to provoke China into entering the war.[72] He was entirely successful. The Chinese openly and massively entered on November 26. The United Nations armies were cut to ribbons. The point of no return had been reached; the real bloodletting and destruction had begun. As the decimated United Nations forces moved South through December and January, they adopted a scorched-earth retreat leaving millions of Koreans homeless and hungry.

At his press conference November 30, President Truman stated that "we will take whatever steps are necessary to meet the military situation." When asked if that included the atomic bomb, he said: "that includes every weapon we have" and added that "there has always been active consideration of its [the atomic bomb's] use."[73]

The Chinese response to MacArthur's attack convinced the National Security Council, according to the Alsops, that the Soviet Union (!) had moved the "time of utmost peril" when it would be

---

[69] Fleming, p. 621.

[70] Ibid., p. 621.

[71] Spanier, op. cit., p. 122 (emphasis added).

[72] Neither our own policy nor that of the United Nations required his mad dash to the Manchurian Border, "and this MacArthur knew. . . . The decision was his; it was provocation." McGeorge Bundy, "Appeasement, Provocation and Policy," *The Reporter,* January 9, 1951; cited in Fleming, p. 622.

[73] Truman, *Memoirs,* II, p. 395.

ready for major aggression up from 1953–1954 to 1950–1951, so that the United States government leaders "expect major Soviet aggression now, today, tomorrow, next month, next spring, next summer." It was no use "pretending that much can be accomplished" before the crisis, but every man and weapon "will surely be needed somewhere, somehow and soon."[74]

The Chinese, "dizzy with success," crossed the 38th Parallel south in late December, committing the same fault as that of the United Nations forces before.[75] They were stopped and stalemated in mid-January. The New Year brought world-wide appeals for negotiation from such leaders as the Pope and nine ministers of the British Commonwealth. The problem of peace, they said, was that of removing the causes of war; of easing tension and promoting understanding; and of "being at all times willing to discuss our differences without foolishly assuming that all attempts to secure peace are a form of appeasement."[76]

But US leaders were hardly in a state of mind to concern themselves with the discussion of differences. They were off on a new, solemn, freedom-advancing crusade: *to brand China the aggressor.* On December 20, Herbert Hoover demanded that the United Nations "declare Communist China an aggressor" and on January 5, the United States sent notes to 29 governments warning that the United Nations might collapse (!) unless China were so branded. Nehru cautioned that such a branding would "bolt and bar the door to a peaceful settlement in the Far East" but this did not faze the American leaders.

On January 19, the House of Representatives, with only two dissenting votes, passed a resolution demanding that the United Nations name China an aggressor and bar it from membership. Four days later, the United States Senate passed a similar resolution.

On January 11, a proposal for the withdrawal of all foreign troops "by appropriate stages" and for a conference between the Great Powers had been introduced in the United Nations and was being discussed. The Chinese had sent a reply to this proposal which the

---

[74] Fleming, p. 626.
[75] Ingram, op. cit. Chou En-Lai recognized the existence of a "boundary" when on October 1, 1950, he announced that his government "would not stand idly by when the territory of its neighbor [North Korea] was wantonly invaded."
[76] Fleming, p. 630.

United States termed a rejection. But most of the Arab–Asian bloc
and some of our European allies held that it was not a rejection, but
a bargaining step.[77]

United States pressure on the United Nations to act built up to
the point where "United States Ambassador Austin refused to agree
to a forty-eight-hour postponement in the debate to allow the Indian
delegate to get information which the latter thought was vital to the
decision." (James Reston.) The Indian delegate, Sir Benegal Rau,
wanted the time to get added information concerning a new two-step
settlement proposal from Mao Tse-Tung which had been sent through
the Indian Government in response to a direct appeal from Nehru.

In the debate that followed this proposal the United States maintained its demand for action against the Chinese, opposing and
defeating an Asian–Arab resolution proposing talks. Finally, the
United States rammed through the resolution declaring China an
aggressor, the Western Allies, as the *Wall Street Journal* put it,
voting "under the lash."[78]

These events reminded Walter Lippmann of September, 1950 when
Mr. Acheson "ordered Mr. Austin to mount his white charger and
lead the hosts of righteousness across the 38th Parallel" having no
clear idea of what would follow after the United States had lined up
the votes. Noting the Asian opposition, Lippmann called the vote
a "self-inflicted defeat" because the United States had "used the
whole apparatus of the United Nations to make a spectacular demonstration that Asia is not with us."[79]

The United States then switched from its offensive in the United
Nations to a military crusade on the battlefield, calling its new
Korean policy "Operation Killer," slaughter without end and without
purpose, which, as Pearl Buck wrote, "lost us what we cannot afford
to lose—the mind of man in Asia."[80]

---

[77] *The Nation,* January 27, 1951; also cf. Fleming, p. 631.

[78] "None [of the European nations] could afford to alienate the US in a showdown,"
commented the *Journal,* "but few hid their opposition."—Cited in *The Nation,* February 10, 1951. Cf. Sherman Adams, *Firsthand Report,* 1961, p. 127: In 1954, when
the British were pressuring the Eisenhower Administration to recognize China, and
support its admission to the UN as a measure which would reduce tension and the
danger of war, Eisenhower demurred saying: "How can we agree to admit to membership a country which the UN has branded an aggressor?"

[79] Cited in Fleming, p. 632.

[80] Cited in Fleming, p. 633: Pearl Buck, "What Asians Want," *Christian Century,*
June 27, 1951. Cf. also James Michener in *Life,* June 1951: "Never in our national

But the actual destruction of the Korean peninsula had preceded the Chinese entry. General Emmet (Rosie) O'Donnell, who was head of the Bomber Command in the Far East, put it succinctly: "I would say that the entire, almost the entire Korean peninsula is just a terrible mess. Everything is destroyed. There is nothing standing worthy of the name. . . . Just before the Chinese came in we were grounded. There were no more targets in Korea."[81]

When the Chinese came into the war, General O'Donnell wanted to use the A-bomb on them at once. "They'll understand the lash when it is put to them."[82] The US–UN forces did not get to use the A-bomb, but they did experiment with a new weapon in Korea: napalm (jellied gasoline). The effects of these bombs were described by the Korean correspondent of the BBC.

In front of us a curious figure was standing a little crouched, legs straddled, arms held out from his sides. He had no eyes, and the whole of his body, nearly all of which was visible through tatters of burnt rags, was covered with a hard black crust speckled with yellow pus. . . . He had to stand because he was no longer covered with a skin, but a crust-like crackling which broke easily. . . . I thought of the hundreds of villages reduced to ash which I personally had seen and realized the sort of casualty list which must be mounting up along the Korean front.[83]

After it was all over, *Time* magazine summed the human cost of the war to the Koreans in macabre (but for that magazine, not uncharacteristic) terms:

The war to save Korea has also killed 400,000 [South] Korean civilians, left 500,000 homes wrecked beyond repair. One-fourth of all Koreans are homeless, and 100,000 are orphans; all are underfed. In North Korea, 40 percent of all habitations are destroyed, and of military targets—factories, power plants, etc.—UN airmen agree there is not much left to destroy. . . . South Korea, likewise, is a war-wrecked shell: 75 percent of its mines and textile factories are out of action, two-thirds of its schools unusable.

history have we been so feared and despised. . . . China, India, Burma and Indonesia today condemn us as reactionary and imperialistic. We . . . are ourselves branded as willful aggressors."
[81] I. F. Stone, op. cit., p. 312.
[82] Cited in Fleming, p. 630.
[83] René Cutforth in the Manchester *Guardian,* March 1, 1952. Cited in Marzani, op. cit.

> *But out of disaster has grown a tough army of 16 divisions, and a sense of manhood.*[84]

One cannot even say that the reckless waste of human life caused by the attempt to "liberate" North Korea advanced Western security interests. In fact, the invasion of North Korea cost the West dearly in the power struggle:

> *. . . The final stalemate was a victory for the Communist powers, because Oriental troops had thrown back and held the troops of the greatest power in the West, with full control of the air at its disposal . . .*
>
> *China was built up into a major military power. Her peasant troops out-dug us, fought us on fully equal terms and learned to use every kind of weapon except atomic bombs, including jet planes . . . She was welded closely to Russia, to her great profit in military and industrial development, and to the long term gain of both countries. . . .*[85]

If Western security was hardly advanced by the protracted war, neither was freedom. For those South Koreans who survived to live under the Rhee regime, life was hardly "free" after the struggle was over. Rhee's concern for Korean welfare can be gauged by his persistent opposition to a negotiated settlement which would have meant the ending of bloodshed. His resistance to the truce was broken down only under US pressure and with the assurance that economic and military support would be forthcoming to his government afterwards.

After the war, Rhee visited the United States and pressed home the cause of "liberation." Addressing a joint session of Congress on July 28, 1954, he called on the United States to join him in a war on Red China. In Philadelphia, Rhee urged the United States to overcome its fear of the atomic age and stand up to Russia as the "positive and fearless" leader of the free world.[86]

---

[84] *Time*, June 29, 1953, p. 18. Cf. Fleming, p. 615 n: "Seoul was recaptured on September 30 [1950] and the liberators received a cool welcome because of the damage done to every part of the city by planes and artillery. Army and Marine commanders protested that the damage and heavy casualties were useless. They contended that 'a triumphal entry into the city' was ordered 'as soon as possible and we gave it to them, but it cost us and the Koreans plenty.' " *New York Times*, September 9, 1950.

[85] Fleming, p. 656.

[86] Cited in Fleming, p. 653. *New York Times*, July 29, August 1 and 2, 1954.

Back in Korea, Rhee moved relentlessly against his opponents. On October 14 he proposed to reduce the number of newspapers by 85 percent because they were too critical of his administration. On November 28, he forced through the Assembly an amendment to enable him to remain as president for life. An attempt by his henchman to prevent the clerks from announcing that the proposal was one vote short of the necessary two-thirds majority produced a fist fight, but the life term for Rhee went through.

Rhee's police machine held the people in a firm grip,[87] which he maintained in 1958 and 1959 "by ejecting the growing opposition from parliament and jamming through additional 'laws' to perpetuate his rule."[88] In the spring of 1960, "a wave of popular unrest" sparked by student demonstrations, toppled Rhee from the pedestal where the United States had put him.

The new government of John M. Chang, which introduced some limited but necessary reforms, was soon succeeded by a military junta, after a successful coup d'etat on May 16, 1961. In a Seoul dispatch on January 31, 1963, the veteran correspondent A. M. Rosenthal described a growing struggle for power within the junta, and the effort of United States officials to prevent the outbreak of civil war (in the South). As for the United States' attitude towards the military junta itself, Rosenthal observed:

> *Ever since the coup the United States has been working hard for the success of the junta Government. This was calculated risk. It involved sacrificing the respect of some Koreans, who bitterly accused Washington of financing a dictatorship.*
>
> *But the United States believed that the junta Government, particularly General Park, represented the only available choice for building stability and progress and moving gradually into a relatively free society.*[89] *With*

---

[87] South Korean "justice" under Rhee has been described by William J. Lederer in *A Nation of Sheep*, 1961: "Once in Seoul I was present when a Korean thief was caught stealing a pair of pants from an army truck. Brought before the Korean magistrate, the culprit was called upon to confess. He pleaded innocent. One by one, the magistrate had the thief's fingers broken in an effort to make him confess. He never did. . . . They are a fierce lot, these Koreans" (p. 54).

[88] Fleming, pp. 653–654.

[89] But cf. E. W. Wagner, "Failure in Korea," *Foreign Affairs* (October 1961), p. 133: "The record of the first months of military rule offers little hope that here at last is the kind of leadership South Korea has been crying for. . . . All executive, legislative and judicial powers are lodged in General Parks' Supreme Council for National Reconstruction. Not only the National Assembly but all deliberative bodies,

Communist North Korea within binocular range of United States troops stationed here, the country's stability is a military as well as a political matter.

If such thinking had any possible validity fifteen years before, when the United States Military Government helped Syngman Rhee to form a police state in the South,[90] subsequent history had made this line of reasoning possible only for the self-deceived or the deeply cynical. For years of police state rule had left the country economically as well as politically in ruins.

Despite two and a quarter billion dollars in United States economic grants since 1954, unemployment in 1960 was estimated to be as high as 25 percent of the labor force. Gross national product was less than 2 billion and per capita income well under 100 dollars. Exports averaged 20 million dollars per year. The average farm household, consisting of over six members, worked just two acres of land and 40 percent of farm families had to subsist on one acre or less.[91]

By contrast, the Communists' reconstruction effort since the end of the Korean War had achieved some notable successes:

True, the North Korean authorities publish economic information in a form calculated to impress; but confirmatory evidence from other sources lends credibility to many North Korean claims. In some key areas, such as output of electric power, North Korea has approached the per capita levels of Italy or Japan. Production in all sectors of the economy has surpassed previous totals, in most cases by wide margins, and an unusually rapid pace of economic growth has been attained. The fruits of this advance have been utilized to give the 10 million inhabitants of North Korea a higher standard of living than they have ever known. And as these people have never lived under free institutions as we know them, the harsh features of Communist rule must seem less crucial to them than their material progress.[92]

Indeed, according to the distinguished Cambridge economist,

down to the village level, have been disbanded and all elected officials discharged." Cf. also Reeve, op. cit., pp. 151 et seq. "Administratively the *junta* brought into being a more authoritarian regime than that of Rhee."
[90] Wagner, op. cit., pp. 129–130.
[91] Ibid., pp. 130–131.
[92] Ibid., p. 132.

Professor Joan Robinson, "All the economic miracles of the postwar world are put in the shade by [North Korea's] achievements."[93]

These facts, while relatively unknown in the West, have not been missed by Koreans. Some 70,000 Korean residents in Japan have chosen repatriation to North Korea.[94] Moreover, "all but a fraction of those accepting repatriation to the North originated in the South. The choice they have made, therefore, in a very real sense reflects their judgment as to which half of the divided peninsula offers the better hope for the future."[95]

In a tragic afternote to all the destruction wreaked upon this unhappy land and underscoring the total failure of United States policy there, Professor Wagner concludes, "The Communist threat to South Korea today is the threat of subversion by invidious comparison. In the long run South Koreans will not choose between Washington and Moscow but between Seoul and Pyongyang."[96]

[93] "Korean Miracle," *Monthly Review* (January 1965).
[94] Ibid., p. 128.
[95] Wagner, op. cit., pp. 132–133.
[96] Ibid., p. 135. Wagner is Assistant Professor of Korean studies, Department of Far Eastern Languages, Harvard University. Cf. Joan Robinson op. cit.: ". . . great pains are taken to keep the Southerners in the dark. The demarcation line is manned exclusively by American troops, down to the cleaners, with an empty stretch of territory behind. No southern eye can be allowed a peep into the North. There is no postal connection. *This* wall is not opened at Christmas for divided families to meet."

Seyom Brown

KOREA AND THE BALANCE OF POWER

Tracing American foreign policy from 1945 through the Administration of Lyndon Johnson, Seyom Brown finds in the Korean War an illustration of his thesis that conceptions of the balance of power have been the leitmotiv of American diplomacy. In the years immediately preceding the Korean War, the Truman administration assumed a bipolar conflict with the Soviet Union, which was characterized as an aggressive, expansionist force that had to be,

From Seyom Brown, *The Faces of Power: Constancy and Change in United States Foreign Policy from Truman to Johnson* (New York: Columbia University Press, 1968), pp. 47–62, by permission of the publisher.

in the phrase of George Kennan, "contained." Military policy, in the face of the assumed threat, was set forth largely by a paper issued by the National Security Council—NSC 68. This document urged the expansion of American capabilities for nuclear and conventional war, but the Truman Administration found itself constrained by fiscal considerations and had already decided that the nation was unable to afford the kind of defense the National Security Council advocated. Brown's discussion of the Korean War places it in this military-political context.

1948–1950: Internal Dialogue on the Components of the Balance of Power

> *God knows I am fully aware of the terrific task which this country faces if it is to keep a free economy and a free society. But to . . . deny Marshall the cards to play, when the stakes are as high as they are, would be a grave decision.—James S. Forrestal.*

Kennan's article displayed important premises about Soviet intentions on which there was an emerging consensus among Truman Administration officials. Nor was there any important disagreement with the policy consequences of these premises as broadly formulated by Secretary of State Marshall in a report to the Cabinet in early November 1947. Marshall stated, according to Forrestal's account, "that the objective of our policy from this point on would be the restoration of the balance of power in both Europe and Asia and that *all actions would be viewed in the light of this objective.*"

There was still a significant lack of consensus on the *components* of either Kennan's "counterforce" or the "balance of power" that Marshall wanted "restored." The Administration was divided, broadly, between those who regarded the industrial strength of the United States, based on a sound economy, as the weightiest ingredient in the global balance, and those who regarded the extension of Soviet control over new areas of the globe the most important factor. In the pre-Korean War period, the Bureau of the Budget, the Council of Economic Advisers, and the White House staff tended to stress economic considerations, whereas State and Defense tended to emphasize stopping the Soviets.

But even among those who were most oriented toward a global, geopolitical view of the power rivalry with the Soviet Union there was an important divergency of premises concerning both the components of the balance of power and of the American strategies required to stop Soviet expansion. The divergent points of view in 1947–1948 clustered around Secretary of State Marshall and Secretary of Defense Forrestal.

Marshall's most passionate commitment now was to the success of the European Recovery Program. But he did concede that a militarily strong Western Europe was essential to right the global balance of power and provide the means locally to dissuade the Russians from attempting an easy fait accompli, either by political subversion or military aggression. Western Europe itself could not contain the Soviets in a major war, but it could provide the front line of defense. The United States would have to come to the direct aid of Europe in any such war, but, as in the Second World War, the full weight of American power would be felt in the later stages of the war as mobilization went into high gear. Marshall favored Universal Military Training in the United States to provide the base for such mobilization should it ever be required, and to signal in advance the refusal of the United States to tolerate Soviet aggression; but he did not view Soviet aggression as sufficiently imminent to require a major increment to ready forces-in-being. Even in response to the Soviet provocations around Berlin in the spring of 1948, and the blockade of 1948–1949, Marshall pressed for priority to be given to *European* rearmament. Marshall, of course, was sensitive to the strong political motivations in the White House and Congress for keeping the lid on expenditures, and very likely saw UMT plus European rearmament— neither of which would require any sudden major increases in the US budget—as compatible with continued Congressional financing of the multi-billion dollar project for rebuilding Europe's economy just getting under way.

Secretary of Defense Forrestal gave priority to the rearmanent of the United States as the most effective means of preserving the balance of power against the Soviet Union. To procrastinate on the buildup of an effective United States military posture would be to "deny Marshall the cards to play" in current crisis situations. Strengthening European military capabilities was important, but Forrestal was skeptical of the Europeans' ability to sustain their level of effort on economic reconstruction and simultaneously build the kind of military establishments needed to balance Soviet military power to Europe. In the meantime—he wrote in late 1947—under current budget allocations, reflecting the existing policy of assisting European recovery before American rearmament, we were taking a "calculated risk." That risk involved reliance on the American *strategic* advantage, consisting of: American productive capacity, the predominance of American sea power, and the exclusive possession of the atomic bomb. But the last factor, he warned, would have an "indeterminate" duration. "The years before any possible power can achieve the capabilities to attack us with weapons of mass destruction are our years of opportunity." It was clear that had Forrestal been given his way he would have attached greater urgency to a buildup of a balanced United States military posture, which did not bank too heavily on either the perpetuation of the atomic monopoly or the rapid attainment of a level of recovery in Europe which would allow Europeans to assume the major burden of sustaining the balance on the Continent.[1]

This difference between Marshall and Forrestal over the components of effective international power was in fact resolved in favor of Marshall by the White House and the Bureau of the Budget. Considerations of domestic political economy rather than a systematic analysis of the capabilities needed to carry out the nation's foreign policy commitments seemed to determine the Executive choice to stick with military budgets well below $15 billion a year, until the Korean emergency revised the prevailing priorities.

Actually, a systematic appraisal *was* called for by the President and undertaken by a special State-Defense task force months before the North Korean invasion of South Korea. The Soviet blockade of Berlin during 1948–1949 and the collateral negotiations of the North Atlantic Treaty had focused attention in the State Department and the White House on the limitations of the usable military power at

---

[1] There was yet another consideration that may have weighed heavily with Forrestal. In contrast to the services over which he presided (as the first Secretary of Defense), Forrestal appeared to be more interested in a general increase in the military budget and capabilities rather than the implementation of any particular strategic doctrine. He seemed to regard some of the esoteric strategic debates of the military as responses to low budget ceilings, and the consequent need to convince their political benefactors that security could be had only through the provision of capabilities required by their particular functions. Apart from this specious quality, these debates were a severe source of embarrassment to Forrestal's attempts to achieve harmony within the Defense establishment. Higher budgets would put him in a position to mitigate the intensity of interservice rivalry.

the disposal of the West in case of major conflict in Europe. The Soviet atomic bomb detonation in August 1949, three years ahead of United States intelligence estimates, gave immediacy to alarms Forrestal had been sounding on the temporary nature of our strategic advantage. And the final fall of China to Mao Tse-tung the next month, placing the bulk of the Eurasian heartland under Communist control and raising the specter of a division of the world's population into two halves was suddenly seen by many in the Administration, as it could not be when only hypothetical, as an immense strategic fact of life. The convergence of these events with the need for Truman to say yes or no to an H-bomb program produced a requirement for some kind of coherent doctrine on our military capabilities, just as the withdrawal of the British from Greece in 1947 produced the need for a doctrine on our intentions. Truman's decision in January 1950 to give the green light, tentatively, to the H-bomb program was accompanied by a directive to the Secretaries of State and Defense to make a comprehensive review of United States foreign and defense policies in light of the developments just mentioned.

In the process of preparing the general strategic appraisal called for by Truman a dialogue on the components of the global balance of power, analogous to that conducted between Marshall and Forrestal in the 1947–1948 period, was now reenacted within the State Department between George Kennan and Paul Nitze.

Kennan laid greater stress on the nonmilitary components of the bipolar struggle, and felt that the Soviets had such a great reluctance to become involved in a major war against the United States that the most important fact in the strategic equation was a clear *resolve* by the United States not to tolerate piecemeal opportunistic extensions of Soviet control. Translating this into military terms was difficult, and apparently uncongenial to Kennan. However, he is reported to have urged the organization of mobile, quickly deployable United States task forces which could be rushed to the scene of "brushfire" conflicts and thus confront the Soviets with the choice of desisting from their provocation or engaging the United States in a military clash which might expand to a major war. Kennan's analysis of the Soviets convinced him that when confronted with such a stark choice the Soviets would back down. Kennan thus did not feel that a general rearmament program was necessary. Moreover, rearmament would stimulate further the undesirable focusing of national energies on the cruder means of waging the Cold War, in opposition to flexible and subtler forms of diplomacy and stress on improving the quality of life of the Western nations.

Paul Nitze, who was given responsibilities for effecting greater liaison between State and Defense when Acheson became Secretary of State in January 1949, gave greater weight than did Kennan to the overall balance of military force between the Soviets and the United States. As Director of the Policy Planning Staff in 1950, and chairman of the ad hoc study group which produced the strategic paper requested by the President, Nitze's views were critical in shaping the advanced planning concepts being developed at the time. Kennan retained major influence as State Department Counsellor, and his knowledge of the Soviet Union was influential in the deliberations of the study group. But Nitze was known to have the full support of Secretary Acheson, who was taking the study very seriously. Forrestal was no longer at Defense, and his economy-minded successor, Louis Johnson, was a weak Secretary who provided little support or guidance to Defense Department participants in the study. Any initiative, or major departures in overall strategic planning, then, would be responsive to the momentum generated by Nitze in fulfilling Truman's desire for a new strategic appraisal.

Nitze felt that the nation's military planning was seriously constrained by the strict budgetary limits imposed by the White House and the Bureau of the Budget. In light of the emergence of a Soviet nuclear striking capability, the United States would need not only to improve its massive destructive capabilities (as was contemplated in the H-bomb program), but also to balance the Soviet capabilities for conventional war. These ideas emerged as major premises in NSC-68 (the paper's file number upon referral to the National Security Council).

But they were only a part of a set of premises designed to give coherence to national security policy. For the first time since the war, military planning concepts were tied to an explicit body of assumptions about the political and technological state of the world. On the basis of an analysis of Soviet economic strengths and weaknesses, the study projected that in four years the Soviets would have a nuclear capability sufficient to neutralize the function of the United

States nuclear capability for deterring local wars. Moreover the Soviets would build this capability without any diminution in their local-war capability. Thus, by 1954, if the West did not take significant compensating measures, the balance of military power would have shifted in favor of the Soviets. When this happened economic and technical assistance would be insufficient to contain Soviet expansion.

A challenge to prevailing premises about the US economy was also leveled by the Nitze group. They argued that the nation could well afford to devote 20 percent of the gross national product to national security purposes as compared with the 5 percent then being spent. In budget terms, defense expenditures could, and ought to, rise to possibly as high as $60 billion a year, from the $15 billion then programed. Nitze and his staff economist, Robert Tufts, had an important ally in Leon Keyserling of the President's Council of Economic Advisers. (Keyserling had been consistently urging "expansionist" policies against the views of the Council's chairman Nourse. Nourse had resigned in October 1949, and from then on, first as acting Chairman, and as Chairman from May 1950, Keyserling dominated the Council and was an increasingly persuasive force throughout the Administration.) In retrospect it is not possible to say whether this alliance of Nitze and Acheson at State and Keyserling's Council of Economic Advisers would have been able to move Truman away from his natural economic conservatism and political responsiveness to "welfare" demands, and provide a convincing Presidential rationale for *implementing* NSC-68, had the Korean invasion not taken place in June 1950.

Acheson had begun to lay the groundwork with his talks in February 1950 on the need to create "situations of strength" vis-à-vis the Soviet Union prior to attempting any kind of global settlement (as was then being suggested by Churchill). But as yet these declarations did not go much beyond making the aspiration explicit to wider public audiences. An implementation of the aspiration through a diversion of a larger portion of the nation's resources to affect the global balance of military power was still not Administration policy. Truman understood that such a shift in the allocation of resources would have to rest on popular consent; and the people, he believed, did not yet appreciate the current function of the military balance of power in global diplomacy.

The Communist North Koreans, by suddenly taking advantage of a local disparity of military power on June 24, 1950, finally gave Truman a sufficient basis for asking the people to approve militarily "rational" national security policies worked out by his professional foreign policy advisers.

The Primacy of Balance-of-Power Considerations during the Korean War

Instead of weakening the rest of the world, they [the Communists] have solidified it. They have given a powerful impetus to the military preparations of this country and its associates in and out of the North Atlantic Treaty Organization.—Dean Acheson.

NSC-68 became the conceptual framework on which the rapid expansion of United States armed forces was hung during the first months of the Korean War. Before the war was over military spending had reached a peak of $50 billion a year. The 1,461,000 men in the United States armed forces in June 1950 were more than doubled in two years, with the Army accounting for the largest increase. As compared with 48 Air Force wings in 1950, the Korean Armistice in 1953 left the United States with nearly 100 wings, with another 50 expected to come into the inventory over the coming four-year period. The Navy was floating 671 ships on the eve of hostilities in 1950, and over 1100 by the summer of 1952. But merely from the fact that Administration spokesmen before Congress defended their early Korean War budgets with reference to NSC-68, and from the fact that there was an across-the-board doubling of military capabilities, it cannot be inferred that the original premises advanced by the Nitze group about the emerging balance of power now constituted the doctrinal bases of the Truman Administration's new basic national security policy. The Korean War rapidly began to generate its own priority requirements, and the critical question put by Congressmen to any budget proposal was: how does this help us in Korea?

On the more conceptual military planning level, the Korean War heightened differences rather than produced a consensus. For some the Korean War confirmed the thesis that the Western Alliance needed permanent and large-scale conventional armies to deter the Communists from future aggression. This view was reflected most clearly in the NATO force goals formulated during the Korean War, the high point of aspiration being the February 1952 Lisbon ministerial meeting which set the number of divisions to be ready and/or deployable for a European conflict at ninety-six. But the Korean experience also gave stimulus to advocates of the doctrinal antithesis: namely, that Korea was a model of how *not* to fight a war; that to allow the Communists to engage us in conventional land warfare was to allow them to choose the grounds and weapons most favorable to them; that the superior mode of warfare for the technologically advanced West was strategic, relying mostly upon air power to strike deep at the sources of enemy power with weapons of mass destruction; that the way to preserve the balance of power (as the Soviets built up their strategic capabilities) was not to dissipate our resources in an effort to redress the imbalance in armed manpower, but to enhance our capabilities for strategic warfare. The resolution of these antithetical military doctrinal reactions to the Korean War had to await a change in Administrations.

Yet the Korean War—the way it was fought by the United States, and the force-posture planning decisions made at the time—left a material and institutional legacy of programs in-being not significantly different from those implied in NSC-68. And programs in-being tend to shape fundamental policy premises just as much as, if not more than, premises tend to shape programs. The perpetuation of existing programs often becomes a psychological, no less than bread-and-butter, commitment for those with the responsibility for their administration. The fact of the matter was that the Korean War *institutionalized* a set of operational (though not necessarily intellectually held) premises:

A. The Soviet Union would resort to military expansion if it were not checked by visible countervailing military power.
B. Local imbalances of military power which favored the Soviets or a Soviet satellite would lead to further "Koreas."
C. The most appetizing local imbalance to the Soviets was in Central Europe.
D. The global balance of power would shift in favor of the Soviets

if they were able to swallow the rest of Central Europe, namely West Germany and Austria. No other area on the periphery of the Communist world, except for the Greco-Turkish flanks (which were already being buttressed) had such a critical function for the balance of power. The next most critical area on the Soviet periphery was Japan.

E. But while attending to the power ratios focused on the prime military-industrial regions, we must not neglect local imbalances in secondary and tertiary areas. The capability and clearly communicated will to defend whatever area the Communist powers might choose to attack, regardless of its intrinsic geopolitical weight in the overall balance, was necessary to prevent the Communists from picking and choosing easy targets for blackmail and aggression. And a number of small territorial grabs *could* add up to a critical alteration of the global balance. Moreover, our failure to defend one area would demoralize nationals in other such localities in their will to resist the Communists. Even in Western Europe people would wonder under what circumstances we might consider them dispensable.

Similar premises, to be sure, antedated the Korean War. But their existence, even in the person, say, of Secretary of State Acheson, did not make them the basis of government policy. It took the Korean conflict to give "validity" to these premises—not in the sense of proving their correctness, but in making them the assumptions on which important wartime and planning decisions were reached.

The overriding fear in the White House was not simply that the loss of the Korean peninsula would encourage the Soviets to embark on further aggressions. Rather, it was that the Soviets were embarked, *now,* on some pattern of military aggression to pin down the resources of the United States in peripheral battles, and then to move, when the right moment arrived, virtually unopposed into Western Europe.

In his *Memoirs* Truman divulges how the strategic (United States-Soviet) situation limited his flexibility in the tactical (Korean) campaign. It was his intention, Truman recalls, to take all necessary measures to push the North Koreans back behind the 38th Parallel. But he was unwilling to commit the United States so deeply in Korea that we would not have the resources to handle other situations. The strategic prize was Western Europe, with its skilled manpower and industrial infrastructure. Truman was convinced that Europe was still at the center of the Soviet design for world domination, and he, for one, was not going to allow our attention to be diverted from this dominant feature of the global power contest.

When the Communist Chinese armies intervened, the prospect of becoming bogged down in a huge war in Asia became more immediate, particularly in light of pressures from General MacArthur to attack the Communist staging bases in Manchuria, even at the risk of a general war with China. The Administration's view was articulated by Dean Acheson at a November 28, 1950 meeting of the National Security Council. The Soviet Union was behind every one of the Chinese Communist and North Korean moves, said the Secretary of State. We were in competition with the Soviets all around the globe. Thus Korea was a world matter, not merely a regional matter. If we were to lose sight of this fact, he warned, and allowed Russia to trap us on the Asian mainland, we would risk sinking into a bottomless pit.

The American Secretary of State presented a similar case to the British a few weeks later during the President's Washington conferences with Prime Minister Attlee. The central enemy was not China, stressed Acheson, but the Soviet Union. The aggression by the North Koreans was not a local, spontaneous maneuver. It was a part of the larger Communist design to get us preoccupied in Asia so the Russians could have a free hand in Europe. We must not and would not distort our global priorities.

This Europe-first emphasis was of course congenial to the British, who were, if anything, afraid that the United States might have already become overcommitted to an increasingly costly Asian conflict, and might engage in rash action—such as nuclear bombardment of China. Attlee kept on raising reservations about the value of attempting to defend Formosa. Acheson thereupon was forced to refine the Europe-first emphasis, by pointing to strategic interdependencies among the various forward positions then being sustained. He explained to the British leaders that, apart from how we might feel about Chiang Kai-shek, we could not, for geopolitical reasons, allow Formosa to fall into Communist hands. The fall of Formosa would raise severe problems for us in Japan and in the Philippines, contended Acheson; and these countries, being the sites of our bases for conducting operations in the theatre, had become essential to our survival as a Pacific power.

General Marshall, present during one of these exchanges, added his weight to the strategic evaluation of Formosa: it was of no particular strategic importance in our hands, but it would be of disastrous importance if it were held by an enemy.

But if hard choices did have to be made in Asia, there was little doubt that priority would have to be accorded the defense of Japan. Such an eventuality was in the minds of the Joint Chiefs during the bleakest days following the Chinese intervention. In the third week of December 1950 they suggested to Truman that consideration ought to be given to ways of withdrawing from Korea "with honor" in order to protect Japan.

The Administration's view of the global geopolitical interests and risks involved in the Korean struggle ran head on with General MacArthur's view that decisive military victory in the theatre of operations was of overriding importance. But this very intensity of the disagreement between Truman and MacArthur had the effect of producing within the Administration a greater self-awareness of its own objectives and the policies it deemed necessary to implement them.

The much-quoted testimony of General Bradley (to extend the fighting to the mainland of Asia would "involve us in the wrong war, at the wrong place, at the wrong time, and with the wrong enemy") capsules the operational effects on the prosecution of the war itself of the premise that the Soviets really had their military sights focused on Western Europe. The effects on future-oriented military planning and alliance diplomacy were no less significant. As Truman telegraphed MacArthur near the final stages of their controversy: "In reaching a final decision about Korea, I shall have to give constant thought to the main threat from the Soviet Union and the need for a rapid expansion of our armed forces to meet this great danger."

The Europe-oriented consequences of these premises were visible in the rapid efforts to transform NATO from a security guaranty pact into an international regional theatre army, most heavily deployed at the spot of critical vulnerability in the global balance: the Central European front. This in turn meant that our European diplomacy was to be oriented toward gaining acceptance from the North Atlantic Alliance partners of the rearmament of West Germany. And the rearmament of West Germany, in its turn, would require—largely to reassure the French—a United States commitment to the principle of supranational (or "integrated") commands, in which the German units would be unable to take independent action.

Although the stimulus of the Korean crisis was short-lived, and, by late 1951 the Europeans returned to their pre-1950 emphasis on economic recovery, an institutional framework was created for redressing the Central European balance in a future conflict. A Supreme Commander over allied forces was created, and provided with a large international (NATO) staff and planning organization, for the purpose of implementing NATO directives on force posture and strategy. A major responsibility was accorded to Germany for providing troops for a "forward defense" under a multination command directly subordinate to the Supreme Allied Commander (Eisenhower). An American military presence—not just bases for the strategic arm, but an overseas army in the forward defense apparatus—was accepted by United States planners as necessary for the indefinite future. (There was some ambiguity with respect to the function and eventual size of these overseas United States deployments, however. Both General Eisenhower and Secretary of Defense Marshall, in urging Congressional authorization for an additional four divisions for Europe in 1951, attempted to delimit their function as largely that of a catalyst for European contributions to a forward ground defense force, in which the Europeans were expected to assume the major burden.)

Moreover, the United States view of the altered scale of priorities, now giving first place to the military components of the power balance, was made explicit to recipients of Marshall Plan assistance. Further economic assistance was to be made contingent upon the alliance partner's conscientious attempt to fulfill its NATO rearmament obligations. By 1951, the European Recovery program was formally subordinated to "security" considerations under the omnibus Mutual Security Act.

The *way* the United States fought the Korean War—particularly our willingness to allow sanctuary status to Communist China even after she became an active belligerent—did confirm and sharpen the pre-existing official premise that mainland Asia was a secondary weight in the balance of global power as compared with Western

Europe. But the fact that we were willing to fight a high-cost war to keep South Korea out of Communist hands also gave impetus to the emerging realization that the power contest could be won or lost in the secondary theatres when there was a stalemate in the primary theatres.

The Korean War thus marked a globalization of containment in terms of operational commitments as well as rhetoric. The United States finally "intervened" physically in the Chinese Civil War by interposing the Seventh Fleet between Mao Tse-tung's forces and Chiang's last island fortresses. Despite our anticolonial protestations, we now put our money behind the French efforts to suppress the Ho Chi Minh Communist-nationalist insurgency in Indochina. And although the United States *formally* intervened in Korea under a United Nations mandate (by virtue of the absence of the Soviet delegate from the Security Council at the time the votes were taken), henceforth our plans and public commitments and material undertakings would no longer convey to our global adversaries the impression that we would hestitate to act unilaterally. As with Europe, Article 51 (the self-defense provision) of the UN Charter now became the operative legal instrumentality of our "collective security" arrangements in the secondary as well as the primary theatres.

The globalization of containment—the notion that practically all pieces of territory now had significant, if not decisive, weight in the power balance, that the reputation for being willing to defend each piece was a critical ingredient of our maintenance of allies and deterrence of enemies—rested on solid bipartisan support. The Republican challenge was not to these fundamental assumptions. Rather, it was a charge that the Truman Administration was first of all too late and then too restrained in countering the threat of communism in Asia.

The forum for the partisan rallying was the 1951 Senate investigation of Truman's recall of General MacArthur from his command. It was here, for the first time, that the bipartisan Europe-first policy was made the subject of a great debate between the two parties. It was only now that Secretary of State Acheson's January 1950 statement omitting South Korea from our "defense perimeter" in the western Pacific was held up to scorn by the opposition (who neglected to note that General MacArthur traced a similar line in March 1949), the charge being that Acheson's statement constituted an "invitation" to Stalin to attack. It was now that it became a Republican article of party faith that the Truman Administration, out of nearsightedness as to the ultimate power stakes involved, "lost" China to the Communists.

But this breakdown in the domestic consensus over where the stakes in the global power balance lay was a *retrospective* cleavage. In 1948 no prominent United States politician or China expert rose to challenge Secretary of State Marshall's assessment that:

> China does not itself possess the raw material and industrial resources which would enable it to become a first-class military power within the foreseeable future. The country is at present in the midst of a social and political revolution. Until this revolution is completed—and it will take a long time—there is no prospect that sufficient stability and order can be established to permit China's early development into a strong state.

Nor had the critics of the Truman Administration's China policies been willing to go so far as to support United States *combat* operations against Mao in 1948 and 1949 when it became clear that military assistance alone would not suffice. Only marginal increments in aid were offered by Congressmen in the China Aid Act of 1948. The statement of Representative Walter Judd (one of Chiang's staunchest supporters) was typical: "Not for one moment has anyone contemplated sending a single combat soldier in. . . . So it is important to make clear when we speak of military aid . . . it is supplies, training, and advice, nothing further."

This had been the period when our rapid postwar military demobilization was in high gear. It was the same atmosphere that led Truman to defer approval of the NSC-68 recommendations, even though he appreciated their strategic soundness.

When the Korean War allowed Republicans and Democrats alike to loosen the purse strings a bit for military rearmament, many in the opposition party, now urging a decisive victory in Korea, and willing to follow MacArthur into a general war with China, were ready to claim superior wisdom from having been Mao-haters since the middle 1940s. This was virtue through hindsight only. Their new charges that the Truman Administration had been overly feeble in its approach to the China problem a few years back were regarded by Administration policy-makers as gratuitous. These charges conveniently overlooked the fact that the critics themselves cooperated in the enfeeblement process. General Marshall later recalled how he was pressed ad nauseam in the early postwar period to give the Communists hell. ". . . I am a soldier and know something about the ability to give hell," he told a Pentagon audience. "At that time, my facilities for giving them hell . . . was [sic] 1⅓ divisions over the entire United States. That's quite a proposition when you deal with somebody with over 260 and you have 1⅓."

Significantly, Marshall did not count among his hell-giving facilities the atomic bomb. If there was to be a military contest with the Chinese Communists, the bomb apparently was of little military utility, nor evidently could it be used as a threat to forestall counter-intervention by the Soviets. This was also a part of the atmosphere of the times—especially with respect to any official contemplation in public of its use against Asians so soon after Hiroshima and Nagasaki.

However, the Korean War also eroded this constraint on United States calculations of usable power in conflict situations. Truman did not unequivocally rule out the use of the bomb. And the Eisenhower Administration went further in actually hinting that it would have to resort to nuclear weapons if the war resumed due to a breakdown in peace negotiations.

If the NSC-68 planners had their way, Korea would have marked the transition to a new era of higher peacetime military budgets, aimed centrally at rectifying local imbalances of power between the Communist and non-Communist nations. The Eisenhower Administration also felt it was beholden to a popular mandate against further Koreas. And alterations in the existing local military imbalances would be an essential requisite for the maintenance of our global commitments and preventing Soviet miscalculations such as Korea. But the plans of the Truman Administration for rearmament were seen to be incompatible with the conventional Republican philosophy of reduced government expenditures.

The most appropriate kind of military power for implementing our now globalized "containment" policy was to remain the primary subject of policy-level debate. But for at least another ten years, the policy itself (however much the Republicans disliked associating themselves with the word), and the premise that an advantageous military balance of power was its essential prerequisite, was taken as fact in official Washington.

The weight of the non-Communist nations in the global balance of power was to be defined, predominantly, as the product of three variables: United States military forces-in-being, United States industrial-economic strength, and the indigenous military forces-in-being of allies of the United States. Significantly, the *economic* strength of other non-Communist nations was not to be directly taken into account, in terms of requiring significant outlays by the United States. To the extent that balance-of-power considerations would suppress other considerations in United States foreign policy, policies whose rationale was the socioeconomic development of other nations would receive only marginal attention by top United States decision-makers.

Adam B. Ulam

WASHINGTON, MOSCOW, AND THE KOREAN WAR

Writing with the double detachment of a European-born scholar and an analyst with the advantage of somewhat more hindsight than previous commentators on the Korean War, Adam B. Ulam attempts to set forth the assumptions, decisions, calculations and miscalculations of both the USSR and the United States as these two superpowers worked out their rivalry in the postwar period.

The relative clarity with which American interests and commitments were defined in Europe contrasted with the hopeless confusion in which both friends and protagonists of the United States foundered when it came to deciding what America would or could do in Asia. This relative clarity on Europe, let us note, was due to the *tacit*

From *The Rivals: America and Russia Since World War II* by Adam B. Ulam, pp. 166–190. Copyright © 1971 by Alan B. Ulam. Reprinted by permission of the Viking Press, Inc.

acknowledgment, much as the phrase would never pass the mouths of the policy-makers, that Europe was now divided into spheres of influence: while the United States could not do anything about Poland, the USSR would not dare to intrude into the West. But in Asia there was this weird jumble of crumbling imperial positions, Communists, nationalists, corruption, American and Soviet bases, all of which seemed to defy any rational approach. One may forgive America's spokesmen for stressing the complexity of the situation and the impossibility of defining America's response to *every* threatening contingency. What could be the US attitude toward an India-Pakistan war? What should the United States do if *Trotskyite* Communists should seize Burma or Ceylon? (For some strange reason this exotic ideological offshoot has flourished in those countries!) But one is much harder pressed to excuse Acheson hailing this appalling and dangerous situation as a hopeful start of a new era: "I believe that there is a new day which has dawned in Asia. It is a day in which the Asian people are on their own, and know it, and intend to continue on their own." And he had just finished saying that Asia's largest country had become a dependency of the Soviet Union!

From Moscow, needless to say, the Asian picture looked quite different. Perhaps it was in view of his own experiences with Asian Communists and nationalist potentates in the 1920s that Stalin in his last years adopted a rather conservative and cautious attitude on the chances and potential benefits of victory of communism in various Asian countries. The prospect of the Red East did not fascinate him as it had Lenin and Trotsky: in each case the question was, what will it be worth to the Soviet Union? To give Acheson his due, there were some indications that the Russians expected the regimes in Manchuria and Sinkiang to be autonomous and tried to deal with them directly. It was publicly announced in Moscow at the time of the Sino-Soviet negotiations in 1949–1950 that representatives of those provinces joined them, a needless humiliation one would think to Mao and his friends and one they would not forget. That Stalin made demands on China of a "colonial nature," as Khrushchev was to say, is thus perfectly obvious. Yet in the very same negotiations, the Russians had to promise to release the large industrial complex of the Manchurian Railway, Port Arthur, and Dairen from their greedy grasp. As to the Communist guerrillas fighting in Malaya, the Philippines, etc.,

Moscow saw their main value in engaging and weakening the West's resources. In January, 1950, the USSR acknowledged Ho Chi Minh in Vietnam. This was undoubtedly prompted by the Chinese, who had done so some days *before* Moscow's action. But a continued civil war in Indochina would tie down the bulk of France's best troops. While much of French public opinion would be outraged, an effective Western military force would be still further delayed.

The momentous fact of the passing of the British Empire in India in 1947 created little excitement in the USSR. Anything marking and contributing to the decline of British power, of the British willingness to hold, at least, to the shadow of their former imperial position, was of course very welcome. But the two successor states were viewed as still within the British sphere. Stalin's Russia did not reciprocate the warm feelings some Congress leaders felt toward her, and their ideological antecedents made the Soviets dislike and distrust Gandhi. For the moment, the Soviets were only too content to leave to the United States the task of nudging the colonial powers to grant independence to their colonial possessions. The US attitude was decisive in the Dutch acquiescing in the loss of their Indonesian possessions and in the sequence of events leading to the British withdrawal from Palestine and to the birth of Israel. For American public opinion and government held, to quote Acheson, that the old relationships between East and West "at their worst were exploitation . . . at their best were paternalism." Here again what seemed then and sometimes still does seem harmless and decorous rhetoric was to cost the American people dearly.

Soviet fears and interests were centered on Europe. There, what the Russians believed to be the key part of the American plot was visibly evolving, to be sure with agonizing slowness. In September 1950, the three Western powers decided to revise the Occupation Statute of Germany and opened the way for eventual West German participation in the NATO defense force. The Federal Republic had been fully launched: it now exhibited political stability, its two major parties were firmly pro-Western, and it had made economic progress and become a major industrial power. Compared with it, the German Democratic Republic was an anemic child. East Germans, especially those in the most sought-after occupations and in their most productive years, were "voting with their feet"[1] by leaving the oppressed and impoverished zone for the West.

From the Soviet viewpoint, then, the fall of 1949 to the spring of 1950 was thus a period of mounting if still not imminent peril. The Russians had just exploded their first atom bomb, thus jostling the Americans out of their complacency. The main danger was still thought to be that of an indirect American response, of a greatly speeded and intensified effort to build a NATO force. Leaders of the main Communist parties in the West were made to declare that in the case of war with the USSR, they and their followers would oppose the governments of their own countries. This was thought in Moscow as bound to inhibit the willingness of the French and Italian governments to enter upon a massive military buildup and to make Washington think twice about the advisability and expense of equipping their forces. The French and Italian Communist parties accounted for between 20 and 30 percent of their respective electorates. Presumably one in four recruits in the French and Italian armies would be a Communist sympathizer. Thus one had to ponder the risk that any vigorous effort to arm Italy and France might incur the risk of civil war.

In 1949, a vast peace movement was also launched to which the European Communist parties were told to devote most of their energies. This worldwide propaganda campaign culminated in the Stockholm Peace Appeal, which demanded "unconditional prohibition of the atomic weapon as a weapon of aggression," and was subsequently signed, according to the managers of the campaign, by more than 500 million people.

All those steps proceeded logically from the conclusion the Soviets had reached more than two years before: that both the Marshall Plan and NATO were instruments for indirect aggression against the Soviet Union, for abetting and helping "wars of liberation" in Russia's European satellites. The average State Department official no doubt simply prayed for a quiet life free from persistent crises erupting suddenly all over the world; certainly the most bumptious American officials still thought in defensive terms, forestalling or reacting to

[1] The phrase used before the November, 1917, Revolution about Russian soldiers who were deserting *en masse*.

Soviet moves. Typical of them was Secretary of Defense Louis Johnson, who wanted Joe Stalin to know that if he started something at
four o'clock, America's power would be on the job at five. (He thus
joined illustrious company. Some of its members include the French
minister of war who in 1870 announced that his country was entering
the war with Prussia with a light heart; Neville Chamberlain who
thought aloud in April 1940 that Herr Hitler had missed the bus; and
Walt Rostow, who expressed his belief in 1967 that the lesson of
American intervention in Vietnam would make the Communists for-
swear "wars of national liberation.")

But the Soviets were not fooled by such rhetoric. In various purge
trials in East Europe between 1949 and 1952, the scenario of Soviet
fears and American villainy was painted in lurid colors: through their
Zionist agents and Titoist allies, the American ruling circles were
preparing uprisings against local governments, and new Yugoslavias.
Those were the plots to which the accused, in some cases until quite
recently the highest officials of Communist parties and governments,
were compelled to confess before being sent to the gallows. Behind
such fantasies there was a real fear of various contingencies the
USSR might have to face: the spread of Titoism to Bulgaria or Hun-
gary; an anti-Communist plot engulfing Czechoslovakia and proving
too strong for the local Communists. The Red Army stood ready to
intervene, but what if the United States, with its atomic superiority
and with NATO forces no longer merely on paper, declared the intervention an act of war?

European fears also prompted a basic re-examination of policy
on Asia. The Chinese Communists became, not for the first or last
time, beneficiaries of Soviet fears about what the Americans might
do. The treatment accorded to the Chinese Communist delegation
when it reached Moscow in December 1949 still eloquently testified
to China's subordinate status: apart from the matter of separate
Sinkiang and Manchurian delegations, which stayed on in Moscow
for some time after their Chinese superiors left, Mao himself, notwith-
standing the multitude of problems he faced at home (especially after
so recent a victory), was made to spend two months in Russia, something which could not be of his own preference. For all such galling
details, the Chinese did obtain a number of concessions and a small
loan. Beginning with the new year, Soviet references to their Chinese

allies grew warmer and more respectful. China was obviously treated differently than the small Communist states of Eastern Europe, and obvious as this might seem to us, it was a marked departure for the Soviets.

The Sino-Soviet alliance was finally signed on February 14, and Mao was free to set out on his long journey home, which he did prudently by train.[2] The treaty spelled out clearly the focus of Soviet fears insofar as Asia was concerned. It pledged mutual assistance "in the event of one of the High contracting Parties being attacked by Japan or States allied with it and thus being involved in a state of war." Curious language which could not have been of great assurance and comfort to the Chinese. The most obvious danger facing *them* was that of Chiang's launching, with American help, an attack upon the mainland from the islands of Formosa and Hainan (then still in his hands) and American air and naval units bombing Chinese cities. That would not have been an attack by Japan or technically a state of war and would not have required Stalin to come to Mao's help. The danger to the Soviet Far East, on the other hand, could come only from a rearmed Japan instigated by the United States to attack Vladivostok and Sakhalin. This curious disparity in obligations assumed by the two allies again seems to have passed unnoticed in Washington.

Everything then seems to indicate that Moscow expected that the American response to the Communist conquest of China would be an abrupt reversal of the policy toward Japan. Nothing of the kind happened. In view of this American equanimity over major setbacks to their position in Asia, it must have occurred to some ingenious minds in Moscow that the Americans could be pushed still further. The logical place was Korea.

What could the Russians have hoped to accomplish by allowing— indeed if not ordering—their North Korean vassals to attack? It is still very difficult to answer this question. The likeliest explanation is that additional evidence of America's inability to protect its friends and clients in Asia was thought to be a good lesson for Japan. There the Communists late in 1949 increased their militant and disruptive tactics against American occupation. The fall of still another Asian

[2] He had not hesitated, during his abortive negotiations with Chiang, to entrust himself to American-piloted aircraft.

country would have a profound psychological effect even on non-Communist Japanese. Perhaps the Americans would feel constrained to withdraw their forces, sign a peace treaty which would leave Japan defenseless. A Communist Japan would offset the power of Communist China, thus enabling Russia to play the classical balance-of-power role in the Far East. Or conversely, the Americans would desperately cling to Japan. This would mean a considerable increase in their military forces there, which in turn would force the Americans to re-examine their military commitments in Europe

It would also make Mao think twice about defying the USSR. In the Sino-Soviet treaty, Moscow promised to release Port Arthur and its properties in Manchuria by the time the Japanese peace treaty was signed, but in no case later than 1952. The latter date was certainly inserted at Mao's insistence, for he could not reasonably hope to live to see the day when the United States and the USSR would agree on a treaty short of the United States packing up and leaving Japan. By the same token, the Russians undoubtedly counted on something happening before 1952 which would make the Chinese Communists appreciate the presence of Soviet soldiers on their soil.

The American reaction to the North Koreans' invasion of South Korea on June 25 must have been one of the greatest surprises of Stalin's life. Having acquiesced in the loss of China, these unpredictable people now balked at the loss of a territory they themselves had characterized as unimportant to their political and strategic interests. The Soviet Union was completely unprepared for this: had there been an inkling of it, the Soviet delegate would not have boycotted the Security Council since January (on the grounds that Communist China should be seated there), and Moscow would have been ready with diplomatic notes and propaganda campaigns about South Koreans invading the North, etc. Between June 27 and July 3, the news from Korea was tucked on the back pages of the Soviet press while the Kremlin obviously meditated over what to do. It was not until a week after the Security Council's action and Truman's ordering armed help to South Korea that the Russians recovered their poise and began to denounce the United States in their usual workmanlike fashion.

There is a strong presumption that the Soviets must have been tempted to call off the whole thing. This would have been relatively easy: having chastised the "invaders," the North would virtuously return where they came from. From this temptation the Soviets were probably rescued by the perceptible apprehension and disarray which lay behind the seemingly resolute American and UN action.

In the first place, the Americans were utterly unprepared. The mistress of the seas and air did not have so much as one combat-ready division to throw immediately into action, and the unprepared units taken from pleasant occupation duty in Japan did not appear capable of stemming the North Korean tide. It was not Stalin but Louis Johnson who had to eat crow and make his exit from the Administration and public life.

Two other factors were of greater importance. No sane person could doubt the ultimate Soviet responsibility for the attack.[3] But the first American move vis-à-vis the Russians was so expressive of Washington's fears of an all-out war that it relieved the Soviets of any apprehension of an immediate confrontation. The American "note of record," so labeled to avoid any implication of an ultimatum, asked Moscow to disavow its responsibility for the aggression. The Russians, needless to say, were glad to oblige. It also asked them to use their influence with the North Koreans to persuade them to stop the invasion. Moscow gravely declared this was beyond its powers and would constitute meddling in the internal affairs of a sovereign state.

The Soviet rejoinder of June 29 was mild and polite by the usual standard of Soviet behavior on such occasions: no talk about "responsibility of the imperialist circles" and "incalculable consequences" which might follow from unleashing aggression.

The other, probably decisive, factor which made the Russians go on with the enterprise was Truman's order for the Seventh Fleet to quarantine Formosa, i.e., to bar any invasion from the mainland or in reverse any attack from the island on the Chinese Communists.

No reason of logic or policy could justify that decision as being in any sense connected with the need to save South Korea. On the contrary, if one assumed that the Chinese were somehow responsible

---

[3] Thus it would be superfluous to discuss the contention that the North Koreans attacked without explicit Soviet permission or orders, and absurd to deal seriously with the charge that Syngman Rhee's government was responsible, as claimed by official Communist sources.

for the North Korean actions then the quarantine increased the chances of their armed intervention in the peninsula. Their best armies were being assembled for the invasion of Formosa; frustrated in that, they would be able to shift to the borders of North Korea. Also and gratuitously, the Seventh Fleet was now protecting them from any forays from the island.

But quite apart from such reflections, there was no reason for the assumption that the responsibility for the June 25 attack rested in Peking. The relations between the Chinese Communists and North Koreans were known to be strained. The main figures in the North Korean regime were clearly Soviet creatures. And it was not until August that an official representative of Communist China arrived to open diplomatic relations with its Communist neighbor. In the summer of 1950, Peking's main objective was to consolidate its rule on the mainland and to conquer Formosa and Tibet. They could not have wished for any major diversion or adventure *at that time* which would interfere with their most urgent tasks.

The real reasons for the strange decision must be sought in the complexities of American domestic politics. Five months earlier, Senator Joseph McCarthy had made his dramatic entrance into world history by declaring that the State Department was teeming with Communist agents.[4]

The hue and cry was on. To a large proportion of the American public, the vicissitudes of American foreign policy during and following World War II were now explained in terms of treason on the part of highly placed officials within the State Department. But prior to the Korean War, this campaign had not constituted a very serious challenge to American foreign policy and its bipartisan underpinnings, although to the occasional shouts of "treason" were joined more serious accusations about blindness of American policies, especially in Asia. It was a real tragedy that following the outbreak of the war the two were to become merged, and that serious critics such as Senator Taft could not resist the temptation of tolerating and profiting from the irresponsible forays of figures like McCarthy and Sena-

---

[4] Their exact number as given in McCarthy's celebrated speech in Wheeling, West Virginia, in February was to be variously remembered, some adducing the figure to be 57, others, 205. But whatever the number, they were "card-carrying" members of the party. Someone should have told the Senator that it was a capital offense for Soviet spies to advertise their political affiliation.

tor Jenner. Instead of a rational reappraisal of America's policy in
Asia, similar to one which in the case of Europe had led to the Truman Doctrine and the Marshall Plan, there was now an emotional
outcry against the country's foreign policy as a whole. Instead of a
a search for and removal of those who had proved incompetent and
naïve, there was a frenzied chase after the wicked and the treason-
ous. Again one finds a melancholy parallel to the debate on Vietnam
in the late 1960s. Here, too, those who started a rational inquest
could not refrain, when dismayed by the casualty lists and a frustrating war, from blaming the moral depravity rather than the intellectual
shortcomings of the policy-makers. A democracy forgets quickly.
But does it ever learn?

When the American policy-makers had to decide what to do about
the invasion, the shape of the things to come—the fury of the electorate at being thrust into a confusing and distant war—was already
discernible. It was also perceived dimly that somehow all the Asian
elements were connected. The assumption of the China White Paper
of less than a year before that the United States could and should
await the working out of the forces of history had just collapsed. The
American people who would be fighting Communists over South
Korea could not be expected to continue to tolerate the explanation
that a *complete* victory of Chinese Communists was of no importance. There was need, it was confusedly felt, for a move against the
Chinese Communists, but one which was not likely to bring on an
American military confrontation with them.

Thus in the course of a few hours' conferences in the National
Security Council on June 25 and 26, the course of American policy
in Asia was drastically changed. The President decided also to expand American help to the French in Indochina and to increase
American forces in the Philippines.

Historically, the decision on Formosa, thrown in largely for complex domestic reasons, came both to overshadow the one on Korea
and to transform the character of the Korean conflict itself. On
January 5, President Truman had declared that the United States
would not provide military aid or advice to the Chinese forces on
Formosa and that it would not interfere in the civil conflict in China.
Now on June 27, in his quarantine order, he declared that the occupation of Formosa by "Communist forces would be a direct threat

to the security of the Pacific area and to the US forces performing their lawful and necessary functions in that area."[5] It would be foolish to argue that without the American move on Formosa, the Chinese Communists' attitude toward the United States would have been one of friendship and gratitude. But by thus interposing American power between Peking and Formosa and denying the Communists a try at the consummation of their victory, Washington gave them a greater stake in the Korean conflict than they had had before, and by the same token the Russians could now, so to speak, sit back and relax.

Yet the Russians could not afford to be entirely complacent. The Americans had surprised once; they might surprise again. The Soviet note of July 4 denounced the American intervention in strong terms but contained no hint of a Soviet counteraction; instead, it called on the Security Council to procure an immediate American withdrawal. The American desk of the Soviet Foreign Ministry distinguished itself in the preparation of the note by its keen historical sense: "The Soviet Government holds that the Koreans have the same right to arrange at their own discretion their internal national affairs in the sphere of uniting South and North Korea into a single national state as the North Americans had in the 'sixties of the last century when they united the South and the North of America into a single national state."[6] But Stalin did not rest content with this appeal to Civil War buffs, and few Americans were ready to identify Kim Il-Sung with Lincoln and Syngman Rhee with Jefferson Davis. It was in the United Nations that the Soviets could find more fruitful ground for their appeals for moderation and restraint.

The fact that the American counterintervention had official blessing from that organization was a handicap as well as an advantage for Truman. As the latter it helped rally public opinion at home and in the first instance was undoubtedly a propaganda asset. But the actual aid in fighting furnished by other UN members was of symbolic rather than quantitatively significant value. And it did not take much foresight to predict that the original resolution and virtual unanimity of the UN in supporting the American actions would not be long-lasting. Very soon India recalled that in view of her superior virtue she was to be a bridge between the East and West rather than take

5 *Documents on International Affairs,* 1949–1950, p. 632.
6 Ibid., p. 654.

sides. Britain's Labour government could not conceal its apprehensions about Douglas MacArthur. Europeans in general reflected unhappily about the US preoccupation in Asia and possible repercussions on Western Europe. For the Third World members of the UN, support for a Western, thus basically imperialist, power ran against the grain. And thus, after the initial exhilaration that the UN because of the Americans was proving effective, everybody began reverting (to be sure slowly and rather shamefacedly) to traditional postures.

Apart from the diplomatic and military complexities of the situation, there was another decisive factor in the Korean drama. This was the personality of General MacArthur. To his detractors, MacArthur appeared as the very embodiment of militaristic megalomania, a man who for all his great gifts was a constant threat to the constitutional concept of civilian supremacy. To his admirers, he has remained a unique man of destiny, the tragedy of whose life really was that of America, which, having scorned his advice, was bound to lose Asia and perhaps more to communism.

Both judgments ignore one trait of the General, which, while it contributed to his greatness as a man and military leader, handicapped him as a statesman. This was his strong emotionalism, which tended to make him concentrate his drive and dedication on the task at hand, and while often this was responsible for his great successes, it made him oblivious of the broader setting of world politics. Even the most thoroughgoing pacifist could not have thrown himself so earnestly into the task of building a new Japan, of transforming that country's society, even the nation's psychology, in the direction of peaceful and democratic pursuits. By the same token, he lacked that dash of cynicism and calculation which in this sinful world remain as necessary ingredients of statesmanship.

With greatly insufficient forces at his disposal, MacArthur was given the task of first stemming and then reversing the North Korean advance. Few generals in his position in June 1950 would have acquiesced in having troops from their command committed to such a seemingly hopeless venture, let alone have recommended it, as he did. In September, after some near desperate moments, MacArthur, by a brilliant and most dangerous maneuver, landed troops at Inchon, far behind the North Korean lines, and soon the rout of the invader was on.

In the meantime, MacArthur had paid a visit to Formosa. From his "quarantined" island, Chiang on August 1 issued a statement that "the foundations were thus laid for a joint defense of Formosa and for Sino-American military cooperation." This action of MacArthur's created both surprise and dismay in Washington. As Acheson says revealingly, "explicit orders then went to him emphasizing the limits of our policy regarding Formosa, and Harriman followed to enforce them."[7] If MacArthur's trip was unauthorized, then one must still wonder at the disarray of the Administration which, having ordered a quarantine, failed for more than a month to explain to the general commanding US and UN forces in actual combat in Korea what were "the limits of our policy regarding Formosa." MacArthur then compounded his error by issuing a grandiloquent statement stressing the importance of Formosa, which was published and later repudiated by the President and at his order withdrawn by MacArthur.

A remarkable document submitted to the UN on August 25 purportedly defined the US position on Formosa. Considerations of space forbid a full reproduction, but a few excerpts must be quoted:

> *The US has not encroached on the territory of China. . . . The action of the US in regard to Formosa was taken at a time when that island was the scene of conflict with the mainland. More serious conflict was threatened by the public declaration of the Chinese Communist authorities. . . . Formosa is now in peace and will remain so unless someone resorts to force. . . . The actual status of the island is that it is territory taken from Japan by the victory of the Allied Forces in the Pacific. . . . Its legal status cannot be fixed until there is international action to determine its future. The Chinese government was asked to take the surrender of the Japanese forces on the island. That is the reason the Chinese are there now. . . . The US has a record . . . of friendship for the Chinese people. We still feel the friendship and know that millions of Chinese reciprocate it. We took the lead . . . in the last United Nations General Assembly to secure approval of a resolution on the integrity of China.[8]*

In his letter to the US delegate to the Security Council Truman threw his authority behind the declaration and repeated, for some bizarre reason, the gist of the statement. He did so, he wrote, "to the end

---

[7] Dean Acheson, *Present at the Creation* (New York, 1969), p. 422.
[8] *Documents on International Affairs,* 1949–1950, pp. 664–665.

that there be no misunderstanding concerning the position of the Government of the US with respect to Formosa."

With UN forces pursuing the utterly defeated and demoralized remnants of the North Korean army north of the 38th Parallel, it became clear that all of Korea would soon be theirs and the world would witness the liquidation of a Soviet satellite without its protector doing anything about it. It was hardly the kind of lesson which Moscow had in mind when it allowed (or ordered) the hapless North Koreans to start the venture.

The repercussions of Korea were undoubtedly seen also in the more vigorous pace of the Western defense effort in Europe. The NATO Council in September issued a statement envisaging West German participation in the planned European army. General Eisenhower left his safe haven (such was a university presidency in those distant times) at Columbia to head once more the combined forces of the Western Alliance. The unforeseen course of the war probably deflected the Russians from an attempt at a military solution of the Yugoslav problem. By 1950 it was clear that Tito's regime would not collapse because of any internal subversion; at the same time "frontier incidents" with Yugoslavia's Communist neighbors grew in frequency and intensity. There is a strong presumption that had not the world situation become so thoroughly muddled through the Americans' unexpected action, the summer of 1950 would have witnessed yet another invasion across the Hungarian and Bulgarian frontiers.

In fact when it became clear that the Americans not only would not be forced out of Korea but would march beyond the 38th Parallel, the kind of situation rapidly evolved which it had been the cardinal point of Soviet policy ever since 1944 to avoid: the revelation of Soviet caution and bluff, of how behind the tough talk lay a real fear of confrontation with the awesome power of the United States. The relaxed and humorous Soviet diplomacy of a few weeks before was giving way to visible anxiety. In August, the Soviet representative returned to the Security Council. In October, a hastily arranged meeting in Prague of the representatives of the USSR and the people's democracies formulated a proposal for a resolution of the German problem which would allow a withdrawal of all occupation forces within a year. For a change the proposal did not contain a single word of abuse of the United States, nor the by now ritualistic phrases about imperialists scheming to rebuild the Wehrmacht and unleash war. It was amazing how, once a danger seemed imminent, the USSR would remember its manners and frame its proposals in irreproachably diplomatic language.

The danger was thought to be considerable. For the moment the American mood was one of combined resolution and exasperation, so that no contingency, however drastic, could be precluded. In August there were isolated voices crying that "one should be done with it": the Secretary of the Navy talked of preventive war, an Air Force general stated his readiness to drop atomic bombs on the source of all trouble, Moscow. The politician was banished to the embassy in Ireland and the general was retired, but there must have been some uneasiness in the Kremlin.

One would give a great deal to read even one of the messages which passed in those weeks between Moscow and Peking. From the Russians' point of view, the great consolation was that the American moves were still more threatening to the Chinese than to them. It was being demonstrated how easy it was to beat *Asian* Communists. Who could believe that with US troops on the frontier of Manchuria and Chiang proclaimed an indispensable ally, America would return to its attitude of "wait till the dust settles" in Asia? And Communist rule on the mainland was far from firmly consolidated. Those warlords who had deserted the Kuomintang and who still controlled some provinces might now decide that the Mandate of Heaven worked the other way.

The Chinese Communists could not view the prospect of their intervention in Korea with wild enthusiasm. They were to enter the war with obsolete military equipment (the North Koreans when they attacked had up-to-date Soviet weapons, but only after their struggle with the Americans began did the Soviets *sell* the Chinese modern arms); and the possibility that the Americans would resort to the atom bomb could not be discounted. There was no public commitment from the USSR that she would aid Peking in such an eventuality. If there was a secret Soviet stipulation to that effect, Mao and his government must have still been dubious that Stalin's Russia would depart from its peace-loving ways even if Peking were bombed and civil war were rekindled on the mainland. But such unhappy reflections may have been somewhat balanced by the elation, partly nationalist and partly ideological, felt at the prospect of humiliating the American imperialists, and the pride that it was China that had become the forward wall of the Communist world.

In October there were repeated Chinese warnings that if the *American* troops crossed the Parallel and moved toward their border, Peking would be compelled to intervene. The American reactions were ambivalent. The fact that the warnings had been conveyed through India decreased their credibility. (The State Department was in one of its frequent moods of irritation over the Indians' nervousness combined with Nehru's "holier than thou" attitude.) On the other hand, the possibility of Chinese intervention was not being discounted. Directives to MacArthur suggested that military operations north of the Parallel should be conducted by South Korean units. But the American commander was at the height of his glory and popularity. The Joint Chiefs of Staff—who had been junior officers when MacArthur was already a national figure, whose fears about the Inchon landing had been so recently confounded—could not bring themselves to *order* MacArthur in direct and unambiguous terms. With Congressional elections but a few weeks away, the President had to ponder the repercussions of a public disagreement with the legendary warrior. There was also a natural temptation to crown what had begun as a military and political calamity with a resounding lesson to the aggressor and his sponsor. (Here one might consider a few "ifs." What if with the crushing defeat of the North Koreans by the end of September the United States had lifted the quarantine of Formosa? What if the response to the Far Eastern aggression had been at least a *threat* of vigorous German rearmament, rather than a halting and uncertain one envisaging German units of batallion strength within a special European total force not surpassing 100,000 soldiers? What if the President had seized this moment of American success and Russian confusion to propose a summit meeting with Stalin?)

It would have been awkward to ask MacArthur to come to Washington: he could plead the impossibility of absenting himself from the theater of war; or if he came, his public reception would be tumultuously friendly. Alexander I and Napoleon solved a somewhat similar problem by meeting on a raft in the middle of a river. Truman and MacArthur met in the middle of the Pacific on Wake Island. In terms of clarifying overall strategy, the meeting could accomplish little. MacArthur's assurance that the Chinese would not intervene and even if they did would be trounced could have been conveyed by telegram. But politically the meeting could be interpreted as a democracy paying overdue tribute to a hero. On his return to Washington, Truman hailed MacArthur as "loyal to the President . . . loyal to the President in his foreign policy,"[9] a rather unnecessary statement, one should think, for the President of the United States to make about a soldier on active service.

On October 7, the UN Assembly authorized the establishment of a "unified independent and democratic Korea." As to the means of achieving this happy situation, it recommended appropriate steps to assure stability throughout the peninsula. This euphemism, endorsed by a large majority of the Assembly (the Security Council could no longer be relied upon since the Russians were back with their veto), meant a fairly clear mandate for MacArthur to sweep into North Korea and to finish off its army. This he proceeded to do, disregarding the suggestions (or was it orders?) from Washington to employ only South Korean units in the provinces bordering on Chinese and Soviet territories. Washington's policy was in line with a sound and cautious strategy which urged that the neck, or as it is sometimes called with less anatomical justification, the pinched waist of the peninsula, some fifty miles north of Pynzyang, be recognized as an ideal defense line if superior forces were thrown in against the UN. It would also have been a cautious response to the Communist Chinese intimations that they would not feel it necessary to intervene if only South Koreans would advance beyond the Parallel and toward their border.

It was subsequently to become a heated political issue whether and how far MacArthur violated explicit orders. There were orders, but were they explicit? Washington's views on the subject prior to the November debacle remind one of the considerations which in the old Austro-Hungarian Empire governed the award of the Order of Maria Theresa: The military commander who violated his instructions and lost the battle was, of course, court-martialed; but one who won

[9] Rovere and Schlesinger, op. cit., p. 133.

while disobeying a higher authority was given this highest military award of the Empire. (It was but rarely granted, since throughout the nineteenth century and World War I, Austrian commanders invariably both obeyed their orders and were defeated.) The general, on the other hand, believed that he understood Oriental psychology. It was palpably foolish for the Chinese to intervene at this late stage; had they done so in the beginning or at the crucial stage after the Inchon landing, they would have tipped the scales. On grounds of military logic and of the celebrated Oriental psychology those were perhaps sound considerations, but the decisive element was neither. The Chinese venture proceeded from a very complicated relationship between Moscow and Peking. Another factor was the Chinese Communists' understanding of *American* psychology: once North Korea was erased, they believed, the United States would not be able to resist some further temptation.

The Chinese Communists attacked first at the end of October, and in early November inflicted significant setbacks on the US forces. On November 7 they broke off action and insofar as MacArthur and Washington were concerned vanished for about twenty days. Here came the really inexcusable action by MacArthur and the equally inexcusable acquiescence in it by his superiors. The Chinese move should have been interpreted as an unmistakable indication, and such it was, that they planned to make good their threats but still hoped to avoid prolonged armed conflict with the United States. If it were otherwise, why give the United States an opportunity to change its plans? Why destroy the surprise element and hold off *continuous* blows until later? But after momentary hesitations, rather than holding to his positions or withdrawing to more defensible lines, MacArthur unleashed his offensive to the border of North Korea, utterly disregarding the possibility of a new and massive Chinese counterattack. Again, as Acheson feels constrained to admit in his memoirs, the Joint Chiefs urged caution and did not countermand MacArthur's orders and insist on a tactical withdrawal. On November 26, large Chinese forces fell upon the exposed and divided UN units. It was the beginning of the new war, which between November 16 and January 25, 1951, resulted in American defeats and a precipitous withdrawal not only from the North but once again from part of the South and its capital, Seoul.

A democracy often performs more creditably faced with a stark defeat than in moments of triumph or apparent peace. The initial panic and deep humiliation felt at the first news of the rout soon gave way in Washington to what under the circumstances was probably the balanced and correct response: the determination to hold on to South Korea at the same time eschewing the temptation to broaden the war with China.

We cannot follow here the subsequent history of the war: the United States' recovery in the spring of 1951, the sporadic but still bloody fighting which went on for two years while the armistice negotiations dragged on, etc. But we may ask, what were and should have been the lessons of America's near triumph and near catastrophe, and of the concluding and frustrating settlement which left the 38th Parallel as one of the leading danger spots in the world? These lessons can hardly be gleaned from the lengthy hearings before the Senate Armed Services Committee, which in 1951, following MacArthur's dismissal, sought to apportion blame for US policies in Asia during and since World War II. In the most succinct form the clashing viewpoints were expressed by Generals MacArthur and Bradley. In war there was no substitute for victory, said the former. What MacArthur wanted, said the latter, would have led to a war with China—"the wrong war, at the wrong time, with the wrong enemy."

MacArthur's formula would hardly be borne out by history, but his sentiments were the reflection of a very basic trait in American psychology: with a job at hand one does not rest until it is completed. Certainly the US victory over Japan had been as complete as any in history. But it was largely due to the completeness of that victory and to the disregard of the wider setting of world politics that within a few years the United States found itself confronted with another and more intractable danger in the Far East. Moreover, an all-out American effort against China would not have been viewed in Moscow with undue dismay. Once the Korean situation became "stabilized" in the spring of 1951, the USSR could view the resulting deadlock with some equanimity. Considerable US forces were tied down in the Far East. The Soviet stock of atomic weapons was growing, and since the USSR was ultimately protecting China as well, she obviously had to retain Port Arthur beyond the scheduled time for evacuation. America's European allies were grumbling. It could not be ruled out that the Americans in one of their incalculable moods might raise the specter of actual war, but those agonizingly inconclusive truce negotiations could then suddenly become fruitful and produce a quick settlement. If Stalin had not died in March, 1953, it is quite likely that the impasse would have continued beyond the date of actual signing of the truce on July 27, 1953.

Stalin's successors were not of the same mettle. They had less confidence in their ability to gauge American reactions and were diffident about pushing the United States too hard. The same applied in regard to the Chinese Communists. Hardly were the obsequies over when the Malenkov-Beria regime proceeded to sign a trade and technological agreement with China which pledged considerable technical and economic aid. V. V. Kuznetsov, then high in the Soviet hierarchy, was dispatched to Peking, replacing as ambassador a career diplomat who had been there only a month. These moves had an eloquence of their own. The magic of Soviet dominance was broken: China was now a partner, even if still a junior one.

It is mostly in its effect on the Chinese Communists that the Korean venture must be considered as one of the most profound blunders of postwar Soviet foreign policy. On the surface it appeared as a master stroke to make Peking the lightning rod for America's wrath and frustration while the Soviet Union remained a sympathetic bystander. In fact, those two years when the Chinese had to assume the burden of the fighting marked their psychological emancipation and speeded up the process of equalization between the two states which had begun with the Mao-Stalin negotiations in Moscow. They acquired not only modern equipment but self-confidence and reliance. Their ability to fight the United States to a stalemate brought them dividends of nationalistic exultation and of speedier and firmer consolidation of their rule on the mainland than would otherwise have been the case. From now on, China would be very careful not to lend itself to any situation where she would be required to pull Soviet chestnuts out of the fire, not to be pushed again into the position and danger she endured from 1951 to 1953.

For the United States, the lessons of Korea were ambiguous. The decision to counter Communist aggression appears, in retrospect, both justified and necessary. Soviet hopes of loosening America's hold on Japan were frustrated. In September 1951, the United States rushed through the Japanese peace treaty (which Russia did not sign), which then was followed by a security pact between the two countries. The United States retained bases and armed forces and the agreement stipulated that the latter could be used at the request of the Japanese government to suppress any internal revolt instigated by an outside power. The two documents marked a decisive defeat of the Soviet design to have in Japan a Communist or at least a neutralist power to balance Communist China in the Far East.

At one time the Korean War promised to become a heartening demonstration of how the United Nations could be resolute and effective in stopping aggression. By the time of the armistice, little remained of such high hopes. Technically the side fighting the Communists was the United Nations; in fact, the United Nations label was not significantly less fictitious than the volunteer status of the Chinese fighting on the other side. Many nations contributed small units, some of them (notably the Turks and the British) fought most gallantly, yet in numerical terms it was clearly an American force. Even more significant and lamentable, though predictable, was the discord within the UN, once "its" forces were attacked by the Chinese, and the mounting criticism of American leadership and aims. In fact if a proof was needed that the UN could not perform its primary function of guaranteeing international peace and security, then the Korean conflict offered fairly convincing evidence. The original approval of other UN members for the American initiative soon turned into a rather ill-humored acquiescence, and that only on the assumption that the predominant share of fighting and casualties would be borne by the United States (apart of course from the South Koreans). There grew on the other hand a bitter feeling among many Americans that countries bearing little or no share of the responsibility and fighting sought to influence or dictate American strategy. There was an element of cruel irony in the drama, and one which was to recur in the years to come. When the responsibility had not been hers, the United States had repeatedly criticized the British, French, Dutch, etc., for their insensitivity to Asian nationalism, their reluctance to make timely concessions to the new and dynamic forces in the Orient. Now this criticism was vented on the United States. The shock of the Chinese intervention brought Prime Minister Clement Attlee to Washington. In his lugubrious manner, he expounded the necessity of appeasement: "He believed," Acheson tells us, "that withdrawal from Korea and Formosa and the Chinese seat in the United Nations for the Communists would not be too high a price. There was nothing, he warned us, more important than retaining the good opinion of Asia."[10] The Americans could not help being chagrined and infuriated. They had borne the burden of fighting, they had poured billions into the recovery of Western Europe, yet their West European allies, some of whom recognized Communist China and traded with her, while clamoring for American help and support showed reluctance even for diplomatic support of the Korean action. American soldiers, it was believed, were providing a defense against new despotisms, while the Europeans assumed the role so recently occupied by the American spokesmen: pleading for an understanding of Asian nationalism, justifying its excesses and its suspicions of the West, calling for patience and sacrifice of Western pride. Nobody could expect Acheson to appreciate the irony of this reversal in the traditional roles. And indeed he did not.

The disappointments and setbacks of the latter phase of the Korean conflict compounded the difficulty of designing and maintaining an over-all policy of containing communism (or was it the Soviet Union?) throughout the world. The impetus to create an effective NATO force and some form of West German rearmament which appeared so strong in September, 1950, had visibly weakened toward the end of the year. A Soviet note of November 3 proposing yet another meeting of the Big Four ministers to consider the German question, and its rather conciliatory tone, were undoubtedly prompted by the prospect of *imminent* West German rearmament. But at the December meeting of the North Atlantic Council, it became dismally clear that West German rearmament was *not* imminent. Hence it seemed there was no reason for the USSR to offer any tangible concessions, and this was to be confirmed at the foreign ministers' deputies' conference which met in March 1951, and dragged on until June 21, producing absolutely nothing. The American diplomats had by now an almost superstitious fear of negotiations with the Russians: meetings led nowhere, they increased the West European governments' procrastination about defense and produced first false hopes and then exasperation at home.

[10] Acheson, op. cit., p. 481.

The British and the French clung to the meetings with equally super-stitious hope. Negotiations, they felt, decreased the chances of the Americans doing something rash and just *might* produce some dra-matic Soviet initiative which would spare them from German rearm-ament and from increased exertion on behalf of joint defense. The Europeans were for negotiating, the Americans for *doing* things. That the two could be combined, that in fact negotiations could be suc-cessful only if the European defense effort was proceeding well and rapidly, does not seem to have occurred to either.

The reverberations of the double impasse in Korea and in Europe echoed angrily in the halls of Congress and on public platforms throughout the United States. There was an impulsive reaction on the part of a large part of the public, in many respects resembling that which was to rage some fifteen years later on Vietnam. Much of the debate concerned not logical alternatives but a search for a magical solution and invocation of moral and philosophical verities inherent in each choice. Europe, it was argued, was being ungrateful and unwilling to assume the burden of its own defense. The British and French were criticizing and quibbling while American boys were dying in the Far East. British intrigues were to blame for the restraints put upon MacArthur and, consequently, for the American defeats and the costly stalemate. The United Nations, some argued, was a hoax which was costing the American people dearly. There was more than a grain of truth in such charges. But they tended to disregard the harsh realities and thus contributed to confusion and certain hysteria rather than to a rational re-examination of the US role and capabilities in international affairs. For all the very considerable criticisms which one can make of the Truman-Acheson management of foreign affairs in 1950–52, one must credit it with not allowing itself to be deflected from the goal of organizing a viable West European defense and political system. But this vital enterprise moved slowly compared to the feverish tempo of modern politics and modern technology. What would the Russians not have given in 1949 in order to avoid a sizable West German force! By 1954, with their nuclear arsenal, they were willing to give much less; and the Russia of the 1960s, with its inter-continental missiles, etc., was not unduly concerned, despite all the propaganda campaigns to the contrary, about a West German *land* force.

In addition to an actual war, the Truman administration in its last two years had two other battles on its hands. It had to assault French obduracy and British fears to get a measure of agreement on European defense. At the same time it had to beat off the persistent attacks of conservative critics at home. From them—people as diverse as ex-Ambassador Joseph Kennedy, ex-President Herbert Hoover, and Senator Robert Taft—came insistent voices that the United States was overextending itself by assuming obligations that created inflation at home and would bring about eventual bankruptcy, and most of all by pledging to rush troops into every threatened breach. In 1947, Taft had warned that America could not help the "free world" unless she remained "solvent and sensible." Korea was a warning and Vietnam was to provide an ample demonstration of how hard it is for a democracy to remain solvent and, even more, sensible when caught in a situation which is neither full-fledged war nor peace. And Taft's call in 1951 for the Congress to reassert itself in foreign-policy matters and to curb the President's powers there, then decried as new isolationism, would be repeated in fifteen years' time.

Caught in the crossfire between faint hearts in Europe and the Republican Jeremiahs at home, the Administration at times seemed oblivious that its real antagonist was the Soviet Union and its real aim a diplomatic victory leading to a solution of the German problem. In 1952, yet another Soviet initiative on the latter threw the State Department into a tizzy. The Russians went beyond their previous tantalizing proposals by expressing readiness to have unified Germany free to rearm, and proposing free elections in East Germany under the supervision of the four occupying powers. This was, at least, a hint that in return for having Germany neutral they might be willing to throw the East German Communist regime to the wolves, or rather to its own people. Again there was an imminent threat: the West was about to grant the Bonn Republic sovereignty—a European Defense Community with German participation was to be set up. Another American Presidential election was in the offing, and prudence dictated yet another friendly approach in Europe. But to Washington the Soviet proposal was the ultimate in unsportsmanlike behavior. The Europeans had been cajoled into doing something—the NATO table of organization had been painfully worked out—and now here were the Soviets ready to spoil everything. Acheson, even before studying the Soviet note, was sure that it "had the usual hooks in it." *After* a careful study he described the Soviet moves as "the golden apple of discord tactics . . . tossed over the Iron Curtain in the hope of causing discord among the allies."[11] The apple was never picked up, and once again the Americans failed to ascertain whether they could cash in on Soviet nervousness. The EDC was to crumble within two years.

The effect of the Korean War was thus to expose and enhance the fragility of the Western alliance. Economically the Marshall Plan had contributed to a near miracle of West European recovery and prosperity. That and the heartening prospect of West European political (as well as economic and military) unity appeared as a splendid vindication of American foreign policies. But undermining this success were the baffling problems of the Third World. The French were fighting in Indochina; their position in North Africa was becoming more precarious. The British were in similar troubles in Egypt and Iran. In practically every case the European power was fighting a rear-guard action against local nationalism. The electorates of the Western nations had become weary of their imperial burdens and eager to enjoy the benefits of the welfare state and the American way of life; they did not want their resources and attention diverted to distant affairs in Cyprus or Tunisia. But the American attitude of anticolonial condescension was bound to irritate, and not only those who clung to the shreds of former imperial grandeur. However greatly Acheson had been disenchanted with India, he still somberly lectured the French ministers (with words that have a pathetic ring in the midst of the Vietnam imbroglio) that the Americans could not help feeling sympathy for *any* people which claimed to be oppressed and that it made little difference "whether or not the allegedly oppressed were, in fact, oppressed." The French were gently chided for their reluctance to have their North African troubles aired in the United Nations, though on legal grounds their position was unassailable.

In fact, the refrain ever so discreetly repeated by Washington to its European allies bears a striking resemblance to the lesson read some years later to the United States: there is no disgrace for a major power in making concessions or even capitulating to colonial nationalism, or in giving in to a small state; on the contrary, such admission

11 Ibid., p. 632.

of political or military defeat would be applauded as a wise and generous step enhancing that power's moral prestige. But the American attitude changed drastically when a conflict involved Communists. There was support for the British action in Malaya against the Communist guerrillas, and the French in Indochina were recipients of considerable US aid. Still, even there American help and support were tinged with condescension and criticism.

It is not that the American attitude was basically wrong or that specific criticisms were not justified. But discretion and restraint are necessary ingredients of a successful alliance. A critical and carping ally in many ways builds up more resentment than a forceful or even bullying one. The United States expected Britain and France to give up long-standing interests and obligations at the same time that it expected them to expend men and resources against every hypothetical Communist threat. It was immoral to use power to protect centuries-old French interests in North Africa or British investments in Iran, yet at the same time the French army was to be expanded and British defense budgets increased to appease an American obsession (as it was being increasingly viewed) about the danger of communism. Washington stubbornly refused to reconcile itself to the fact that Communist China was now a reality, while every predatory Near Eastern politican, every non-Communist rebel movement, was seen to embody irresistible national aspirations. Thus mutual disenchantment and irritation grew. The Western alliance limped on. But what could have been achieved had there been more unity and expedition!

Mounting frustrations over the European alliance and the Asian war thus ended much of the public enthusiasm and unity behind American foreign policy which had been generated by the inception and success of the Marshall Plan. Continued prosperity (which moved a rueful Democratic politician to observe callowly, after the 1952 election, "We have run out of poor people") did not cancel the effect of continuing casualty lists. A complex and lingering crisis which calls for patience and measured response rather than widely shared sacrifices and all-out effort can be more dangerous to democratic institutions than an all-out war. This was perhaps the most important lesson of Korea, yet it was largely ignored.

Legally, the United States was not at war. The kind of patriotic elation which in "real" war silences partisan criticism could not assert itself. The issue at stake, clear to some, was and had to be puzzling to most of the people. Whom‚was the United States fighting? Obviously *not* the North Koreans, for they could be and were defeated with little trouble. The Communist Chinese? But then why not bomb their bases and cities? The Soviet Union? But the United States had diplomatic relations with that state, joined with it in international conferences, etc. Was the United States merely fighting as one of the United Nations and at its behest? Why then was the participation of other members at most only token? The principle at stake also appeared fuzzy. The aim of the US actions and sacrifices was to teach the lesson that "aggression does not pay." But then the real instigator of aggression was not affected and it could hardly be claimed that this was the intended lesson.

"There shall always be a Korea," said some wiser and more pessimistic people, implying that just as the British soldiers throughout the nineteenth century intermittently fought at the northwest frontier in India, so in this strange world the American soldier would always have to watch over some border of the non-Communist world. But this threatened to be a shattered psychological if not a material burden. Britain's little wars of the nineteenth century were fought by a small professional army. A dictatorship, especially a Communist one, is always in a state of emergency, *psychologically* always on a war footing. But America? Korea could not be compared to the Indian wars, nor was it a "police action" as Truman once incautiously characterized it. "Laws become silent when arms begin to talk" was an old Roman maxim. But that was an insufferable prospect. Politicians, newspapers, and television (still in its infancy) were free to portray horrors of actual fighting, impugning the purpose of the whole enterprise, questioning motivations of the leaders, while *some* young Americans were required to risk and give their lives. Truman's administration was wiser than Johnson's in a similar predicament, when in December 1950, it proclaimed a state of national emergency and followed with some economic controls, for these at least created the appearance of the nation sharing in the purpose and the sacrifice. Still, this was merely "tokenism."

These troublesome paradoxes were not without their effect on and beyond the battlefield. The American soldier performed creditably, and the Communist expectation of widespread demoralization of the American fighting men, of actual mutinies, etc., was disappointed, whatever the painful facts which were established later on about the behavior of Americans in prisoner-of-war camps. The Soviet and the Chinese managers of the Korean enterprise were too sophisticated to share Hitler's contemptuous delusions about the worthlessness and lack of tenacity of the American soldier. Yet if one studies their moves and propaganda, one gets a clear picture of their hopes that disgruntled soldiers would blame their government for incomprehensible conflict and might become susceptible to revolutionary appeals; that a democratic community would not have the endurance to sustain the "neither war nor peace" situation; that the resulting frustrations, guilt feelings, and disenchantment with the ineffective and undemocratic South Korea regime would turn into dissent and then widespread defeatism, eroding social cohesion and setting the stage for anarchy. At the time, however, the scenario was not to be acted out.

Suggestions for Additional Reading

The best comprehensive history of the Korean War is probably David Rees, *Korea: The Limited War* (New York: St. Martin's Press, 1964). Rees, who is a British subject, includes excellent discussion of the role played in the war by Great Britain. T. R. Fehrenbach's *This Kind of War: A Study in Unpreparedness* (New York: Macmillan Co., 1963) is somewhat tendentious in its argument. Nonetheless, the book is a good journalistic account of the military action.

For the "revisionist" critique of American policy, discussed above (pp. 216–217), numerous sources are available. General revisionist analyses of postwar American policy can be found in William Appleman Williams, *The Tragedy of American Diplomacy* (Cleveland: World Publishing Co., 1959); Edmund Stillman and William Pfaff, *The New Politics* (New York: Coward-McCann, 1961), and *Power and Impotence* (New York: Random House, 1966); Ronald Steel, *Imperialists and Other Heroes* (New York: Random House, 1971), and *Pax Americana* (New York: Viking Press, 1967); Richard M. Freeland, *The Truman Doctrine and the Origins of McCarthyism* (New York: Alfred A. Knopf, 1972); and Joyce and Gabriel Kolko, *The Limits of Power* (New York: Harper & Row, 1972). Antedating these books and anticipating much of their argument is I. F. Stone's *The Hidden History of the Korean War* (New York: Monthly Review Press, 1952).

The political process that led to Truman's decision to intervene is extensively analyzed in Glenn D. Paige, *The Korean Decision* (New York: Free Press, 1968).

For the military side of the war as seen by those who made the decisions, see MacArthur's *Reminiscences* (New York: McGraw-Hill Book Co., 1964); Courtney Whitney's *MacArthur: His Rendezvous with Destiny* (New York: Alfred A. Knopf, 1956); Mark W. Clark, *From the Danube to the Yalu* (New York: Harper & Bros., 1954); Matthew B. Ridgway, *Soldier: The Memoirs of Matthew B. Ridgway* (New York: Harper & Bros., 1956); and J. Lawton Collins, *War in Peacetime* (Boston: Houghton Mifflin, 1969).

MacArthur's *Reminiscences* and Whitney's biography (which was written from MacArthur's papers) together provide a full account of MacArthur's side of the controversy with Truman, whose own version of the events should be read in full as it appears in his *Memoirs* (Garden City, New York: Doubleday & Co., 1956). Three further stud-

219

ies of the controversy are important. Richard H. Rovere and Arthur
M. Schlesinger, Jr., *The MacArthur Controversy and American Foreign Policy* (New York: Farrar, Straus, & Giroux, 1965), is a retitled
and somewhat revised version of a highly readable and very partisan
account first published in 1951. The book also contains a number of
useful appendixes that reproduce some of the documentary material
of this pamphlet. Trumball Higgins, *Korea and the Fall of MacArthur:
A Precis in Limited War* (New York: Oxford University Press, 1960),
is a good brief analysis by one who received his Ph.D. in military
history. The best study of the dispute between the general and the
president is, however, John W. Spanier, *The Truman-MacArthur
Controversy and the Korean War* (New York: W. W. Norton & Co.,
1965). This is a paperback revision of the 1959 edition, with an an-
notated bibliography. The full five-volume collection of the *Hearings*
(*The Military Situation in the Far East*) and the *Congressional Record*
(1950–1953) contains a great deal of significant material (and a great
deal of the trivial and repetitive).

For the Korean War as a case study in limited war, see in addition
to the articles reprinted in this pamphlet, Martin Lichterman, "Korea:
Problems in Limited War," in *National Security in the Nuclear Age,*
ed. Gordon B. Turner and Richard Challener (New York: Frederick
A. Praeger, 1960), pp. 31–56. Allen S. Whiting, *China Crosses the
Yalu* (New York: Macmillan Co., 1960), is the standard analysis of the
Chinese decision to intervene.

For limited war and other concepts of modern strategy, the fol-
lowing books are useful: Bernard Brodie, *Strategy in the Missile Age*
(Princeton: Princeton University Press, 1959); Morton H. Halperin,
Limited War in the Nuclear Age (New York: John Wiley & Sons, 1963);
Henry A. Kissinger, *Nuclear Weapons and Foreign Policy (*New York:
Harper & Bros., 1957); Robert E. Osgood, *Limited War* (Chicago: Uni-
versity of Chicago Press, 1957); and Maxwell Taylor, *The Uncertain
Trumpet* (New York: Harper & Row, 1960). An excellent study of
American defense policy since 1945 is Samuel P. Huntington, *The
Common Defense: Strategic Programs in National Politics* (N.Y.:
Columbia University Press, 1961).

Higgins, Rees, and Spanier all have selected bibliographies. The
standard inclusive bibliography is Carroll Henry Blanchard, *Korean
War Bibliography and Maps of Korea* (Albany, N.Y.: Korean Conflict
Research Foundation, 1964).